CENTRIFUGAL EMPIRE

CENTRIFUGAL EMPIRE

Central–Local Relations in China

Jae Ho Chung

Columbia University Press
New York

Columbia University Press
Publishers Since 1893
New York   Chichester, West Sussex
cup.columbia.edu
Copyright © 2016 Columbia University Press
Paperback edition, 2019
All rights reserved

Library of Congress Cataloging-in-Publication Data

Names: Chŏng, Chae-ho, 1960– author.
Title: Centrifugal empire : central–local relations in China / Jae Ho Chung.
Description: New York : Columbia University Press, 2016. | Includes bibliographical
references and index.
Identifiers: LCCN 2016002533 | ISBN 9780231176200 (cloth) |
ISBN 9780231176217 (pbk.) | ISBN 9780231540681 (e-book)
Subjects: LCSH: Central-local government relations—China. | Decentralization in
government—China. | Chinese autonomous regions—Government policy. | Local
government—China. | China—Ethnic relations—Political aspects. | China—
Politics and government—2002–
Classification: LCC JQ1506.S8 C46 2016 | DDC 320.80951—dc23
LC record available at http://lccn.loc.gov/2016002533

COVER IMAGE: © sylverarts/iStockphoto
COVER DESIGN: Milenda Nan Ok Lee

Contents

CONTENTS

Figures and Tables

FIGURES

TABLES

Preface

This is my third single-authored book in English. Sixteen years since the publication of my first book on central–local relations with the case of rural reforms of the early 1980s, I am both happy and relieved to come back to the subject of my lifelong passion, which is also one of the most crucial and cross-cutting themes in Chinese politics. Particularly given that the number of books devoted to China's central–local dynamics has been on the decline since the late 1990s, I harbor some modest expectations that this volume will contribute to a better understanding of complex central–local relations in the past three decades of system reforms.

Many individuals and institutions provided invaluable support and encouragement in the long process of research and publication of this book and deserve thankful acknowledgment. Anita Chan, Bruce J. Dickson, Tao-chiu Lam, Kenneth Lieberthal, Margaret Pearson, Sangbum Shin, Dorothy J. Solinger, Jonathan Unger, and Yukyung Yeo offered critical but useful comments on different parts of the draft manuscript. Three chapters of the book were originally presented at the Asian Network for the Study of Local China (ANSLoC), which was established in 2006. I am thankful to its cofounding members and good old friends—John Donaldson, Phil Hsu, Tse-Kang Leng, and Long Yang in particular—for having been indispensable sources of encouragement and inspiration for the entire period of research and writing for this book.

The rewriting, editing, and refining of the manuscript benefited enormously during my third sabbatical leave (2014–2015) from Seoul National University. Several institutions provided financial and logistical support for research stay, as well as valuable venues where draft chapters were presented and commented on. My sincere gratitude is due the East Asian Institute (Singapore), and Gungwu Wang and Yongnian Zheng; Singapore Management University and James Tang; the University of Hong Kong, and John Burns and Peter T. Y. Cheung; Fudan University's School of International Studies and Zhimin Chen (I am also thankful to Ruichang Li, Yalin Tang, and Lixin Wang for offering useful comments and providing additional materials for the paper I presented there in October 2014); the Institute for Political Science at the Academia Sinica and Yu-Shan Wu; and the Samsung Economic Research Institute and Ki-Young Chung.

Some portions of chapter 3 are adapted from "China's 'City System' in Flux: Explaining Post-Mao Administrative Changes," *China Quarterly*, no. 180 (December 2004), and chapter 5 is a modified version of "China's Local Governance in Perspective: Instruments of Central Government Control," *China Journal*, no. 75 (January 2016).

I must also acknowledge the invaluable support (including one term of the Hysan Lee Fellowship) I received over the years from the Universities Service Center for China Studies at the Chinese University of Hong Kong. Without the archival research conducted there, this book could not have become what it is now. I thank the former and current assistant directors, Jean Hung and Gao Qi, for their unstinted support. I would also like to thank my former students Yongkai Liu, Jieun Kim, and Jongyoon Baek for research assistance. Thanks are also due three anonymous readers who read the entire manuscript for Columbia University Press. Anne Routon, my editor, was indispensable as a manager, supporter, and good friend for the entire, often painstaking process.

Last but not least, I am grateful to my wife, Hye Kyung, whose unpunctuated prayers for the last twenty-seven years made all this possible. I hope my daughter, Jean, whose interest in China and the Chinese language has been increasing over the past years, may also appreciate this book in due time.

CENTRIFUGAL EMPIRE

1

China as a Centrifugal Empire

Size, Diversity, and Local Governance

All modern states are constructed within sovereign territories that are in principle politically monopolized, economically sustained, socially integrated, diplomatically safeguarded, and even militarily defended if necessary. Because modern states must carry out a wide range of socio-economic functions catered to the indispensable needs of their populaces, certain degrees of political-administrative penetration—ranging from nationwide taxation and conscription to public services delivery and welfare provision—are a prerequisite.[1] The principal mode of organizing and regulating territorial jurisdictions, however, differs widely among states as history is bound to shape distinct patterns and cultures of local governance.[2]

States differ considerably in their physical size. In terms of total area (i.e., land area plus water area), Russia, Canada, China, the United States, Brazil, and Australia boast continental sizes, ranging from 7.7 million to 17.1 million square kilometers. Of over 240 countries on the globe, on the other extreme, Vatican City and Monaco occupy merely 0.4 and 2 square kilometers in total, respectively. States also have vastly different sizes of population—ranging from China (1.36 billion), India (1.24 billion), and the United States (318 million) to Palau (20,901) and Nauru (9,945).[3] There is no doubt that history and culture have long conditioned and sustained such wide variations in the size of modern states. Some scholars suggest that certain trends of globalization (i.e., lowered barriers of trade and other exchanges), democratization (i.e., delegation of political accountability), and increasing bottom heaviness in social interactions (i.e., the rise of more heterogeneous preferences from the society at large) appear to be key determinants of the size and number of modern states.[4]

Nearly 20 percent of all states in the contemporary world have opted for a variety of federal structures in which "dual (central and local) sovereignty" is to be constitutionally safeguarded for the sake of protecting regional autonomy, sustaining local diversities, and coping with tensions that come with multiethnic and multicultural heritages. These federal states are generally huge in physical size, large in their population, and/or multiethnic and multicultural in their domestic compositions. Most notable examples include the United States, Russia, Canada, Brazil, and India. Despite its continental size, the world's largest population, and highly multiethnic and multicultural attributes, the People's Republic of China has all along been a unitary system that allows more power for the central government at the expense of local autonomy.[5]

One cannot help but wonder at this juncture: Why is China a unitary state after all?[6] Some may argue that, in the absence of rule of law, the constitutional provisions for a federal structure (i.e., safeguarding dual sovereignty) cannot be properly sustained in China anyway. True. But, then, why did China not even pretend to adopt a sort of federal structure in nominal terms just as the Soviet Union did in the 1920s? What has been pulling China away from even a "federalist" way of thinking, if not the structures and processes as such? What has made China so stuck on a highly centralized unitary system despite the so-called "diseconomies of scale" deeply embedded in its sheer magnitude in size?[7] Furthermore, what is constantly driving China and its leadership to pledge to safeguard domestic stability and territorial integrity even at the expense of almost everything else? What are the drivers behind China's perennial preoccupation with effective control over localities?

This book seeks to find some answers to the daunting questions outlined above. It is suggested here that China—the People's Republic and its dynastic predecessors alike—has been deeply immersed in the ultimate task of preventing *centrifugal* forces from threatening and toppling the center, whether it was ruled by emperors, generalissimos, or general party secretaries. Since the Qin dynasty (221–206 B.C.E.) nearly 44 percent of China's two-millennium-long history was under a divided center, with its throne often usurped by regional armies, local dukes, or peasant rebels.[8] Intergenerational transmissions of such memories, history, perceptions, and preoccupations have kept them still much alive in the minds of Chinese leaders residing in the *Zhongnanhai*.

The goal of this book is to identify, substantiate, and reconstruct such resilient perceptual undercurrents (i.e., national identities of local governance), as well as their behavioral manifestations, in the People's Republic, particularly during the post-Mao reform era. For that, this volume seeks to reconstruct, empirically, how the central leaders of the People's Republic have thought about localities and gone about designing modes of local governance. The key argument of this study is that the Communist leaders are as preoccupied as their imperial predecessors with local governance and devote as much effort to improving their capacity to control regions and provinces.

SIZE MATTERS!

Modern states, by definition, are inclined to expand and "thicken" as they constantly seek out more material and human resources, larger organizations, bigger budgets, and wider territories to work with.[9] Imperial expansion and colonial acquisitions worldwide, up to the Second World War, illustrate such insatiable drives embedded in modern states. Whereas rulers would generally prefer to enlarge the territories under their jurisdiction, the overall size of a state might actually be inversely correlated with the effectiveness of sovereign control—hence the diseconomies of scale. Yet, the "big is beautiful" mindset was perhaps ubiquitous among many great powers despite history's unequivocal lesson that most empires fall from within. The Roman and Mongol empires and the Soviet Union all imploded, thereby highlighting the crucial importance of internal cohesion and local governance.[10]

The very large size of a state poses a wide array of problems with control and regulation—often fatal. What can be termed here as a three-pronged problem of governance refers to (1) difficulties in exercising effective political control and maintaining domestic stability in a large territory due to high costs of administrative monitoring and law enforcement, (2) complexities involved in regulating and enhancing the efficacy of economic-social development due to high transaction costs and diverse externalities, and (3) challenges of safeguarding sovereign territories and protecting citizens from external threat due to the burdens of high defense spending required for expansive defense along extralong borders.

The Soviet Union is a vivid case in point. With its ever-dwindling resources spread thinly over often wasteful schemes of strategic competition with the United States and of national defense against China and Western Europe, Moscow had little interest in paying due attention to the livelihood of its own citizens for an extended period of time. With its "shortage economy" further aggravated over time, thereby alienating increasing portions of the populace, including diverse ethnic groups, fatal seeds were planted for failed local governance and an eventual implosion of the empire.[11]

How different is today's China? China certainly is much more affluent now than the Soviet Union in the late 1980s, and, overall, Beijing's defense spending has not been as aggressive as the Soviet Union's or as its economic growth has indicated over the past thirty-some years, although there now emerges a sign that such a trend might be reversed. However, that does not necessarily mean that the Chinese people are more or less happy with their lives and its ethnic groups generally content with the status quo. Despite being in a relatively better-off situation than leaders of the Soviet Union, Chinese leaders are by no means free from the perennial concern with local governance that has always been lurking in the back of their minds.[12]

Let us consider some notable episodes from contemporary China, all of which seem to highlight the central leaders' continuous—often excessive—preoccupation with governance and stability even during this more affluent and peaceful post-Mao era. Internal records of the central leadership's thinking and activities in the midst of the Tian'anmen tragedy in 1989 vividly illustrate how paranoid central leaders indeed were during that extreme turmoil and that they collectively attributed the popular outburst in large part to a conspiratorial mastermind by some antagonistic external forces (the United States in particular).[13]

The infamous cases of fallen Bo Xilai and Zhou Yongkang are also illustrative of the extent to which functional bureaucratic systems [xitong], regional elites, and occupational networks [tonghang] could be intricately interwoven to pose a formidable challenge to Beijing's effective governance. Available evidence suggests that the so-called public security [gong'an xitong] colluded with some provincial-level officials from Chongqing, Sichuan, and Shanxi, as well as with the Oil Faction [shiyoupai; i.e., petroleum industries] and the Secretaries Clique [mishubang], to get around and interfere with what the center was doing.[14]

In China these days, it is not so hard to hear about the so-called "three evil forces" [sangu heieshili] as imminent and fatal threats to

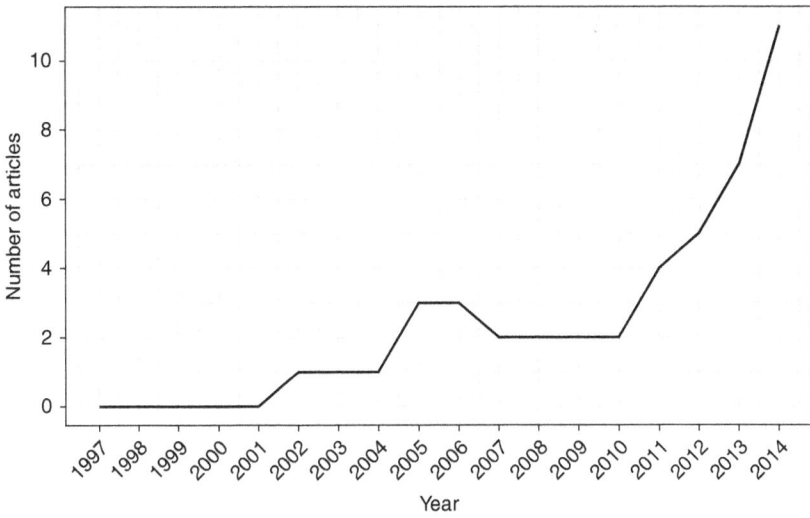

FIGURE 1.1 Level of academic interest in "local autonomy," measured by number of scholarly journal articles published in China. *Source*: This chart is based on the author's search by way of http://trend.cnki.net using the key term "*difang zizhuxing.*"

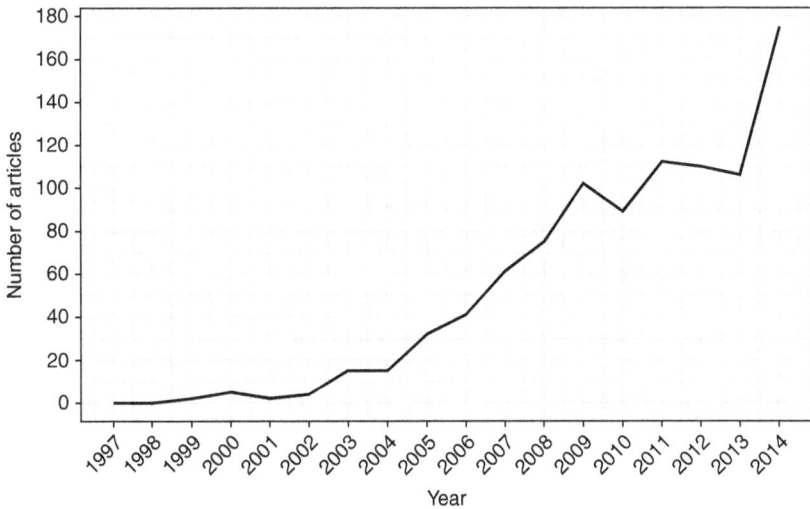

FIGURE 1.2 Level of academic interest in "local governance," measured by number of scholarly journal articles published in China. *Source*: This chart is based on the author's search by way of http://trend.cnki.net using the key term "*difang zhili.*"

stability. They refer specifically to terrorist forces, religious extremists, and ethnic separationists, and most of them are—like the followers of *Falungong* and Tibetan and Xinjiang Uighur activists—generally viewed as coming from localities and therefore centrifugal in nature. Hence, it is no coincidence that the State Security Commission [*guojia anquan weiyuanhui*], newly established in 2013 with Xi Jinping, Li Keqiang, and Zhang Dejiang designated as its top three leaders, is to focus as much on safeguarding domestic security against these centrifugal forces as on coping with external security threats.[15]

The growing concern in China with the issue of local governance is well reflected in the trend of scholarly research. Figures 1.1 and 1.2 show the increasing number of articles specifically on the themes of local autonomy [*difang zizhuxing*] and local governance [*difang zhili*] published in academic journals in China during the period of 1997–2014. Given the highly authoritarian (even self-censored) system that China has, these could be crucial indicators for the regime's preoccupation with the imperative of containing provincial assertiveness and local deviations.

SO DOES HISTORY

Nothing is created in a vacuum. Certainly, history is one of the most powerful factors in shaping and conditioning territorial dynamics and central–local relations. That is to say, precedents and modes of central-local interactions—and records and memories of them—are just as important as the physical endowments (i.e., land mass, population, topography, etc.) of a state. Whether a state is federal or unitary has its historical roots, but even among the unitary states, variations are readily discernible in the ways in which the specific mode of local governance has been structured. For instance, in terms of how many tiers were established between the central/federal-level government and the grassroots administration, some states chose one, whereas others did more than three. Yet, nearly two-thirds of the modern states opted for two- or three-tier systems of local administration, demonstrating the adaptive work by history over time. The impact of history—i.e., the power of path dependence—can also be seen from the cross-national variations found in the total number of highest subnational units, whether they are called provinces, states, oblasts, or cantons.

Although the so-called "watershed moments" are mostly the reconstructions of human interpretation of history, some "events" (i.e., crucial changes with lasting impact) do occasionally generate important triggers for altering institutions, perceptions, values, and even power relations between territorial jurisdictions. In decoding such elusive work of history, it seems, two approaches are particularly useful: (1) tracking down certain key patterns or recurring cycles in organizational and behavioral modes of local governance; and (2) identifying, often retrospectively, the imperative of the times (the "historical atmosphere," or *Zeitgeist*). Expectedly, neither is an easy task because neither renders itself to readily available empiricism or easy quantification.

Let us now look at the case of China, whose history of more than two millennia is replete with oscillations between three-tier systems of local administration and others. As table 1.1 illustrates, the recurring cycle in this case denotes the following three that all eventually reverted back to three-tier systems: (1) from the Qin and Han toward the Wei/Jin, (2) from the Sui and Tang toward the Song/Jin, and (3) from the Yuan and Ming toward the Qing and after. At the same time, a significant degree of institutional stability is discernible from the highest level of local administration [i.e., *sheng*], and the durability of the county [*xian*] is also equally, if not more, noteworthy. Problematic were the intermediate "county-ruling units" [*tongxian zhengqu*] where the extent of institutional change was the greatest, in addition to the frequent changes in their name.

What merits our attention is the fact that the cycle repeated itself during the sixty-some years of the People's Republic. The Communist leaders in the Zhongnanhai were by no means free from the perennial dilemma of deciding how many tiers should be built into the system of local administration and which level/unit should be in charge of governing the counties. As will be discussed in more detail later, the People's Republic initially had the provinces (by way of utilizing the prefectures as their field offices) rule the counties. In the post-Mao reform era, the cities-ruling-counties [*shi lingdao xian*] policy was adopted in the mid 1980s, thereby allowing the prefecture-level cities to rule the counties. During the 2000s, however, the policy faced a serious challenge as the provinces-directly-ruling-counties [*sheng zhiguan xian*] scheme was being popularized.[16]

The People's Republic faced an additional challenge—penetrating further down to the local hierarchy by seeking to rule townships/towns, a task that their dynastic predecessors had not even dreamt of. Here, too,

TABLE 1.1

China's Local Administration in History

	Highest level[a]	County-ruling unit[b]	County-level unit	Number of tiers
Qin	–	*jun*	*xian/dao*	2
Han	–	*jun/wangguo*	*xian/dao/yi*	2
Wei/Jin	*zhou*	*jun/wangguo*	*xian/guo*	3
Sui/early Tang	–	*zhou/jun*	*xian*	2
Late Tang	*dao*	*zhou/fu*	*xian*	3
Liao	*dao*	*fu → zhou*	*xian*	4
Song/Jin	*lu*	*fu/zhou*	*xian*	3
Yuan	*sheng*	*lu → fu → zhou*	*xian*	5
Ming	*sheng*	*fu/zhilizhou → zhou*	*xian*	4
Qing	*sheng*	*fu/zhilizhou*	*xian/zhou/ting*	3
Republican	*sheng*	*dao*	*xian*	3
PRC	*sheng*	*diqu/dijishi*[c]	*xian*	3 (4)[d]

NOTES: (a) The highest level refers to *gaoceng zhengqu*; (b) County-ruling unit refers to *tongxian zhengqu*; (c) This refers to the situation after 1983; (d) In the People's Republic, the township/town level constitutes a formal layer of local administrative hierarchy, but *diqu/dijishi* does not, although it did rule county-level units. Therefore, the total number is between three and four. Slashes refer to the same administrative level, and arrows denote hierarchical relationships.

SOURCE: Zeng Wei and Luo Hui, *Difang zhengfu guanlixue* [Local government management] (Beijing: Beijing daxue chubanshe, 2006), 57; and Zhou Zhenhe, *Tiguo jingye zhidao—Zhongguo xingzheng quhua yange* [The way of zoning and ruling the nation—Changes and continuities in China's administrative zoning] (Shanghai: Shanghai shudian chubanshe, 2009), 30.

a mini-cycle was produced where rural townships were initially reorganized into self-ruling people's communes during the late 1950s but later reinstated as a formal tier of local government by the post-Mao decollectivization of the early 1980s. In the 2000s, particularly since 2006 when the agricultural tax was totally abolished nationwide, townships/towns became increasingly hollowed out with their finances subject to county management, posing the possibility of yet another institutional change or reversal down the road.[17]

SPATIAL VARIATION AND ISSUE VARIANCE

China is no Monaco or Singapore. The sheer magnitude of China's physical size necessitates that regional variations and local diversities are bound to be important ways of life there.[18] Yet, out of their perennial concern with effective local control, the leaders of the People's Republic have been nearly obsessed with treating the whole of China as one "unified" entity by, say, adopting a single time zone for the entire nation, which actually spans five-hour differences.[19] Although China has sought hard to popularize one standardized language [*Putonghua*] to minimize the divisive effect of the prevalence of local languages and regional dialects, it is obviously easier said than done. According to a 2004 nationwide survey, only 53 percent of the Chinese population was able to communicate in *Putonghua* effectively.[20] Furthermore, after all the construction and infrastructure building for the past six decades since 1949, according to a 2005 report, only 65.8 percent of the villages in China were connected to the outside by roads, reflecting the impact of size and underdevelopment on local governance.[21]

The leaders of the People's Republic—whether Mao, Deng, Jiang, Hu, or Xi—all agonized on the task of keeping an intricate balance between "promoting national goals" [*quanguo yipanqi*] and "safeguarding local interests" [*yindi zhiyi*]. The most troublesome practice of the Maoist era had, in fact, been the imposition of one single policy or a standardized model for the country as a whole—often sarcastically dubbed as "cutting with one knife" [*yidaoqie*] or "boiling in one pot" [*yiguozhu*]—without taking into account different regional conditions and local endowments. As the post-Mao decentralization reforms more or less put an end to such malpractices and transformed the key norms of policy implementation from "blind commandism" and top-down imposition to local experimentation and bottom-up diffusion, a new type of problem has emerged—namely, excessive degrees of variation, including some acts of defiance, among localities.[22]

To the extent that local discretion and provincial diversity were emphasized in the overall policy process, the line between legitimate regional variation and willful foot-dragging became increasingly blurred in the post-Mao era. Distinguishing one from the other got more complicated in a continent-sized nation like China, with limited capabilities for administrative monitoring.[23] If the issue-area dimension—i.e., how the extent of local discretion is related to the type of policy under implementation—were added, the equation would certainly become even more complex.[24] Yet, this is precisely what has been happening in today's China. That is to say, thanks to measures of administrative and fiscal decentralization, localities have actively sought to take full advantage of the newly transformed environments by maximizing the boundaries of their discretion, depending on the policy issue at hand. All these pose some practical difficulties for the central government, which has to evaluate the implementation outcome both nationally and regionally, as well as for scholars who need to appraise the policy process from an academic perspective.

ON LEVELS OF ANALYSIS AND
VERTICAL–HORIZONTAL AXES

Much of the scholarly literature on central–local relations is largely abstract on what the "local" actually denotes. Strictly speaking, the term local in China refers to all subnational units that are administratively higher than the self-ruling [*zizhi*] units at the grass-roots level. Excluding such short-lived units as the "great administrative region" [*da xingzhengqu*] and "special districts" [*zhuanqu*], the local units include provinces (and province-level units like centrally administered municipalities, ethnic minority regions, and the special administrative regions [SARs]), prefecture-level cities and prefectures (and prefecture-level ethnic districts), county-level cities and counties (and ethnic minority counties as well as county-level urban districts), and finally, towns, townships, ethnic minority townships, and street-level administrative offices.[25]

Many studies treat villages as if they fall under the domain of local governments, but, in fact, they do not, because they are officially self-ruling units [*zizhi danwei*]. In most cases, even counties and townships rarely come into direct contact with the central state except for some extraordinary circumstances where top leaders and special delegations from the center make purposive visits to these lower-level units for specific reasons.[26] Therefore, provinces and provincial-level units, and deputy-provincial cities, to a lesser extent, are the only units that constantly and directly interact with the central state on a daily basis. In this regard, identifying and distinguishing pertinent levels of analysis in conducting research on central–local relations and local politics becomes crucial. In this volume, the level of analysis is specified whenever possible and necessary.

It should be noted at this juncture that the term local does not refer only to top-down vertical dynamics, although the literature in the field is predominantly concerned with that alone. It is suggested here that the term local also denotes a wide range of horizontal and lateral interactions among different local units.[27] Although the prevalent imagery of a centralized socialist dictatorship too often makes one overlook this intriguing—but currently fast-growing—dimension, much has indeed been happening in terms of horizontal liaison, lateral competition, and interlocal cooperation in today's China.[28]

INTERWEAVING THE SPATIAL, TEMPORAL, FUNCTIONAL, HIERARCHICAL, AND HORIZONTAL

In answering the challenging question—how the leaders of the People's Republic think about localities and seek to design modes of local governance—five analytical axes are interwoven in this volume: namely, the spatial, temporal, functional, hierarchical, and horizontal. *Spatial* refers to the extraordinary size of China's territory and population and the resultant extent of regional diversity, both of which generate a myriad of problems for local governance. Analytically, the axis stretches from standardization to variation. *Temporal* denotes historical continuities and institutional resemblance in China's mode of local governance. The analysis along this line focuses specifically on recurring cycles and institutional similarities over time. *Functional* here means that specific balances of power in central–local relations tend to differ among different issue areas concerned. Key analytical components in this regard include policy scope, policy nature, and the level of urgency. *Hierarchical* refers to differing or even conflictual perceptions and interests among different levels of government. *Horizontal*, on the other hand, denotes lateral interlocal dynamics that range from competition to cooperation.

In addition to this introduction (chapter 1), this book consists of seven other chapters. Chapter 2 tackles a functional-hierarchical question: Has the post-Mao decentralization generally favored the localities or not? In contrast with the Maoist era (1949–1976) when the totalitarian awe had temporarily put a halt on China's centrifugal tendencies, the post-Mao reform era has seen China "go local" again. In efforts to gauge the extent and impact of decentralization, the chapter first surveys the principal changes in both economic (planning, fiscal, budgetary, investment, and foreign economic relations) and noneconomic (personnel, ideology, legislation, administrative monitoring, etc.) issue areas and then explores their implications for the central–local balances of power and influence. The chapter concludes that although the overall extent of local discretion has increased considerably in the economic issue areas, the same cannot be said of the noneconomic issue areas where the central state, preoccupied with local governance, still enjoys considerable commanding power.

Chapter 3 examines a spatial-temporal-hierarchical theme of institutional changes and continuities in China's local governance. Linking China's two millenniums of experience in searching for optimal institutional designs for effective local control with that of the People's

Republic, this chapter suggests that the Communist regime is by no means much different from its imperial predecessors and probably fares no better on average. As a matter of fact, it argues, the daunting task of economic modernization has brought additional factors of complications into the entire equation of local governance.

Chapter 4 examines a temporal-hierarchical question as to the central state's evolving perceptions of the local bureaucracy. In illustrating the trajectory in which the role of China's local bureaucracy has evolved over time, a triple concept of "agents" (i.e., localities performing as the center's loyal agents), "representatives" (i.e., localities articulating and defending societal interests in the face of the central state), and "principals" (i.e., localities becoming defenders of their own interests as opposed to national or societal interests) is employed. The chapter, then, looks into Beijing's variant perceptions toward different levels of the subnational administration—namely, the provincial, the prefecture-level, the county-level, and township governments.

Chapter 5 takes on a spatial-temporal-hierarchical question: How similar are the present-day instruments of local control to those of the imperial past? In stark contrast with the prevailing official rhetoric, the chapter suggests the People's Republic's principal mode of local control resembles that of traditional China more than that of the pre-1949 revolutionary era. In terms of preventive mechanisms, investigative instruments and tools of suppression, high levels of historical continuity and institutional adaptation are discernible, highlighting the fact that the dilemmas of local control that the People's Republic is facing today remain more or less the same as those of the traditional times.

Chapter 6 tackles a spatial-functional-hierarchical question: What factors condition and determine the extent of local discretion in policy implementation? This chapter presupposes that, with other things (i.e., patronage networks and societal demands) being relatively similar among different regions, the level of local discretion permitted in implementation is likely to vary with different *types* of policy issues. Using three subdimensions—policy scope, policy nature, and the degree of urgency—the chapter compares a total of six cases (the household responsibility reform of the early 1980s; the measure of taking Hainan out of Guangdong in 1988 to make it a province-level unit; the "tax-sharing reform" in 1994; the "Revive the Northeast" scheme since 2004; the provinces-directly-ruling-counties policy since 2009; and the stability maintenance policy during the 2000s) to see if the expected level of discretion matched the actual level measured by the overall time taken for complete implementation.

Chapter 7 examines a spatial-hierarchical-horizontal dimension of central–local relations. That is to say, compared with vertical control and support by the central state, how important and useful is horizontal cooperation in coping with regional disparities? Much of the scholarly discussion overlooks the fact that interregional lateral networks and linkages have always been on Beijing's menu for policy choices. This chapter seeks to fill the void by assessing the relative importance of the central state's vertical resource and policy support during different periods, as well as the evolving roles of vertically induced and voluntarily formed horizontal cooperative networks. The key argument here is that, whereas Beijing's policy support and centrally induced horizontal networks were important in the early phases of the reform era, the center's resource support and voluntarily formed lateral linkages have become increasingly crucial in recent years.

In chapter 8, the tightly organized empirical discussions provided in the previous seven chapters are brought together in a more macro-historical reflection on the future of China as a re-emerging empire. It is suggested here that the lapse of time will invariably dilute the socialist or Communist flavor, thereby further accentuating the Chinese nature of the system that continues to be centrifugal. Hence, history will become more useful and handy by offering invaluable insights and by guiding us to better understandings of a future of China that is much too uncertain at the time of this writing.

NOTES ON METHODS AND DATA

In answering the key question at hand—how the leaders of the People's Republic think about localities and seek to design modes of effective local governance—chapters in this volume frequently go back and forth between traditional China and the People's Republic, between memories and perceptions, between national trends and provincial cases, between the center's perspectives and local viewpoints, and between narratives and analyses.[29] Historical-analytic narratives with process tracing are particularly appropriate for the purpose of this book as the leaders of the People's Republic—Mao Zedong and, most recently, Xi Jinping—have continuously and actively sought lessons and connections with traditional China. At the 18th Collective Study Session of the Politburo in

November 2014, for instance, Xi remarked: "[We] must respect and reflect more on our 5,000 years of history. We must take successful ancient experiences and improve them for today's system of state governance. . . . History is an echo that travels from the past to the future [*lishi shi guoqu chuandao jianglai de huisheng*]."[30]

Although historical-analytic narratives with process tracing constitute a principal methodology for this study, some surveys (chapter 4) and comparative case studies (chapter 6) are also utilized when necessary. Additionally, fieldwork and interviews are widely used throughout the volume. Most fundamentally, methodological eclecticism is at the heart of this book as it is this author's main conviction that methods and methodologies must cater to the kind of questions that are to be pursued.

This volume grew out of interpreting numerous party and government documents, scholarly journals, media reports, statistical yearbooks, academic books, and other archival resources in Chinese and English languages, which were acquired over a period of twenty-some years.[31] We must be keenly aware of the inherent problems that any government statistics and archives may contain.[32] Yet, statistics are used here mainly to highlight overall trends rather than to point to exact magnitude or variations. Archival records were cross-checked with the author's own interviews and other sources whenever necessary and possible. Positivism has always been a guiding light for the research on this volume, but persuasiveness is invariably the most crucial criterion for pertinent arguments provided.

2

China Goes Local (Again)

Assessing Post-Mao Decentralization

Fatal challenges to the "mandate of heaven" [*tianming*] and resultant dynastic cycles were familiar themes to the rulers of the Chinese empire. The recipe for such dynastic changes consisted of some combinations of the eruption of peasant rebellions, the rise of local strongmen, and foreign aggression or invasion. As the later years of the Qing dynasty and the Republican era forcefully demonstrate, the Taiping and Nian rebellions, the rise of provincial armies and regional warlords and later of the Red Army, and the Western and Japanese encroachment since the Opium War jointly contributed to their demise or debacle.[1] All these historic episodes took place as spatial competitions in which alternative military forces sought to attain bases of opposition to the imperial throne or the central government in power.

Chinese history is replete with dynastic cycles of unification and disintegration during the period spanning over two millennia, as few dynasties managed to last longer than three hundred years. The centrifugal tradition has long been an integral part of the Chinese empire, waiting to resurface whenever the conditions were ripe. As Owen Lattimore once observed, "Old China was a decentralized country in which every province had a life of its own."[2] What, then, about the new China? Despite its socialist and modern outfit, there is no special reason to assume that the People's Republic is either immune or insusceptible to the dangers of disintegration or local defiance, although it has clearly commanded tighter control over localities than any of its imperial predecessors.

This chapter examines two questions in particular: (1) how to characterize the totalitarian Maoist era (1949–1976) in terms of local governance and (2) how to assess the key changes in China's central–local relations during the last thirty-some years. As for the former, the chapter suggests that this specific—and brief—period constitutes a sort of exception to China's centrifugal tradition, due mainly to the highly dogmatic and ideological nature of the Communist rule. As for the latter question, it is suggested that a myriad of measures of post-Mao decentralization—both fiscal and administrative—has once again made China go local, rendering the task of local governance more difficult. At the same time, however, this study argues that the center still commands quite effectively in many of the issue areas, both economic and noneconomic.

ASSESSING THE MAOIST ERA: THE PUNCTUATED TRADITION OF LOCALISM

Prior to 1949, no single regime in China had ever been able to rule the nation below the county [*xian*] level effectively. Thanks to the land reforms and associated political struggles, the millennium-old system of gentry-based local self-rule was broken for the first time, extending the reach of the People's Republic down to the townships [*xiangzhen*] and, very often, to the villages [*cun*].[3] Much of the official historiography of the Maoist era is either overly euphemistic or nostalgic about the revolutionary era (1921–1949), as if that was the most ideal and representative period for local governance. The interpretation provided below, however, counters such views by comparing the revolutionary period with the Maoist era in terms of central–local relations.

Reevaluating the Legacies of the Revolutionary Era

Many Chinese feel nostalgic about the pre-1949 period of revolutionary struggle and find their pride and inspirations from these hard years. It is certainly true that some of the key administrative styles and organizational principles of the People's Republic today originated from this period of extreme hardship, but it is equally important to note that the political circumstances of that period were both special and unique. Therefore, it is argued, applying those administrative principles and organizational styles to more normal circumstances of the post-1949 years was not as easy as it seemed.

During the brief—but important—period of the Jiangxi Soviet (1931–1934), the Communist government had a highly decentralized structure of governance where most policies, except for military-related ones, were decided by the county-level authorities. Given the unique geopolitical circumstances of that period, the provincial level was nearly irrelevant, and consequently, Mao Zedong and the Communist leadership were more interested in managing the counties and the townships. Agrarian policy varied considerably among different counties and townships, and naturally, such distinct styles of local governance as decentralized experimentation, mass participation, and two-way communication (i.e., "democratic centralism") grew out of these special environments.[4] Adaptive and even romantic as they might seem, these experiences were not easily transferable to the enormously enlarged and more normal contexts of the People's Republic after 1949.

Similar assessments may be offered of the experiences of the Yan'an years (1936–1948). The Yan'an era began with a small, geographically remote, and inaccessible area in Shaanxi. Although the size of the region under Communist control expanded over the years, it was still mostly disconnected by the areas ruled separately by the Kuomintang forces, regional warlords, and Japanese armies. Until the mid-1940s, Communist leaders focused more on garnering mass support at the grassroots level and immediately above. Central–local relations were not their key interest yet.[5]

It was during these base-area years that the famous tenet of "implement according to local conditions" [yindi zhiyi] was first developed, but again, this period was more special than normal. Having to carry out a geographically disconnected revolution in widely scattered areas, Communist leaders simply did not have the luxury of blind commandism dictated solely from above. The guerrilla-style policy making thus necessitated flexibility, autarky, a united front, and the securing of mass support. The survival imperative of the Chinese Communist Party (CCP) facilitated due attention to local initiatives and variations while the urge for top-down control and standardization was carefully restrained.[6]

These unusual experiences and legacies of the pre-1949 period were to be remembered and cherished as a successful recipe for local governance of the People's Republic.[7] Whenever hard times fell on the population, these legacies were called upon for inspiration and encouragement. Highlighting local experiments and grass-roots initiatives alone can be misleading, however, as the implementation dynamics were in reality dictated more by Beijing than driven by localities in the post-1949 context. That is, stark differences between the revolutionary and post-revolution years, in terms of their political circumstances and policy environments, need to be duly recognized.[8]

Local Governance in the Maoist Era

The centrifugal tradition was largely suspended during Maoist China (1949–1976) as there were no discernible trends toward local assertiveness vis-à-vis Beijing, not to mention explicit regional defiance under Mao's rule. During this period of less than thirty years in total, the utopian groupthink that both the elite and the masses shared in the frantic processes of policy making and implementation offered little room for local defiance.[9]

In the beginning of the People's Republic, of course, deep-rooted regionalism had to be struggled against, along with the eradication of regional warlords and local bandits. Communist leaders also built extensive roads and railways to overcome territorial fragmentation and cultural parochialism, two key ingredients of China's centrifugal tradition. The interim scheme of six great administrative regions [*daxingzhengqu*] was implemented from 1949–1953 to merge numerous subnational units into the new Communist state.[10] Once the task of territorial incorporation was completed through the great administrative regions, Beijing sought for tight political integration by resorting to centralized command and ideological control in the management of provinces.[11]

Although there were some provincial variations and intergovernmental frictions, especially during the period of 1955–1957 when the provinces were even encouraged to exercise discretion, we hardly know of outright central–local conflicts in the Maoist era. Particularly since 1957, after the traumatic anti-rightist purges against numerous intellectuals and cadres who had voiced concerns about the Communist rule, local voices and regional variations were tightly controlled from above (i.e., Mao and the Party Center). Because of rigid—often black-and-white—ideological norms and severe punishments against local deviation, compliance-in-advance was a popular mode of local response to Beijing under Mao's rule.[12]

The experiences during the Great Leap Forward (1958–1959) and the Cultural Revolution (1966–1976) are also pertinent to the issue of local governance. As a scholar puts it, "Many analysts conclude that the decentralization measures of 1957–1958 led to more provincial autonomy. . . . Instead, the decentralization in 1958 seemed more apparent than real."[13] Due to the sheer lack of local discretion, provincial compliance was generally fast and highly standardized, and provincial deviation was a rarity.[14] The Cultural Revolution is also commonly associated with extensive decentralization. Contrary to such views, even in the midst of organizational breakdown and administrative disruptions, the Party Center was able to whip up "policy winds" to force a controversial policy onto the agenda for the provinces to implement by relying on the ideological control mechanisms highly independent of formal bureaucratic institutions.[15] The self-policing ideology operated effectively enough to ensure local conformity to Mao's policy lines. Furthermore, rival factions took advantage of the ever-changing ideological winds to bring down their foes, thereby preventing local officials from voicing concerns that might be perceived as even remotely contradicting Mao and the Party Center.[16]

During much of the 1970s, despite the prevailing rhetoric on decentralization, the tenet of implement according to local conditions was willfully neglected. Localities only had single national models such as Dazhai and Daqing to emulate. Little room was available for comparative advantage or regional specialization as the nationwide adoption of standardized policy—i.e., "taking grain as the key link" and "mechanization is the only way out for China's agriculture"—was emphasized.[17] Extreme standardization without due regard for local variations led to a nationwide isomorphic structure where provincial per capita agricultural and industrial outputs were increasingly highly correlated (from –0.16 in 1957 to 0.75 in 1980).[18]

In sum, during Mao's rule, successive commitments to decentralization were mostly formalistic, and consequently, localities had little genuine discretion of their own. Beijing's urge to control the localities and pervasive local fears of persecution jointly worked to defeat the revolutionary legacy of *yindi zhiyi*. Beijing was therefore largely able to enforce its preferences with regard to most nationwide policies although the efficacy of such policies remained suboptimal. One crucial lesson can be distilled from these experiences: unless the norms of decentralization were sincerely internalized, local implementers would always view provincial discretion and regional variation as ideologically faulty and politically unsafe.[19]

CHINA GOES LOCAL: ASSESSING POST-MAO
DECENTRALIZATION

Since the Third Plenum of the 11th Central Committee in November 1978, both drastic and far-reaching changes took place in China's central–local relations. Although China's transitional reforms in the past thirty-some years have entailed a wide array of programs catered to de-ideologization, decentralization, marketization, ownership diversification, liberalization, and internationalization, this section focuses specifically on the evolving dynamics of decentralization—defined here as a process of decisional authority being devolved from the central government to the provinces and below in efforts to promote local incentives and initiatives.

In tandem with the crucial changes introduced since 1979, scholarly communities paid much attention to the diverse patterns and evolving dynamics of China's central–local relations.[20] They have indeed grown to become a subfield of contemporary China studies.[21] The research has over the years been increasingly enmeshed with studies on elite politics, government-business dynamics, and state–society relations.[22] The growing number of studies on a variety of themes related to local governance notwithstanding, how to construe the intricate—and still evolving—balance between central control and local discretion in China remains a daunting challenge.

The principal challenge comes from the fact that central–local dynamics continue to change over time, and so do the pertinent discourses in and outside China. Dichotomies of decentralization–recentralization, control–autonomy, unitary–(pseudo) federal, and collapse–integration constitute only a part of the question at hand. Although some may disagree on the extent to which the post-Mao decentralization brought about economic successes, it is difficult to deny its impact on transforming the norms and procedures of local governance in contemporary China.[23] In fact, over the last two decades, a multitude of studies have suggested that the post-Mao decentralization was so extensive in scope and substantive in nature that localities became increasingly and sufficiently empowered so as to defy Beijing on many occasions.[24]

Assessing central–local relations is an inherently complex task not only because pertinent interactions invariably span two or more levels of government (and analysis), but because the relevant dynamics may also relate to a multitude of policy issues.[25] If a historical time dimension is added, the challenge of producing a balance sheet becomes more formidable. It is therefore imperative to take a comprehensive look at China's central–local relations that are multilayered in nature and rapidly diversified over time. Only such an overarching perspective may enable us to draw a picture that more closely resembles the real balance of influence between Beijing and the localities.[26]

The Economic Domain: Overall "De-Centering" with Selective Recentralization

Of many economic realms in which Beijing frequently interacted with localities, planning [*jihua*] was a domain where central power was most consistently and conspicuously weakened since the dawn of the post-Mao reform era. Although the central government "played God" during the Maoist era, due to the sheer lack of an optimal capacity to monitor and assess local performance, central planning more often than not led to frequent plan revisions, rampant inter-unit bargaining, prevalent relational contracting, and the margins of error that were kept as high as 25 percent of the original target.[27]

Crucial changes were introduced to the planning system beginning in the early 1980s. All the planning bureaus within the line ministries were abolished while their counterparts in the provincial governments survived, thus strengthening the horizontal [*kuai*] planning authority of the regions vis-à-vis that of the hierarchical [*tiao*] system. The relationship between the State Planning Commission (SPC) and provincial planning commissions was also transformed from vertical leadership [*lingdao guanxi*] to a relationship of coordination [*yewu guanxi*] at least in principle. Furthermore, "mandatory targets" [*zhilingxing zhibiao*] were sharply cut down and gradually replaced by less binding "guidance targets" [*zhidaoxing zhibiao*].[28] As table 2.1 demonstrates, the total number of plan items controlled by Beijing (i.e., SPC) was drastically reduced over the years.

Rapid marketization across the board further constricted the room for central plans and mandatory targets.[29] The share of the industrial output value generated under SPC in China's gross value of industrial output (GVIO) declined from 95 percent in 1979 to a mere 7 percent in 1993.[30] In 1992, the State Bureau of Commodity Prices liberalized the prices of 571 industrial products, leaving 22 in charge of the provinces. By the end of 1992, the number of industrial production materials whose price was directly administered by the State Bureau of Commodity

TABLE 2.1

Reduction of Central Mandatory Plan Control, 1979–2001

	Agricultural production	Industrial production	Material allocation	Price control	Export control	State procurement
1979	25	200+	256	1,336	900+	65
1985	0	85	20+	1,021	31	n/a
1992	0	59	19	89	29	21
1994	0	33	11	n/a	n/a	14[b]
1998	0	12	5	58	16	n/a
2001	0[a]	n/a	n/a	13	n/a	n/a

NOTES: Figures denote the number of items subject to the State Planning Commission's mandatory planning; and for the price control, the numbers refer to those of production materials controlled by the State Bureau of Commodity Prices [guojia wujiaju]. (a) Guidance planning [zhidaoxing jihua] was still in place for nine items such as grains, cotton, edible oil, sugar, meats, etc; (b) Of these fourteen, all but one were guidance plan items.

SOURCES: Gui Shiyong, Zhongguo jihua tizhi gaige [The reform of China's plan system] (Beijing: Zhongguo caizheng jingji chubanshe, 1994), 7–11; Terry Sicular, "Agricultural Planning and Pricing in the Post-Mao Period," China Quarterly 116 (December 1988): 677; Dangdai zhongguo de wuzi liutong [Materials allocation in contemporary China] (Beijing: Dangdai zhongguo chubanshe, 1993), 103; State Planning Commission, "Woguo zhongyang yu difang jingji guanli quanxian yanjiu" [Boundaries of economic management between China's central and local governments], Jingji yanjiu cankao [Reference materials for economic research], no. 434/435 (March 1, 1994): 5, 19–23; Lu Jiang, ed., Neimao daili chutan [Exploring the agency system in internal trade] (Beijing: Zhongguo wuzi chubanshe, 1995), 17; Wang Shaoxi, ed., Zhongguo duiwai jingji maoyi lilun yu zhengce [Theory and policy in China's foreign economic relations and trade] (Beijing: Zhongguo duiwai jingji maoyi chubanshe, 1997), 255; Wu Shaojun, Guojia fazhan jihua gailun [Introduction to state development planning] (Beijing: Zhongguo renmin daxue chubanshe, 1999), 84–87; Zhang Dexin et al., Zhongguo zhengfu gaige de fangxiang [Direction of China's governmental reform] (Beijing: Renmin chubanshe, 2003), 100; Zhou Lianshi, Zhengcexing jihualun [On policy-oriented planning] (Shanghai: Shanghai renmin chubanshe, 2003), 33–34; Yao Kaijian and Chen Yongqin, eds., Gaibian Zhongguo—Zhongguo de shige wunian jihua [Changing China—10 Five-Year Plans in China] (Beijing: Zhongguo jingji chubanshe, 2003), 229; Liu Guoguang, ed., Zhongguo shige wunian jihua yanjiu baogao [Research report on China's 10 Five-Year Plans] (Beijing: Renmin chubanshe, 2006), 472; and Chen Jiagui, ed., Zhongguo touzi tizhi gaige 30nian yanjiu [Study of the thirty-year reform of China's investment system] (Beijing: Jingji guanli chubanshe, 2008), 207, 209.

Prices and other ministries was reduced from 737 to 89.[31] Table 2.2 highlights the predominant role that market played in setting the prices of various products that had formerly been controlled solely by the central government.

The SPC, often dubbed the "little State Council," in charge of imposing both macro-plan items and micro-quotas on local units and state enterprises, was steadily curtailed during the 1990s and eventually overhauled in 2003 as the State Development and Reform Commission [guojia fazhan he gaige weiyuanhui; hereafter SDRC].[32] Annual quotas became less important and mid- and long-term planning [zhongchangqi jihua] came to receive higher priorities. The 11th Five-Year Social/ Economic Plan for 2006–2010 was for the first time officially designated as guiha [i.e., directional guidelines] as opposed to jihua [i.e., operational

TABLE 2.2
Share of Market-Set Prices (%)

	Retail commodities	Agricultural products	Industrial products	Industrial production materials
1979	3	7.4	–	0
1986	–	–	35.8	–
1990	53	51.6	45.6	36.4
1993	91.4	87.5	–	81.3
2000	95.8	92.5	–	87.4
2002	97.1	97.4	–	90.3

SOURCES: "Guanyu zhongguo shichanghua jincheng de yanjiu" [Study of China's marketization], *Diaocha yanjiu baogao* [Investigative research report], no. 1747 (July 26, 2002): 5; Liu Guoguang, ed., *Zhongguo shige wunian jihua yanjiu baogao*, 538, 644; Chen Jiagui, ed., *Zhongguo touzi tizhi gaige 30nian yanjiu*, 208; and Wang Haibo, "Xinzhongguo shige wunian jihua de bianzhi shishi yu jingji shehui de fazhan" [The making and implementation of 10 Five-Year Plans and socioeconomic development], *Zhengfu guanli cankao* [Reference materials for government management), no. 65 (2006): 12–13.

plans]. It can be safely suggested that the era of socialist central planning was nearly over, although state intervention in the management of state-owned enterprises is still prevalent.[33]

Investment is another key domain where the impact of decentralization was highly discernible. In spite of intermittent overheating (e.g., during the late 1980s), considerable decisional latitude was granted to provincial and subprovincial units and development zones so that they came to authorize large-scale investment projects without attaining Beijing's prior approval.[34] Owing to the major restructuring of the State Council in 1998, the Ministries of Machinery, Metallurgy, Electricity, Electronics, etc., were reorganized as bureau-level units directly under SDRC and therefore no longer allowed to review and approve investment projects. All these state bureaus [*guojiaju*]—except for the one in charge of cigarettes—were abolished in February 2001.[35]

According to the appendix of the State Council Document [2004] No. 20, all agriculture-related investment was to be approved by the provinces or at lower levels of government. Most of the industrial projects, other than those specifically on nuclear energy, cross-provincial dams, roads and railways, airport construction, and automobile manufacturing, were also to be approved by the provincial authorities instead of the State Council or SDRC. The central government set very high thresholds for the projects that required the State Council's approval, thereby leaving most of the investment projects to be endorsed by the provincial or subprovincial authorities. All foreign direct investment projects of less than $100 million—way up from $30 million during the 1990s—were left for the provincial authorities to decide on their own.[36]

Extensive measures of decentralization often led to "evil" cycles of nationwide investment sprees, which in turn generated successive strings of inflation. In contrast with the late 1980s, however, during which Beijing had serious difficulties with reining in local excesses, the central government's tightened control over investment behavior kept local appetite for overinvestment more or less at bay in the 1990s. Although Beijing's political imposition appears to have mattered somewhat—at least with regard to certain national priorities—scholarly assessments differ concerning the center's control capacity and local discretionary power in the realm of investment, particularly with regard to the widespread use of extra-budgetary revenues and the capture of local banks and other financing vehicles by the territorial administration.[37]

The expansion of local discretion in investment was accompanied by the diversification of funding sources. The post-Mao era witnessed a significant reduction in the share of state budgetary allocation to industrial investment projects. Only 21.3 percent of all investments made in 1990 were financed by the state budgetary appropriation, with the remaining funded by bank loans, foreign investment, and locally raised funds [zichou jijin].[38] By 2002, the share of budgetary appropriation in total fixed-asset investment marked a mere 7.3 percent, whereas that of locally raised funds and bank loans accounted for 52.4 and 20.4 percent, respectively. By 2013, the figures for budgetary allocation, bank loans, and locally raised funds became 4.5, 12.1, and 68.0 percent, respectively.[39] The share of locally invested projects in total projects also rose from 57.3 percent in 1991 to 94.3 percent in 2013.[40] The predominant status that the locally raised funds—more often in the form of borrowings—enjoyed is illustrative of the significantly enhanced financial power of the provinces and other local units in the domain of investment.

The state-capacity argument was nowhere more persuasive than in central–local fiscal relations of the 1980s, which were typically characterized by extreme diversities in the mode of revenue sharing and frequent policy oscillations. As the provinces became adept in taking advantage of dyadic bargaining with the center under the "fiscal contract system" [caizheng baogan zhi], Beijing found it increasingly difficult to accommodate all the demands from the provinces while securing a minimum level of revenues for itself. Not only did the share of state revenues in gross domestic product (GDP) drop from 31 percent in 1978 to 16 percent in 1993, but Beijing's share in total state revenues also declined from 57 percent in 1981 to 33 percent in 1993.

At the Third Plenum of the 14th Central Committee in late 1993, Beijing opted for a nationwide tax-sharing reform [*fenshuizhi*] by reversing its earlier pledge that the fiscal contract system would remain in place until 1995. That is, the center drew its final card to reassert fiscal control over the provinces by standardizing the overly diversified patterns of revenue sharing, thereby constricting the provinces' room for "hidden information." Given that several intermittent ad hoc measures adopted during the 1980s had all proved unsuccessful, drastically altering the ways tax revenues were to be distributed between the center and the provinces was the only option left for the center.[41]

By way of reclassifying the tax categories—i.e., dividing up the consolidated industrial-commercial tax—Beijing managed to take a big bite out of the largest tax item. In January 2002, additional measures were adopted to make the enterprise income tax—regardless of the ownership [*lishu guanxi*]—shared between the center and the provinces evenly in 2002 and in the ratio of six to four since 2003.[42] Furthermore, the recentralization of the privileges to offer tax reductions and exemptions back to the State Council strengthened Beijing's power to plug loopholes in the collection of taxes.[43] After these measures were deployed, the center's share in total budgetary revenue rose from 33 percent in 1993 to an annual average of 52 percent from 1994–2002. The figure for 2003–2010 was 53.2 percent.[44]

Beijing's apparent success in milking the provinces is reflected, though ironically, in the extent to which the fiscal conditions of subprovincial units have worsened over the years. That is, the provinces managed to pay for the increased remittances to Beijing by getting more out of the cities and counties through a wide range of non-tax administrative fees [*feishui shouru*].[45] Cities and counties in turn sought to squeeze their subordinate units to make up for the budgetary shortfalls. Subsequently, township finances hollowed out and peasant riots spread out in protest against the rampant "fee collection" [*ruanshoufei*] on the part of lower-level governments as a last-ditch effort to sustain themselves.[46] This unfortunate linkage between the success of the tax-sharing reform and the diffusion of rural instability was largely unforeseen in 1994 and central–provincial dynamics appear to have produced significant impact on state–society relations in an unexpected way.[47]

From 2011 on, Beijing's share in total budgetary revenues dropped below 50 percent—49.4 percent in 2011, 47.9 percent in 2012, and

46.6 percent in 2013—for the first time since 1994. To cope with these new problems, Beijing adopted several measures, including the Ministry of Finance's decision in June 2010 to include all extra-budgetary revenues—except for fees for education—in the purview of formal budgetary management.[48] Additionally, "stamp duties on securities trading" [zhengquan jiaoyi yinhuashui] had initially been divided evenly between the center and the provinces but, after a few adjustments, are now shared in the ratio of 94 to 6.[49] Furthermore, Beijing took a big bite into what had been originally designated solely as a local income—i.e., "business taxes" [yingyeshui]. After a year of experimentation in ten provincial-level units in 2013, the transportation-related business taxes are now shared between the center and the provinces.[50] The center's ability and privilege to change the rules of the game anytime it wishes matters dearly as Beijing can come up with countermeasures whenever it finds itself in troubles vis-à-vis localities.

One of the most crucial dimensions in post-Mao China's systemic reform concerns the restructuring and "multidirectional opening" of foreign economic relations. By granting drastic preferential policies to coastal regions deemed to possess comparative advantages and developmental potentials, Beijing opted for selective or segmented deregulation.[51] Over the last thirty-some years, provinces, coastal cities, riverine cities, border cities, special economic zones (SEZs), development zones, and rural counties all actively participated in the creation of "outwardly oriented economies" based on opening, trade, tourism, and foreign investment.[52]

In efforts to promote foreign trade and investment, the central ministries' monopoly on external trade was terminated, facilitating a rapid increase in the number of foreign trade corporations that already amounted to over seven thousand in 1994. Provinces, cities, and counties were permitted to retain fixed portions of their foreign exchange earnings generated through exports. Both provincial and subprovincial governments were empowered to authorize foreign-invested projects worth US$30 million in the late 1980s and US$100 million in the late 1990s, and even higher for certain projects. The practice of "splitting up" [qiekuai]—dividing a large project into a few small ones so as to bypass the approval by Beijing—was by no means rare.[53] One notable recent development is the swift increase in China's outbound investment overseas. In early 2014, the ceiling of outbound investment projects that could be approved by the provincial authorities was raised to US$1 billion.[54]

The multidirectional opening had initially been based on the scheme of "regional pairing" between coastal provinces and neighboring countries—i.e., linking Liaoning with Japan, Shandong with South Korea, Guangdong with Hong Kong, and Fujian with Taiwan—thereby prompting the subnational authorities to actively develop overseas economic linkages, sometimes even bypassing Beijing.[55] With the "Develop the West," "Revive the Northeast," and "Raise the Mid-Belt" schemes launched in 2000, 2004, and 2008, respectively, "opening" became a highly competitive game for all the provinces and localities in China.[56] As the internationalization and globalization of China's foreign economic relations intensified (including the accession to the WTO), Beijing's dilemma—i.e., wishing to see foreign economic relations expand further and faster while also wanting to rein in excessive local discretion—deepened too.[57] In sum, long-term implications of the emerging local–global nexuses for China's central-local dynamics remain to be further explored.

The Noneconomic Arena: Beijing Continues to Matter

The extent to which post-Mao decentralization affected the noneconomic domains is undoubtedly more difficult to gauge. Although many changes were introduced to the cadre management system in the last thirty-some years, the appointment, transfer, promotion, and dismissal of provincial officials are still firmly controlled by Beijing so far as the crucial positions are concerned. The drastic revision of the central *nomenklatura* in 1983, by which the personnel management authority of the Central Organization Department (COD) was curtailed from "managing two levels down" [*xiaguan liangji*: roughly thirteen thousand positions] to "managing only one level down" [*xiaguan yiji*: approximately seven thousand positions], did not lead to any significant change in Beijing's ultimate control over key provincial officials. Despite the reduction in COD-controlled *nomenklatura* positions by 46 percent, key appointments such as provincial secretaries, deputy secretaries, governors, and deputy governors were still monopolized by COD. Furthermore, since 1990, the management of key party and government positions at the "separately planned cities" [*jihua danlie shi*] and prefecture-level governments were recentralized back to COD, pointing to further strengthened personnel control by Beijing.[58]

Systematic efforts were made to circulate local officials both vertically and horizontally. Central-level cadres—particularly those on reserve [*houbei ganbu*]—were regularly sent down to serve in local governments and attain firsthand local experiences. Those local officials who had earlier demonstrated their caliber in political and economic management were often recruited into the central stage.[59] Since 1990, local cadres have been horizontally circulated among different regions on a large scale. From 1995–2002, for instance, over ten thousand cadres were cross-appointed, including 96 percent of all county-level party secretaries and 97 percent of the county magistrates.[60]

Because of the decline, if not the demise, of ideology as a core mechanism of inducing local compliance, Beijing substituted local cadres' economic performance as a crucial yardstick for career advancement during the reform era.[61] Of course, there are heated debates on the extent to which economic performance actually shaped the careers of provincial leaders. Some found the two largely unrelated, whereas others were in support of the former's impact on the latter. Yet others took note of the variant influence on the provincial secretaries on the one hand and on the provincial governors on the other.[62] Whether assessed on the basis of ideological allegiance or gross domestic product (GDP) figures, once Beijing was determined to enlist local compliance at all costs, provinces were left with few options but to go along, as the careers of their leaders were at stake.

Closely related to the management of local compliance is the amount of systematic effort Beijing put in for administrative monitoring and performance assessment. Because fabricating performance statistics has long been a "silent weapon" of local officials, the center continuously sought to strengthen its monitoring and informational capacity. By 1995, all provincial-level units stipulated on the penalties against the violation of the Statistics Law [*tongjifa*] promulgated in 1983. More importantly, the State Statistical Bureau sought to create its own vertical system by shouldering personnel appointments and budgetary responsibilities in such a way that interferences by the provincial authorities would be minimized.[63] As of 2009, statistics collection was listed as one of twenty-eight domains where exclusive "vertical-line control" [*chuizhi guanli*]—i.e., permitting no intervention by the respective territorial authorities—was to be implemented.[64]

Despite Beijing's efforts to improve its monitoring capacity, inflated (or deflated) reporting on GDP, total grain output, per capita income, inflation rate, and average birth rate is still prevalent. The widely circulated episode that the sum of all provincial GDP announced surpassed China's total GDP by the margin of 11 percent in 2012 is illustrative of the key problem at hand.[65] In principle, economic decentralization is not mutually exclusive with informational centralization, and China's system of administrative monitoring, if properly improved, may offer Beijing a distinct edge over defiant localities. As it stands now, however, the center does not yet appear to have won the war against fabricated data and hidden information.[66]

Since the granting of legislative powers to the provincial people's congresses in 1982, a total of 2,483 provincial laws were promulgated by 1991. Beginning in 1986, provincial capitals [*shenghui*] and nineteen "relatively large cities" [*jiao da de shi*] designated by the State Council were also permitted to enact local rules and regulations. Qingdao, for instance, enacted a total of 130 local laws during the period of 1986–2001.[67] Additionally, "special zones"—Shenzhen (1992), Xiamen (1994), Shantou (1996), and Zhuhai (1996)—were also provided with a range of law-enacting authority. By the end of 2004, 7,449 local laws were legislated by a total of 233 local people's congresses, although most of them were economic and administrative in nature.[68]

The lack of clear delineation of legislative responsibilities generated serious problems as an increasing number of local laws and regulations proved inconsistent or incompatible with the Constitution or national laws. Some localities even passed local laws to grant special tax reductions and exemptions, in violation of the national law.[69] Although the State Council came up with a remedy in 1990, according to which "in such cases (of conflicting laws between different levels of governments), the National People's Congress (NPC) was to mediate upon requests by the State Council," ample room still existed for jurisdictional disputes. In fact, the Standing Committee of the NPC has rarely annulled lower-level rules on the grounds of unconstitutionality.[70] Although the "Law-Making Law" [*lifa fa*] was promulgated in March 2000 to better delineate the central–local boundaries of legislative power, local people's congresses often performed a dual role of being both the spokesmen for the NPC as well as the remonstrators for local interests.[71] Therefore, grave concerns were often voiced regarding the prospect of "sultanization" [*sudanhua*] of legislative power.[72]

As the respective territorial government authorities were responsible for providing revenues and personnel for the local courts, some degrees of capture were unavoidable. Because the lion's share in revenue support for the local court was provided by the provincial government, local protectionism was pervasive. Many scholars have long proposed that the system of managing the local courts should change from the horizontal-territorial [*kuai*] system to a vertical-centralized [*tiao*] one and that the jurisdiction over courts should not match that of local administration.[73] Some key decisions made at the Third and Fourth Plenum of the 18th Central Committee in 2013 and 2014, respectively, to materialize these changes merit our attention as they stipulated the establishment of supra-provincial courts [*kuaqu fayuan*] and circuit courts [*xunhui fating*] in concrete efforts to mitigate local protectionism.[74]

Compared with the totalitarian Maoist era, localities became more proactive and even assertive in articulating their interest vis-à-vis the center in the post-Mao authoritarian period. Not only did the extensive measures of decentralization curtail the power of Beijing in relative terms, but at the same time the center also became more tolerant of local excesses for the hoped-for gains of the reform at the national level. Although central–provincial dynamics at times resembled a zero-sum game, Beijing's reduced imposition did not always and necessarily result in a corresponding increase of local discretion. Issue areas matter dearly as Beijing's political attention varies significantly from one issue to another.[75]

POST-MAO NORM CHANGES IN
CENTRAL–LOCAL RELATIONS

In addition to the functional devolution and rearrangements discussed above, significant changes were introduced to the norms under which Beijing and subnational units have interacted in the post-Mao era. Just as totalitarian public consciousness could still persist for quite some time in a post-totalitarian society, a genuine devolution of authority must entail systematic and continuous efforts to weaken the dominant norms of centralization that take local compliance for granted without due regard for local conditions.[76] Under the pervasive fears of political persecution, however important local interests might be, they could never become as crucial as the careers of top local officials. Naturally, local implementers would have every incentive to play safe by doing precisely what they were told by the center. As long as compliance and conformity constituted the ultimate criterion for career advancement, everyone sought to detect someone else's deviation so that their own allegiance would stand out. During Mao's rule, therefore, tight ideological control led to uniform compliance, rendering local discretion a dangerous luxury.[77]

The post-Mao reformist leadership deserves credit for its daring efforts for the "emancipation of mind" [*sixiang jiefang*] by way of redressing the pernicious practice of using ideological yardsticks in policy implementation.[78] The reformers' endeavors to transform the Maoist norms of central–local relations were manifested in their consistent and largely genuine emphasis on the principle of "implementing according to local conditions" [*yindi zhiyi*]. Subsequently, the hitherto prevalent malpractice of promoting a single model for the entire country—e.g., the Dazhai and the Daqing—was terminated, and multiple models and local experiments became popular.[79]

The post-Mao leadership's will to transform the dominant norms of central–local relations were both genuine and strenuous as, overall, the provincial and local authorities indeed became more proactive and assertive as far as protecting their vital interests was concerned. The staunch resistance that some provinces put up in 1985 and 1988 against Beijing's fiscal austerity schemes, as well as the unabated efforts to sustain their influence over tax collection and land management throughout the 2000s, are indicative of the rising levels of provincial assertiveness.[80] However, assuming that such changes would be present across the board is faulty because the impact of decentralization is not necessarily indiscriminate among all issue areas.[81] Furthermore, Beijing's intermittent—but all-out—efforts to recentralize and reassert control might also produce some effect of offsetting its own plan to transform the dominant norms of central–local relations.

Beijing announces so many policies and regulations all the time, but it only has limited capacity for performance monitoring and active enforcement at all local levels. When the center's policy was deemed clearly unsuitable for certain local conditions and if it was not officially designated as a national priority, provincial leaders would probably enjoy some leeway and subsequently seek to get around the regulations to protect their interests. In such a contingency, most of the time Beijing would not actively go after and punish them even if it were aware of some local deviations and foot-dragging.[82] In contrast, if the policy was categorized as a national priority and localities became evasive without good reason, then, the outcome would, of course, be quite different. In a nutshell, despite extensive measures of decentralization (and some recentralization), the overall impact of post-Mao reforms on central–local relations has not been uniform or straightforward.

3

The Subnational Hierarchy in Time

Institutional Changes (and Continuities)

The institutional hierarchy of local administration is generally subject to intermittent changes and adjustments due to a variety of factors either common to most states or specific to some. Acute needs for the efficient delivery of public goods and services often brought about new structures of subnational administration, such as the metropolitan government system in many parts of Western Europe.[1] Democratic transitions also led to some decentralizing tendencies, particularly when local actors needed to perform crucial roles inside their political parties.[2] Even within the same state, the dominant structure of local governance has occasionally changed over the course of history, with the complex evolution of the British system of local administration being a good case in point.[3]

China is by no means unique in this regard and has seen plenty of changes in its system of local governance.[4] Despite the abundance of precedents and cases to explore, China's local administrative hierarchy and its historical evolution have to date received relatively scant attention in scholarly literature. The paucity of research on this crucial topic is particularly manifest in Western academia, where, under some heavy influence of the behavioralist tradition, factional dynamics and interactive policy processes were overemphasized while structures and institutions of local governance were largely overlooked.[5] In light of the significant changes (and continuities) under the People's Republic in the last thirty-odd years, it seems both timely and worthwhile to go back to the basics and examine in depth the institutional ingredients of local governance in China.

CHANGES AND CONTINUITIES IN CHINA'S LOCAL ADMINISTRATIVE HIERARCHY

During the past 2,100 years since the first unification of the Middle Kingdom by the Qin dynasty, China's rulers have always been highly sensitive to the task of effectively governing their huge territory and population. Because local rebellions often constituted a crucial ingredient of dynastic collapses in traditional China, how to organize and regulate regions and localities was a daunting challenge, constantly haunting the emperors and their modern-day successors.[6] Although certain variations are clearly discernible from the hierarchies and structures sustained under different dynasties, both changes and continuities aptly characterize the evolution of China's system of local governance for the last two millennia.

Over the course of its long history, China's dynasties largely adopted three types of local administration in terms of how many tiers were embedded in the hierarchy. As shown in table 3.1, the most popular was that of three-tier varieties, accounting for 57 percent of the total years considered here.[7] Because the county [*xian*] was the lowest level of local administration that the power of the imperial court was able to reach in traditional China, the two other tiers refer to the "highest political regions" [*gaoceng zhengqu*], including *zhou, dao,* and *sheng,* and the "intermediate-level areas that ruled the counties" [*tongxian zhengqu*], such as *jun, fu,* and *dao.* With the exceptions of the Yuan dynasty and the dynasties prior to the Tang, the three-tier system was the dominant mode of China's local governance.

TABLE 3.1
Types of Local Administration in Traditional China

Two-tier systems	Three-tier systems	Four or more tier systems
Qin, Han, Sui, early Tang	Late Tang, Song, Liao, Jin, Ming, Qing	Yuan

SOURCE: Zhou Zhenhe, *Zhongguo difang xingzheng zhidushi* [History of China's local administrative systems] (Shanghai: Shanghai renmin chubanshe, 2005), 58–82.

For sixty-some years since 1949, the People's Republic has witnessed a complex path of changes in its system of local administration. During 1949–1953, though short-lived, six supra-provincial great administrative regions [daxingzhengqu] were in operation, as these mega-regions were a necessity for swift centralization of long-divided localities.[8] More importantly, nationwide land reforms, coupled with fierce struggles against landlords and rich peasants, extended the reach of the Communist party-state down to the townships and villages, enabling the central rulers to have control below the county level for the first time in Chinese history. Equally crucial was that the rural prefectures [diqu]—formerly "field agencies" [paichu jigou] of the provincial administration—were gradually reorganized into the prefecture-level cities [dijishi], starting in the mid-1980s, eventually forming an additional layer of China's subnational administration.[9]

According to the Constitution, China's local administration officially consists of three tiers: the province [sheng], the county, and the townships/towns [xiangzhen].[10] As noted above, however, the rise of the prefecture-level cities added another tier between the province and the county, making a de facto four-tier system.[11] In the centrally administered municipalities [zhixiashi], a two-tier system has long been the norm, where the real locus of administrative power resided in the urban districts [shiqu], whereas the street administrative offices [jiedao banshichu] generally worked as field agencies of the urban districts.[12] In some ethnic-minority autonomous regions [shaoshu minzu zizhiqu], even five-tier structures were in operation.[13] The Constitution stipulates the three-tier system, whereas the Ministry of Civil Affairs (MCA) openly recognizes a de facto four-tier system with the addition of the prefecture level.[14] In sum, the local administration of the People's Republic has been a sort of "mixed unitary system" [fuhe danyizhi].[15]

The current layout of China's system of local governance, as of 2013, is shown in table 3.2.

The frequency of institutional changes to China's local administration has been particularly high during the post-Mao reform era. As the Communist regime assigned key priorities to economic development, extensive measures of decentralization were implemented nationwide, as noted in chapter 2, leading to the expansion of functions and powers of the subnational administration. Subsequently, corollary changes had to be made to the institutions of local governance.[16] The scope of the changes, however, varied widely among different layers of China's subnational hierarchy.

TABLE 3.2

The Structure of China's Local Administration (2013)

Level	Varieties and numbers	Total
Province level	Provinces: 22 (excluding Taiwan) Centrally administered municipalities: 4 Ethnic minority autonomous regions: 5 Special administrative regions: 2	33
Deputy-provincial level[a]	Deputy-provincial cities: 15	15
Prefecture level	Prefecture-level cities: 271 Prefectures: 14 Autonomous prefectures: 33 (including *meng*)	318[b]
County level	Counties: 1,442 Autonomous counties and *qi*: 166 County-level cities: 368 Urban districts: 872 Others: 5	2,853
Township level	Townships: 12,812 Towns: 20,117 Street communities: 7,566 Others: 2	40,497

NOTES: (a) Deputy-provincial cities are, in official administrative terms, prefecture-level units but are generally categorized separately from other prefecture-level cities because of their special privileges in many economic domains; (b) This figure of 318 has not changed since 2003.

SOURCES: *Zhongguo tongjinianjian 2014* [Statistical yearbook of China 2014] (Beijing: Zhongguo tongji chubanshe, 2014), 3; Xingzheng quhuawang [Website on administrative zoning] at http://www.xzqh.org/html/show/cn/34652_2.html; and http://www.xzqh.org/html/list/10100.html.

Institutional Stability at the Provincial Level

Whereas fifty-three province-level units directly ruled the counties during 1949–1953, with the abolition of the six great administrative regions in 1954, the number was sharply reduced to twenty-nine. That is, the province once again rose to the top (i.e., the highest-ranked political region) of China's subnational hierarchy. For much of the Maoist era, China maintained twenty-one provinces, three centrally administered municipalities, and five ethnic-minority regions.[17] During the reform era, the province-based system was also highly stable relative to the subprovincial units. Since 1978, only three changes have been introduced to the provincial system: (1) the establishment of Hainan Province in 1988, (2) the designation of Chongqing as the fourth centrally administered municipality in 1997, and (3) the establishment of Hong Kong and Macau as special administrative regions in 1997 and 1999, respectively.[18]

Given China's huge land mass and population, the total number of province-level units—thirty-three as of 2013 (excluding Taiwan)—is by no means large in comparative terms. The figure may even be considered small when compared with the number of highest local units in the United States (fifty), Japan (forty-seven), and Russia (eighty-nine). At this juncture, one cannot help but wonder why the provincial system in China has been sustained with such a high level of stability. Could it be the case that the rulers of contemporary China were still very much concerned about—if not preoccupied with—the centrifugal forces of the Chinese body politic that have constantly haunted their imperial predecessors?[19] Had it not been for such memories and reflections on the part of its leaders, the People's Republic would not have so fervently rejected even the nominally federal structure that the Soviet Union had adopted.[20] The sweeping abolition of twenty-four province-level units during 1953–1954 and the failed effort in 1985 to establish Sanxia Province aptly demonstrate Beijing's proclivity to minimize the total number of provincial-level units it has to rule directly.[21]

Closely related to the perennial concern with the centrifugal tendencies is the establishment of administrative areas designed specifically for the management of ethnic minorities. Whereas the Republic of China [*minguo*] had set up two regions [*difang*] for the management of Mongolia and Xinjiang, full-scale redesigning took place during the People's Republic. A total of five province-level autonomous regions (Tibet, Xinjiang, Inner Mongolia, Ningxia, and Guangxi) were established in 1953. As of 2013, there were thirty-three autonomous prefectures [*zhizhizhou* and *meng*], 117 autonomous counties [*zizhixian* and *qi*], five urban ethnic minority districts [*chengshi minzuqu*], and over 1,034 ethnic minority townships [*minzuxiang*], jointly accounting for 65 percent of China's land mass and 75 percent of the ethnic minority population.[22]

Frequent and Extensive Changes at the Subprovincial Levels

Compared with the province-level units with a high level of institutional stability, subprovincial units went through more extensive and frequent changes during the post-Mao era. Under the circumstances where, as noted earlier, China's leaders were unwilling to increase the number of provincial-level units, the functions of local administration nevertheless continued to expand to cope with newly emerging needs of reforms and opening. Naturally, Beijing found it increasingly difficult to avoid establishing new subprovincial units or adjusting (i.e., increasing or decreasing) the number of already existing ones to meet the new institutional challenges.

Six principal changes are noteworthy in terms of institutional adjustments to the subprovincial levels in post-Mao China. First, the number of rural prefectures—formerly field agencies of the provincial administration—declined sharply from 165 in 1985 to 50 in 2007 and to 14 in 2013. As of 2006, fifteen provinces did not have a single prefecture within their jurisdictions. Instead, the number of prefecture-level cities, which were directly administered by the provincial government and put in charge of managing the counties, increased from 90 in 1978 to 162 in 1985, to 268 in 2007, and to 271 in 2013.[23] Although the total number of prefecture-level units did not change much—from 327 in 1985 to 318 in 2013—the rise of the prefecture-level cities as an additional tier of China's subprovincial administration was a significant development.[24]

Second, important changes took place at the county level as well. Throughout China's history that spanned from the Han to the Qing dynasty, the county was the oldest (with 2,700 years of history) and most durable unit of local administration. As a matter of fact, nearly one-third of the counties in China have more than a thousand years of recorded history.[25] The total number of county-level units [xianji danwei] in China's history oscillated between the lowest of 1,124 (Northern Zhou) and the highest of 1,587 (Western Han), whereas the number of county-ruling units varied much more widely, from the lowest of 103 to the highest of 508.[26]

During the People's Republic, the number of county-level units rose from 2,248 in 1949 to 2,850 in 2013. Compared to those of traditional China, their number increased rather significantly.[27] One crucial reason is that several county-level units were newly created, including ethnic-minority autonomous counties [zizhixian], Mongolian counties [qi], urban districts [shixiaqu], and, most importantly, county-level cities [xianjishi]. Whereas the number of county-level units recorded a sharp increase, the total number of counties continued to decrease from 2,180 in 1949 to 2,046 in 1985, to 1,696 in 1996, and to 1,442 in 2013.[28] The principal reason lay in the reorganization of counties into county-level cities, urban districts, or even prefecture-level cities due to developmental incentives and budgetary considerations.[29] Consequently, the number of county-level cities rose sharply from 66 in 1949 to 368 in 2013. And that of county-level urban districts also increased from 615 in 1991 to 872 in 2013.

Third, crucial changes took place at the lowest level of China's local administrative hierarchy—i.e., townships and towns.[30] Nearly revolutionary changes occurred at this level during the Agricultural Cooperativization Movement (1953–1956) and the Great Leap Forward (1958–1959) as well as during the post-Mao years of decollectivization (1979–1984). All these historic events point to abrupt shifts back and forth between the communes [gongshe] and the townships [xiang]. With a steeply increasing level of urbanization in recent years, reportedly around 40 percent as of 2006, the number of townships decreased drastically from 92,476 in 1984 to 12,812 in 2013. On the other hand, the number of towns rose from 7,750 in 1986 to 20,117 in 2013.[31]

Fourth, the developmental imperative of the reform era facilitated the creation of yet another layer of local administration, most importantly the "deputy-provincial cities" [fushengjishi]. Deputy-provincial cities are in significant ways distinct and economically semi-independent of the provinces where they are geographically located, although they "belong to" [lishu] their respective provinces in administrative terms.[32] There are currently fifteen such cities, including ten provincial capitals of Harbin, Shenyang, Changchun, Jinan, Nanjing, Hangzhou, Wuhan, Guangzhou, Xi'an and Chengdu, and five separately planned cities [jihua danlieshi] of Dalian, Qingdao, Ningbo, Xiamen, and Shenzhen. The mandate for these cities was not provided by the Constitution, but by the central government's pertinent decisions and regulations.[33] In a similar vein, some county-level cities took up the administrative rank of "deputy-prefecture" [fudiji] either on the grounds that they were directly run [zhiguan] by the provincial authorities or that they were selected as "strong counties with extensive power" [qiangxian kuoquan].[34]

Fifth, the reform era also witnessed the birth of various special zones and open regions. During Mao's rule, there were specially designated areas like mining zones [kuangqu], salt-producing zones [yanqu], forest zones [linqu], and mountainous zones [shanqu]. Throughout the reform era, the rapid proliferation of special zones—mostly development-, investment-, technology-, tourism-, and even free trade–oriented—is particularly noteworthy.[35] Two derivatives of this trend merit attention. One concerns the rise of megacities like Shenzhen, which made a successful transition from a small special economic zone to a deputy-provincial city.[36] The other denotes a pervasive trend of administrative upgrading [shengji] among many such cities and county-level development zones. Given that every local unit in China was in for a highly competitive game of administrative upgrading in efforts to render them more attractive for foreign investment, the designation as special zones was indeed a big deal for many local governments.[37]

The return of Hong Kong and Macau in 1997 and 1999, respectively, to China's sovereign rule gave birth to new provincial-level special units—namely, the special administrative regions [SARs: *tebie xingzhengqu*]. Under the "one country, two systems" framework, the SARs provide a sort of semi-federal structure for these two former colonies within a finite period of fifty years.[38] The creation of these two units added an extra category to the institution of China's local governance.

Sixth, one prominent feature that characterizes the evolutionary process of China's local administration during the post-Mao reform era has been frequent debates and experiments, intermittent institutional changes, flooding of new ideas and proposals, combinations of top-down directing and bottom-up fervor, and occasional policy reversals. Overall, compared with the Maoist era, the level of institutional stability has decreased while that of uncertainties has increased.[39] Some key cases of institutional change are examined in detail in the remaining section.

INSTITUTIONAL CHANGES AT THE
SUBPROVINCIAL LEVEL: FOUR CASES

Since the early 1980s, China's subnational governments came to perform an increasingly pivotal role in shaping the developmental processes by substituting for the shortage of bourgeois entrepreneurs and private business groups. In those processes, new local units and special designations were created. Four principal cases are considered here: (1) the creation of deputy-provincial cities, (2) turning prefectures into prefecture-level cities, (3) changing counties into county-level cities, and (4) designating counties and county-level cities as urban districts.

Establishing Deputy-Provincial Cities

Although some precedents were available for the centrally administered municipalities—i.e., eight such cities were in existence in the 1920s—deputy-provincial units had no predecessors.[40] Seeds for the deputy-provincial cities were first planted in April 1981 when Beijing designated fifteen "key economic cities" [*jingji zhongxin chengshi*] in an effort to create regional engines of growth. Of these fifteen, ten (then prefecture-level) cities were later designated as deputy-provincial cities.[41] More pertinent was another designation made by the State Council during 1983–1989 of fourteen prefecture-level cities as separately planned cities [*jihua danlie shi*].[42] In the past, the designation of separately planned cities had occurred at least on two occasions: (1) six large cities like Chongqing and Wuhan were designated as such during 1954–1958; and (2) nine cities, including Chongqing, Tianjin, Shenyang, Guangzhou, Xi'an, and Wuhan, were granted such a status during 1963–1967.[43]

The designation of separately planned cities had entailed a wide range of privileges, many of which deputy-provincial cities later inherited. First, the designation came with provincial-level authority in making economic plans. That is, key planning responsibilities, except for those reserved exclusively for the State Planning Commission, were to be handled directly by the separately planned cities. These cities were also entitled to separate listing in the national economic plan.[44]

Second, the designation was accompanied by economic decision-making power formerly reserved only for the provincial authorities. In remitting revenues and determining exports, the separately planned cities engaged in direct one-on-one negotiations with Beijing. In approving domestic construction projects, the same ceilings as those for the provinces—i.e., 50 million yuan for energy-, raw materials- and transportation-related sectors and 30 million yuan for others—were granted. In endorsing foreign investment projects, the ceiling of $30 million—hitherto reserved only for the provinces—was permitted for the coastal separately planned cities, whereas that of $10 million for their inland counterparts.[45]

The most crucial blessing was the expanded fiscal authority for nine separately planned cities, except for five provincial capitals (Guangzhou, Nanjing, Xi'an, Chengdu, and Shenyang) whose pertinent privileges were withdrawn due to the provinces' opposition. The nine cities were granted provincial-level budgetary powers and authorized to deal directly with the Ministry of Finance. Due to the lifting of provincial interference, these nine cities' revenues increased sharply thereafter.[46]

Third, the designation also came with the transfer of enterprises formerly owned by the central and provincial governments. In principle, all national and provincial enterprises located within the city's premise—except for military-industrial, railway, civil aviation, electricity, and postal ones—were to be turned over to the separately planned cities. Due to the complex webs of interests among different levels of government, however, finalizing the scope and pace of transfer was neither easy nor smooth.[47]

Fourth, most government units within the separately planned cities were administratively upgraded by half a rank. This change originated from a decision by the State Council's Small Group on Reforming the Wage System [*gongzi zhidu gaige xiaozu*] to raise the salary baseline for the separately planned cities.[48] Subsequently, the party secretaries and the mayors of these cities came to hold the deputy-provincial—rather than the prefecture-level—rank. Given that every local unit was in for a game of administrative upgrading in China in the reform era, the designation as such was viewed as a big deal for the recipient localities.[49]

The rise of the separately planned cities enjoying a deputy-provincial status and provincial-level authority in economic management meant corresponding degrees of weakened power for the provinces. The provinces' concern was primarily budgetary as the economic separation of prosperous cities from their jurisdiction, as well as the transfer of profitable enterprises, would induce considerable losses.[50] The provinces' resistance was so firm that Beijing had to adopt some measures to minimize the adverse impact on the provinces. Consequently, Guangzhou, Nanjing, Shenyang, Xi'an, and Chengdu never attained the privilege of "compiling their own budgetary plans" [*caizheng jihua danlie*]. Even concerning the nine cities that did obtain budgetary autonomy, the center adopted some measures to mitigate the negative impact on the provincial coffers.[51]

The paucity of evidence does not enable us to gauge the overall extent of conflict between the separately planned cities and their provincial superiors. Yet, in April 1985—just a year after the designation of six cities—*People's Daily* issued a stern warning against the provincial authorities and the separately planned cities being at loggerheads.[52] Contradictions were more serious with the separately planned cities that were also provincial capitals that housed both the provincial and city governments.[53] After a decade of tension and conflict, the Party Center and the State Council jointly issued Document No. 7 on July 2, 1993, which canceled the separately planned–city status of all eight provincial capitals, leaving only six cities of Qingdao, Dalian, Ningbo, Chongqing, Shenzhen, and Xiamen.[54]

In February 1994, the Central Commission on Public Sector Reform [*zhonggyang jigou bianzhi weiyuanhui*] named sixteen cities as deputy-provincial cities. They were the eight provincial capitals whose separately planned–city status was canceled in 1993, the six remaining separately planned cities, and two additional cities of Hangzhou and Jinan.[55] Because Chongqing was promoted to a centrally administered municipality in 1997, the total number of deputy-provincial cities was reduced to fifteen.[56] Only eleven of the twenty-seven province-level units (excluding the centrally administered municipalities and special administrative regions) have deputy provincial cities. They are more concentrated in the coastal region with ten deputy provincial cities. Two-thirds of them are provincial capitals, although none currently enjoys the separately planned–city status.[57] Their designation was an effort by Beijing in part to console the provincial capitals deprived of the separately planned–city status.[58] Given that Kunming, Yunnan's capital, has striven hard in vain to attain the deputy-provincial status for several years since 1998, the designation as such must have been highly appealing to many prefecture-level cities in China.[59]

Since Dalian, Qingdao, and Ningbo were "coastal open cities," and Shenzhen and Xiamen special economic zones, the retention of the separately planned status made them the most privileged cities in China. Why, then, did Beijing let these five continue with the separately planned status? An answer may be that the center wished to utilize these cities as local engines of growth in the key coastal provinces of Liaoning, Shandong, Zhejiang, Fujian, and Guangdong. The exclusion of Jiangsu is attributed to the dominant power that Shanghai has wielded over the lower Yangzi region.[60] In retrospect, it seems, Beijing's design has thus far worked fairly effectively.

Turning Prefectures Into Cities [Di gai shi]

Prior to 1982, between the province and the county, there were only prefectures, province-administered cities [shengxiashi], and autonomous districts [zizhizhou]. Prefectures were rural field agencies of the provincial government and did not constitute a formal tier of local administration. Province-administered cities—only a few in each province, including provincial capitals—governed very limited space in the urban proper. Except for autonomous districts, none of the prefecture-level units were officially put in charge of ruling the counties. Hence, as the Constitution stipulates, the three-tier structure was formally maintained.

In the post-Mao era, the number of prefecture-level cities rose sharply from 97 in 1978 to 185 in 1990, to 259 in 2000, and to 271 in 2013. In principle, prefecture-level cities refer to the "cities with urban districts" [shequ de shi] because county-level cities are not permitted to establish districts.[61] Prefecture-level cities are therefore either provincial capitals without the deputy-provincial status or the relatively large cities that met certain standards in terms of nonagricultural population, gross value of industrial output (GVIO), gross domestic product (GDP), and revenue income.[62]

Important is the fact that the rise of prefecture-level cities was closely linked to the policy of subjecting the counties to the management by these cities. This policy of having the counties ruled by the cities is not entirely new, as Luda (Liaoning), Nanjing (Jiangsu), and Hangzhou (Zhejiang) experimented with it in 1950, although the practice was terminated in 1954.[63] During the Great Leap Forward, the policy was revived, and as many as 243 counties were directly administered by 48 cities. By 1965, due to the post-Leap retrenchment, only 78 counties were ruled by 24 cities. As of 1981, 147 counties were directly administered by 57 cities.[64]

Although the pre-reform antecedent and the post-Mao scheme were labeled identically as *shi guan xian* (or *shi lingdao xian*), the former was much more limited in its scope as the policy was implemented mainly in large metropolitan centers like Beijing, Shanghai, Nanjing, and Dalian.[65] During the post-Mao era, the policy was carried out nationwide, with few well-defined conditions, so that nearly all the prefectures became eligible to become cities.[66] More importantly, this new development rendered the formal subnational hierarchy—the three-tier system as stipulated in Article 30 of the Constitution—nearly obsolete and gave birth to a de facto four-tier structure.

Given the characteristic of post-Mao policy implementation that localities did not automatically follow Beijing's directives, the pace at which China's prefectures were turned into prefecture-level cities was quite extraordinary. Right after Jiangsu experimented with the scheme in 1982, Liaoning and Guangdong followed suit. By 1991, 170 prefecture-level cities—i.e., 89 percent of all prefecture-level cities in China—ruled 696 counties. Between 1982 and 1998, the number of prefectures dropped from 170 to 66. By 2000, there were 259 prefecture-level cities, accounting for 78 percent of China's prefecture-level units. By 2013, out of 333 prefecture-level units, only 14 were rural prefectures, accounting for 4.2 percent compared to 56.4 percent in 1978.[67]

A close look at the process reveals the extent to which local fervor for an urban status and administrative upgrading played a predominant role. In the initial stage (from 1982 through the late 1980s), the mode of merging a prefecture-level city with a rural prefecture was most popular—i.e., a smaller prefecture-level city came to take in a much bigger rural prefecture and place all the counties under its control.[68] Because prefecture-level cities and rural prefectures often had their headquarters in the same cities, this particular mode clearly had a benefit of "reducing organizational redundancy" [jingjian jigou]. Incorporating prefectures into prefecture-level cities became so popular that even converting the prefectures without organizational redundancy became widespread.

In the second stage (from the late 1980s through the late 1990s), two additional modes were devised to satisfy local officials' fervor for an administratively upgraded urban status deemed conducive to economic development. In so doing, either the existing county-level cities were simply upgraded to become prefecture-level cities, or even rural counties were often directly transformed into prefecture-level cities, largely irrespective of their urban composition.[69] Local fervor for an upgraded urban status, mostly capitalizing on the lack of clearly defined standards and conditions, produced an effect of defeating the original intention of Beijing.[70]

Changing Counties Into Cities [Xian gai shi]

The dramatic increase of county-level cities is another notable development in the post-Mao subnational hierarchy. In 1949, county-level cities accounted for a mere 3 percent of all county-level units in China. After explosive growth during the 1980s and 1990s, the figure rose to 19 percent (393 out of 2,053) in 2001 (see table 3.3). In contrast with the scheme of "turning prefectures into cities" under the auspices of Beijing's directing, that of "turning counties into cities" was more of the center's endorsement of what had already been happening at the local level.

Systemic reform and extensive opening generated popular perceptions that cities—as opposed to rural counties—enjoyed better images

TABLE 3.3
The Number of County-Level Cities in Select Years

Year	1949	1975	1985	1990	1995	1996	1999	2007	2013
Number	66	86	159	279	427	445	427	369	368

SOURCES: Liu and Wang, Zhidu yu changxin, 40; Dai, Zhongguo shizhi, 65; Pu, Dangdai zhongguo xingzheng, 333; Liu, Zhongguo xingzheng quhua de lilun yu shijian, 176; Jingji yanjiu cankao, no. 86 (2000), 40–41; Zhonghua renmin gongheguo xingzheng quhua jiance 2001, 3; Lam, "The County System and County Governance," in China's Local Administration, eds. Chung and Lam, 157; and Zhongguo tongji nianjian 2014, 3.

and more advantages in attracting overseas investment. As early as 1983, thirty-nine county-level cities were already created by way of carving a more developed portion out of rural counties. Provincial governments actively took advantage of a *post-facto* directive issued in 1986 by the Ministry of Civil Affairs (MCA), which laid down only the minimum requirements for a county to be eligible for the city status. In most cases, these minimum requirements set by the MCA were considered too low and vague, making most counties eligible. Although the MCA raised the bar substantially in 1993, even the new yardsticks were set so low that nearly half of the rural counties were entitled to become county-level cities.[71] What further complicated the issue was that the approving authority in Beijing—the MCA in particular—was not in a position to verify the statistics supplied by the counties. Furthermore, the MCA also found it difficult to resist the political pressure coming from the provinces in light of the prevailing developmental logic at the time.[72]

County-level cities were created largely via two channels: (1) carving out a more developed and urbanized portion of a rural county and turning it into a county-level city [*qiekuai sheshi* or *chezhen sheshi*], and (2) turning an entire county into a county-level city [*zhengxian gaishi*]. Although the former had been utilized in the pre-reform era, the latter became the *modus operandi* of the reform period. The predominance of the latter mode is due to the fact that most counties were strongly opposed to surrendering a developed township and that turning an entire county into a county-level city would produce positive effects on reducing organizational redundancy.[73] Naturally, Beijing allowed provincial governments to endorse the transformation of entire counties into county-level cities. Of all the county-level cities newly established during 1978–1997, the latter mode accounted for 86.6 percent.[74]

Unlike rural counties, county-level cities were officially authorized to collect "municipal construction fees" [*shizheng jianshe jingfei*] and make independent decisions on land appropriation, both of which were clearly huge incentives for the counties to apply for a city status.[75] Nationwide fervor for city status led to a dramatic increase in the number of county-level cities, often dubbed as a "blind fever" [*mangmuxing guore xianxiang*]. Eventually, the central government had to intervene in 1997 when the MCA buried as many as five hundred pending applications. Only after the MCA issued a temporary ban on the practice of turning counties into cities did the trend begin to level off (see table 3.3).[76]

The rise of the county-level cities generated a new unforeseen problem. Because the Constitution dictates that "cities cannot rule cities" [*buneng shi guan shi*], the county-turned-cities could only be administered directly by province-level units. Yet, the provincial authorities were practically unable to deal directly with so many county-level cites, and the nationwide adoption of the cities-leading-counties policy necessitated a situation where the prefecture-level cities administered county-level cities "on the provinces' behalf" [*daiguan*], thereby introducing another anomalous mode of local governance.[77] As discussed later, all these problems were to be further entangled with a new scheme of the "provinces directly ruling the counties" [*sheng zhiguan xian*], popularized since the late 2000s.

Redesignating Counties/Cities as Urban Districts [Xian/Shi gai qu]

One additional development concerns the rise of urban districts [*shixiaqu*]. Turning counties and county-level cities into urban districts took place largely in two different settings. One concerns the establishment of urban districts in the centrally administered cities and deputy-provincial cities. With the large-scale redesignation of suburban districts and rural counties as urban districts, China now boasts some of the biggest cities in the world. In 1986, Shanghai's total area had been only 375 square kilometers, but it expanded to 5,155 square kilometers by 2013 (compare with New York's 790 square kilometers). Chongqing even has a "flying" (i.e., noncontiguous: *feidi*) urban district—Shuangqiao District— 162 kilometers away from the city boundary.[78]

The other setting, more pertinent to our discussion here, refers to the cases where prefecture-level cities turned their counties and county-level cities into urban districts. Whereas the total number of urban districts had increased by 41 percent from 275 in 1949 to 388 in 1976, the comparable figure for the post-Mao era was 125 percent from 388 in 1976 to 872 in 2013. This drastic increase is attributed in significant part to the nationwide fervor for turning prefectures into cities. As many rural prefectures suddenly became prefecture-level cities, many of their not-so-urban counties were simply redesignated as districts [*chexian gai qu*] with more urban nuance. Although there were four different ways of creating urban districts in prefecture-level cities, the dominant—and most convenient— mode was simply to redesignate rural counties and county-level cities as districts, although many of these counties were anything but urban.[79]

During the 1990s, the pace of turning counties/cities into districts accelerated in many of China's cities due to three factors. First, it resulted from the fast-growing demand for usable land, not only to accommodate the growing number of urban dwellers but also to devote more land to manufacturing industries and lucrative real estate development.[80] Second, unlike in the case of turning counties into cities, there were no official standards set for the eligibility, naturally providing more room for local maneuvering.[81] Third, the regulation that "(prefecture-level) cities cannot rule (county-level) cities" worked as a catalyst for this change.[82] The tidal wave of establishing urban districts went unabated throughout the 1990s and 2000s because, unlike that of turning counties into cities, the center did not intervene to stop or slow down the process. Between 2012 and 2013, twelve urban districts were newly created, including Wujiang District in Suzhou.

Locomotives for Institutional Change: Local Preferences Prevail

Given that no policies change without good reasons, the question why the number of prefecture- and county-level cities and of urban districts increased so swiftly during the post-Mao era merits attention. In retrospect, these developments have been hinged upon the following four factors: (1) promoting urbanization, (2) mitigating organizational redundancy, (3) increasing local revenues, and (4) cultivating environments conducive to economic development. Overall, in most of these processes, local preferences seem to have prevailed over Beijing's.

It is no coincidence that China's urbanization—as broadly defined— made a huge leap during the reform era at least on official statistics, as the total number of new urban units increased drastically. Ultimately, however, we are confronted with the conceptual issue of what urbanization really stands for.[83] The system of *hukou* [household registration] mattered as the size of nonagricultural population was artificially increased in many localities where rampant selling of nonagricultural *hukou* proved irresistible, not only because it made them eligible for city status but because the sales also provided a windfall.[84] In many relatively large cities, turning counties and cities into urban districts brought down the long-standing rural–urban divide by providing suburban residents with the city *hukou* and corresponding urban privileges.[85]

Although organizational streamlining—cutting down the number of government units and staff—at local levels was also on the central leadership's agenda, pertinent records show that the outcome went quite the other way. When a prefecture was merged with a prefecture-level city, the effect of streamlining was the greatest. When a prefecture was simply redesignated as a prefecture-level city, however, the streamlining effect was less than ideal because it immediately had to set up a local people's congress as well as a people's political consultative conference. Prefecture-level cities, unlike counties and county-level cities, were also allowed to establish urban districts and therefore had substantially more government units under them. The staff size for a prefecture-level city ranged between 700 and 2,100, whereas that for a prefecture remained much smaller at 500 to 900.[86]

As for the county-turned-cities and county- and city-turned-districts, the records were largely negative. Whether the entire county was turned into a county-level city or a portion of a county was taken out to become a county-level city, redesignation was generally not so useful for streamlining because the county-turned-cities had to perform many new activities (e.g., urban construction), naturally demanding more staff and bureaucratic units to house them.[87] When counties became urban districts under the centrally administered and deputy-provincial cities, their staff tended to expand. When counties and cities became districts under the prefecture-level cities, organizational and personnel arrangements remained unchanged or even shrank (at least in principle). Overall, the proliferation of urban units generally contributed to bureaucratic thickening rather than slimming.[88]

If Beijing had the goals of urbanization and organizational streamlining in mind, subnational governments had their own motives: maximizing revenue incomes. Unlike rural prefectures, prefecture-level cities became a de facto independent fiscal regime [*duli hesuan caizheng danwei*] between the provinces and counties. Naturally, they strove hard to maximize fiscal extractions from the counties, county-level cities, and county-turned-districts for themselves, as well as on behalf of provincial authorities.[89] By 1998, about 70 percent of the counties became unhappy with the level of fiscal extractions by their superiors, the prefecture-level cities.[90]

When counties were turned into county-level cities, substantial changes were fewer except for two new sources of incomes—i.e., "urban construction fees" [*chengshi jianshe fei*] and administrative surcharges levied on motorcycle registrations.[91] In contrast, county- and city-turned-districts stood on a revenue-losing side as urban districts no longer constituted an independent fiscal unit. Because no standardized rules were available on turning counties and county-level cities into urban districts, despite the strong opposition by counties and county-level cities affected, centrally administered municipalities and prefecture-level cities usually had their way. The outcry of Kunshan and Panyu against being turned into the districts of Shanghai and Guangzhou, respectively, is illustrative.[92]

From a local government perspective, developmental incentives were probably the most crucial attraction. By attaining a city status, a locality could improve its overall image and policy environments and therefore enjoy an elevated status in the eyes of many who would "value cities more than rural counties" [shi zun xian bei] in locating their investments. The developmental logic embedded in the rise of many new cities is best illustrated by the high representation of cities in China's coastal region: in 1998, 45 percent of China's cities were concentrated in the eastern region, as opposed to 37 and 18 percent located in the central and western regions, respectively.[93] Generally speaking, county-turned-cities, particularly those in Guangdong, Zhejiang, and Jiangsu that enjoyed privileges on a par with the prefecture-level cities, were more appealing to foreign and domestic investors than rural counties.[94]

Another developmental logic embedded in these institutional changes was to increase the so-called "radiation" [fushe] effects of these cities as new local engines of growth. A key problem was that many of the newly created cities possessed neither the abilities nor the conditions to assist the growth of their subordinate or neighboring counties and county-level cities. Worse yet, many of these cities chose to subject the counties and county-level cities to a maximum extraction instead of helping them to grow.[95]

In sum, Beijing was neither highly meticulous in inducing these institutional changes nor able to produce the consequences on a par with its original intentions. Although the center was content with the rising level of urbanization (though mostly administrative rather than socioeconomic), localities were reaping substantial gains such as more bureaucratic units, bigger staff, administrative upgrading, and increased revenues and investment. Overall, local preferences prevailed over those of Beijing's.

THE SUBNATIONAL HIERARCHY UNDER
READJUSTMENT AND RESTRUCTURING

Debates within China on the future direction of reforming the subnational hierarchy were initially a two-way split. Although some scholars preferred to retain the prefecture-level units, others argued strongly for their abolition.[96] The latter was again divided into two groups. One favored a two-tier local system where the prefecture level would be canceled and townships/towns merged into the grass-roots level as self-ruling units [zizhi danwei], leaving only the provinces and the counties.[97] The other group preferred a three-tier system where only the prefecture level would be abolished. Under this latter scenario, prefecture-level cities were to be retained and managed directly by the provinces, but the jurisdiction over counties and county-level cities was to be fully transferred to the provinces.[98]

Initiated as a pilot program in Zhejiang in 1992, the latter scenario—i.e., weakening the prefecture-level cities and putting the county-level units back under direct provincial control—grew in importance over time. Central Document [2006] No. 1 stipulated that "localities with proper endowments [jubei tiaojian de difang] might set up a few experimental sites for the provinces-directly-ruling-counties policy" and, by the end of 2007, twenty-four province-level units set up experimental sites for the scheme.[99] Three years later, Central Document [2009] No. 1 went further by suggesting that "provinces with proper conditions be encouraged to simplify the administrative hierarchy by promoting the 'provinces-directly-ruling-counties' policy." By mid-2009, the new scheme was to be carried out nationwide except in the ethnic-minority regions, and even the target date was set for the end of 2012, thereby virtually abrogating the twenty-year experiences of the cities-leading-counties scheme.[100]

Whereas over 80 percent of China's counties were ruled by prefecture-level cities in 2004, by 2007, a quarter of China's counties were under direct control by the provincial authorities. In 2010, 50.2 percent of the counties (excluding those under the centrally administered municipalities) came under the provinces-directly-ruling-counties scheme.[101] Worth noting at this juncture is that, as of 2014, the original target of completing the restructuring by the end of 2012 was not met, nor did the nationwide process of implementation appear smooth.[102] As a matter of fact, Beijing's stance has changed from active promotion to that of "watching quietly" [jingguan qibian] and "coordinating a gradual path" [shitiao jianjin].[103]

Three problems stood out in particular. First, although the relevant central documents stipulated that localities with proper conditions were allowed [*yunxu*] to experiment with and carry out the new scheme, Beijing never clarified what those proper conditions really were. Consequently, localities exercised maximum discretion in interpreting them either to adopt the new scheme fast or to drag their feet over it. Some transferred only the fiscal dimension of control over the counties to the provincial authorities, whereas others forfeited comprehensive administrative control.[104]

Second, announcing a new policy was one thing, but acting upon it apparently was quite another. As expected, prefecture-level cities, to be most adversely affected by the new scheme, were neither so willing nor eager to relinquish control over the county-level units under their jurisdiction. In the case of Henan, for instance, nine out of the ten experimental counties had serious difficulties with implementing the policy, as their prefecture-level superiors did not wish to transfer key approval authority for license issuing, etc.[105]

Third, perhaps most importantly, the weakening and eventual cancellation of the prefecture-level cities as an intermediate tier of the subnational hierarchy points right to the thorny issue of how broad the geographical scope of provincial oversight should be. Given that the ideal number of subordinate units for effective provincial control is said to range between 24 and 40, the cancellation of the prefecture level would force the provincial governments in Hebei, Sichuan, Yunnan, Shandong, Shanxi, and Hunan to manage 135, 135, 116, 96, 89, and 87 counties, respectively. On average, each province must administer 82 counties, and these were simply too many for a single province to manage properly or effectively.[106]

This in turn brings back an age-old debate on what the ideal (i.e., optimal) number of provincial-level units is for China. As noted earlier, the number of highest local units (thirty-three, including the two special administrative regions) in China is smaller than those of the United States, France, Russia, and even Japan relative to the size of territory.[107] Some even suggested that the optimal number for China should be around fifty.[108] If China should nullify the prefecture-level and increase the number of provincial-level units, where might Beijing look for potential candidates? Some deputy-provincial cities that are not provincial capitals may become the first candidates, such as Dalian for Liaodong Province, Qingdao for Jiaodong Province, or Xiamen for Xiashan Province. Some provincial capitals like Wuhan, Shenyang, and

Xi'an, as well as Shenzhen, may also be upgraded to centrally administered municipalities.[109]

The foregoing discussions demonstrated that China's local administrative hierarchy has undergone frequent and extensive changes in the last sixty-some years. If the past is any useful guide, China's local hierarchy is likely to continue to face important changes. The future evolution of China's system of local governance is likely to be conditioned by the following factors.

First, given that China's local governments are not self-governing units and that the center has the prerogative to alter the status and the scope of local jurisdictions at any time, China's system of local governance—particularly at the subprovincial level—is bound to have a low degree of institutional stability.

Second, much of the important transformation in China's local administrative system was related in one way or another to the processes of economic development and urbanization. Urbanization in particular will continue to be a key driving force behind the tectonic shift from the conventional system of "separate governance of urban and rural areas" [chengxiang fenzhi] toward that of "integrated governance" [chengxiang hezhi]. More specifically, the intricate issues of how to cope with fast-growing urbanization below the county level and of how to manage environmental protection, transport services, and welfare provision will invariably put the current structure of China's local administration to a real test.[110]

Third, the future evolution of China's local governance is likely to be the vector of policy advocacy and the interests of the central and local governments. The gradual process in which such contentious ideas as "placing the counties directly under provincial control" were first hotly debated among academics and, later, their local experimentation and nationwide implementation were endorsed by the central government is a good case in point.[111] In contrast, despite the advocacy for resizing the provinces and making the scope of provincial jurisdiction smaller, China's provincial-level units have shown a remarkable degree of institutional stability.[112] Whereas the center promoted the proliferation of prefecture-level cities, its role was rather limited regarding the rise of county-turned-cities, and much more so concerning that of county-turned-districts.[113] That is, local preferences mattered more in the cases of the county-turned-cities and county-turned-districts policies. As the norms of decentralization were gradually rooted more deeply over time—often referred to as "sinking powers downward" [quanli xiachen]—local interests may play an increasingly crucial role in determining China's local administrative system, often adding fuel to the centrifugal tendencies.

Fourth, path dependence—i.e., a process in which past decisions and present developments have closed certain options for a future action, thereby setting future developments along a particular course[114]—may constitute yet another key conditioning factor. That is, however sensible and desirable they may be, future institutional reforms rarely take place in a vacuum. Most notably, the scheme of placing the counties directly under provincial control was bound to face difficulties due to the very fact that the cities-leading-counties system has already been in place nationwide for more than two decades.

Fifth, one familiar challenge that China's system of local governance faces concerns the vastly different size—in terms of area, population, or both—of government jurisdictions. Geographical boundaries of local governments, whether provincial or subprovincial, have long historical backgrounds and therefore do not render themselves to easy adjustments. Given that the provincial-level units have thus far been remarkably stable and that, despite the vastly different sizes of the counties, the prospect for their wholesale restructuring seems rather unlikely, reconfiguration is perhaps more likely to occur at the intermediate prefecture-level units.[115]

Sixth, in the longer run, even the factor of democratic transition may constitute a key variable as the process as such is likely to interject new structures and logic of local governance.[116] Being a continent-sized nation with abundant precedents of centrifugal tendencies and even of federalist movements during the 1920s, China does not easily allow us to speculate on a future mode of local governance. Given the high level of institutional stability sustained at the provincial and county levels, townships/towns could also be vulnerable to future changes, as they have of late become a relatively weaker level of local governance due to the nationwide abolition of the agricultural taxes.[117]

In sum, short of regime changes of such magnitude, China's local administrative system is likely to endure while adapting here and muddling through there. Changes may still take place intermittently and incrementally in efforts to cope with some of the recurring problems, particularly at the intermediate level. As gradualism lies at the heart of the making and implementation of policy during the post-Mao reform era, reforming China's local administrative system may also be more piecemeal than abrupt. Then, again, we are constantly reminded that it is China that we are dealing with here, a nation so often characterized by high levels of uncertainty and unpredictability.

4

The Center's Perceptions of Local Bureaucracy in China

A Typological First-Cut

Whether between states, groups, or individuals, perception plays a crucial role as it formulates, guides, prompts, and constrains the behavior of actors involved. Despite its importance, perception is generally complex and amorphous and therefore does not render itself to easy deciphering. This chapter takes on the question of how the central state's perception of the local state has been changing in the People's Republic.[1] By way of tracing the evolutionary trajectory of the center's views of local bureaucracy, this study suggests that Beijing's perception of the local state as a principal has been gradually reinforced, while that of an agent relatively diluted and that of a representative still largely underdeveloped. The chapter also posits that the center's view of the local state varies according to the latter's administrative level—i.e., whether the province, the prefecture/city, the county/city, or the township/town.[2]

This chapter consists of the following four sections. The first lays out a typology of three images—namely, the agent, the representative, and the principal—in efforts to conceptualize the central state's view of the local bureaucracy in the People's Republic. The second section examines the process of local empowerment in which Beijing's perception of the local state has gradually evolved from that of agent to principal during the reform era. The third section delves into some discernible differences in the central state's views regarding four levels of the subnational government. The final section offers concluding observations as to what this perceptual evolution implies for China's local governance.

THE CENTER'S VIEWS OF THE LOCAL STATE:
A TRIPLE TYPOLOGY

Numerous vocabularies are used in China to refer to the local state. Some are relatively neutral terms, such as "implementers" [*zhixingzhe*], "local decision makers" [*difang juecezhe*], "speakers" [*chuanshengtong*], and "lower-level governments" [*xiaji zhengfu*]. Others denote some connecting functions that the local state carries out, most notably "bridges" [*qiaoliang*] and "corridors" [*qudao*]. Yet others entail more negative and sarcastic connotations, which include such terms as "regional dukes" [*difang zhuhou*], "local bandits" [*tufei*], "corrupt forces" [*fubai liliang*], and "door locks" [*dingmengang*]. Instead of utilizing all these terms, many of which are neither analytical nor academic, this study presupposes that, from the center's perspective, the first category of vocabularies may be encapsulated within the concept of agents; the second, within that of representatives; and the third, within that of principals.[3]

As noted earlier, perception is often a crucial determinant of action, although concrete evidence is always difficult to secure. Conducting systematic surveys on a sufficiently large number of central government officials is almost impossible, and carrying out in-depth interviews with some of them may pose an intricate methodological question as to the selection and optimal number of the interviewees, not to mention the possible interactive bias embedded in their replies. Granted that these two most popular methods of tapping perceptions are not feasible, the remaining option is to rely on interpreting and inferring from published materials—specialized books and scholarly articles in Chinese, as well as a few rare internal surveys—with some doses of rational-choice reasoning. In doing so, admittedly, what the center views the local state *is* may often get mixed up with what the center views the local state *ought to be*. Wherever necessary and possible, efforts were made to distinguish one from the other, both conceptually and analytically.

In the section below, the concept of the three terms (agent, representative, and principal) and the rationale for the local bureaucracy to take up each of the three roles in dealing with the central state are discussed.

The First Image: Agents

As in many other unitary states, agent is the most widely accepted and popularly subscribed image of local bureaucracy in China. Agent, by definition, refers to "one who acts for, in the place of, or on behalf of another, by authority of the latter."[4] If we choose to adopt this definition, the local bureaucracy is then the one that acts for and on behalf of the central state by authority of the central state of the People's Republic. This particular image presupposes that the local bureaucracy is generally compliant with the central state and its top-down command, that it is vulnerable to a wide range of control instruments in the hands of the center, and that it mostly lacks its own autonomy and discretion in interpreting and implementing central policy.[5]

The image of the Chinese local bureaucracy as a loyal agent is largely a product and legacy of the "totalitarian" era of the People's Republic. Totalitarian control was, by definition, comprehensive in its coverage, omnipresent in its scope, and not only behavior inducing but also thought transforming in its intention.[6] Particularly in the context of Maoist China (1949–1976), due to the chronic eruption of mass political movements closely linked to purges and persecutions, little room was available for the local bureaucracy to interpret or adapt the central policy for the sake of advancing or safeguarding local interests.[7]

Because thought control was the most important means of making the local bureaucracy perform as a faithful agent in Maoist China, in most cases fears of purge and persecution deterred local bureaucrats from taking actions that could be even remotely interpreted as anti-Beijing. Since outright defiance and explicit foot-dragging were politically suicidal and therefore rare, compliance was usually the only option left to the local bureaucracy, and even in-advance implementation (i.e., accomplishing the target way ahead of the original schedule, though often only nominally) was not uncommon.[8]

During Mao's rule, the local bureaucracy lacked financial and material resources to act on its own or defy Beijing in any effective manner. Almost totally dependent on the center's allocation of fiscal and material resources, the local bureaucracy of the Maoist era had no other choice but to be a faithful agent—i.e., one that almost always acted in the interest of the central state.[9] The center's most crucial leverage was, of course, personnel management. Despite some adjustments to the *nomenclature* system during the post-Mao era, assignment, promotion, transfer, demotion, and dismissal of all key local positions were determined through the assessments by the COD and relevant party organizations.[10] Loyalty and allegiance were principally the ultimate criteria in such assessments although local performance—attaining economic growth and, more recently, maintaining social stability—also became important during the reform era.[11] Under the circumstances where popular elections were absent, local bureaucrats looked mostly to the superiors, and consequently, public opinions counted little.

When local agents carried out administrative duties on behalf of the central state, performance evaluation was central to sustaining the efficacy of the hierarchical system of governance. Given the sheer magnitude of China's territory and population, however, monitoring local behavior and assessing local performance has always been a daunting challenge. Lacking sufficient resources and effective mechanisms to beat the chronic problem of information asymmetry between the center and localities, Beijing often resorted to a perverted measure of "quota politics." That is, by imposing standardized targets on the local bureaucracy without due regard for regional variations, the central state managed to get things done at a minimum, though in a very coarse manner.[12]

The agent imagery generates an impression that the local bureaucracy was totally helpless and fully compliant with Beijing. In reality, the local bureaucracy has been a savvy strategic actor in the sense that, despite dire difficulties, it often strove to maximize its own interests either by pretending to accommodate the center's demands or by fabricating local performance statistics. With few exceptions, however, in the end the local bureaucracy was willing or forced to sacrifice everything else for the sake of the center and national interests. The local bureaucracy did so not because it preferred such losing outcomes, but because it did not have other workable choices under the totalitarian reign of the Maoist period or under that of authoritarian control of the reform era.

In the long haul, such commitments to being a faithful agent for the central state produced an irony, particularly during the Maoist era; the more sincere and loyal the local bureaucracy became in serving the center's interests, the more severe policy failures it had to bear locally. In the midst of ideological extremism and frequent policy oscillations, some local officials might have advanced their individual careers, but they did so only at the expense of overall well-being of the localities concerned. This queer contradiction was to be mitigated only after "thought liberation" was carried out after the late 1970s.

The Second Image: Representatives

Viewing China's local bureaucracy solely as Beijing's faithful agent can be misleading because it has also performed the role of a representative. In contrast with the agent imagery described above, this alternative image presupposes that, on some rare occasions, the Chinese local bureaucracy worked in a bottom-up fashion to articulate and represent some views and interests of the populace to the central state [*minyi biaoda*]. Representative, by definition, is "one that represents one or other constituencies," and some precedents suggest that certain representation did take place in central–local relations of the People's Republic.[13]

Three questions are particularly pertinent here. First, in the Chinese context, where no meaningful local elections were permitted, *whose* interest did the local bureaucracy seek to represent? Under Mao's rule, protecting "locally specific interests" [*difang teshuxing*] was often deemed crucial in mitigating the adverse impact of Beijing's imposition of "blanket policies" [*yidaoqie*] without due regard for local conditions. Locally specific interests were not, however, easy to define or justify and, more importantly, very often carried the risk of being branded as "parochial" or "factional" by going against national interests.

Second, given the rigid ideological circumstances in Maoist China, why did the local bureaucracy even attempt to represent local interests? It is not entirely clear why some provincial leaders chose to make a case for locally specific interests at the risk of being stigmatized as counter-revolutionaries.[14] Despite the fact that demonstrating allegiance to Mao and his policy line or to the Party Center in the post-Mao era was more advantageous to one's political career, some provincial leaders were courageous enough to push for local collective interests. Apparently, with certain central patronage or based on limited policy leeway, they went beyond the calculus of personal interests and pushed for some *missions* of their own—safeguarding the people's livelihood by way of policy experimentation or innovation.[15] In most of these cases, provincial leaders' actions were reactive in that they were intended to redress the central policy that did not take into account particular local conditions.

Third, through what procedures did the local bureaucracy represent local collective interests to the central state? The central state might point to the conventional "mass line" [*qunzhong luxian*] discourses, according to which lower-level organizations were entitled to bottom-up articulation and representation of interests of the populace. Such discourses were much too romanticized, because, in reality, the upward flow of articulation and representation was almost always overshadowed by the downward flow of central command and imposition. Efforts by some national leaders to reflect on local conditions met with purges (as in the case of Peng Dehuai), and similar attempts by provincial leaders were branded as factional [*paixing*] and the leaders persecuted. Overall, the cases where the local bureaucracy represented locally specific interests against the preferences of the central state were neither common nor always successful.[16]

The representative role of the local bureaucracy gets highlighted particularly when there is a lack of consensus within the national leadership. Leadership disunity tends to create a widened window of opportunity for local representation in two ways. For one, cracks in the national leadership are likely to activate factional ties down to subnational levels and, based on patron–client networks as political insurance, some local leaders may become tempted to speak out for local collective interests.[17] For the other, leadership disunity may also facilitate a rare environment where multiple localities become horizontally allied to speak with one voice to defy certain central policy.[18]

The Third Image: Principals

Viewing the local bureaucracy as a principal—"one that takes a leading and proactive role in any activity for its own interest"—is relatively new, as the literature on central–local relations generally places the central government in the position of a principal. This imagery presupposes that the local state has its own agenda, interest, strategic calculus, and risk assessment, all independently of the center. As depicted in this conceptualization, the local state is not just some imagined actor who represents at best vaguely defined popular interests, but a substantive entity that gets proactively involved in interactions with both the central state and the society in order to fulfill its own goals.[19] The local state in this case does not merely react to central policy, but it proactively initiates plans and schemes designed specifically to promote its own interests that may be distinct from the interests of the center or the society.

One crucial point of distinction needs to be made at this juncture because viewing the local state as a principal may often be confused with seeing it as a representative. Two main differences—though not always so easily discernible—can be pointed out. First, the nature of local action in the case of principal is more proactive than reactive (or defensive) in the sense that the local state seeks to play a leading part for the sake of expanding—not just safeguarding—the interest of the territorial government at the expense of national and/or societal interests. Second, what can be termed as "meso-politics" (as compared to the dynamics involving mainly "high politics" of central elites) looms large as local strategic thinking and subsequent central–local bargaining determine the costs and benefits for the local state as a principal.

This particular perspective is relatively new because the rise of a proactive entrepreneurial local state is more an outcome of the reform era.[20] As noted earlier, local assertiveness was mostly taboo and very often subject to political persecution during the Maoist era. Hence, viewing the local state as Beijing's loyal agent and, on a few rare occasions, as an imagined representative of the society was more popular. Only when the norms of decentralization—along with thought liberation— weakened those of blind commandism [xiazhihui] and in-advance hasty compliance was the local state in China able to become proactive and assertive vis-à-vis the central state without so greatly fearing political persecution.[21]

In the post-Mao reform era, the central state has come to face an intricate dilemma as the local state was being transformed into a principal with its own agenda, interests, and strategic thinking. On the one hand, Beijing has, since the early 1980s, preferred the local bureaucracy to become more proactive, initiative, and discretionary, because the locomotives of economic modernization could not be fully harnessed with the localities shackled by top-down norms of centralization.[22] After thirty-some years of reform, the overall extent of local discretion in the realms of fiscal and implementation control reached a stage where the central state often had to adopt some drastic measures of recentralization.[23] On the other hand, the necessity and duration of the systemic reform set clear limits as to how far Beijing could go back in reining in the localities. That is, local initiatives and discretion could not be completely abrogated because such an act would undoubtedly dampen the overall atmosphere for reform, thereby slowing down the pace of growth and raising the specter of social instability.

It was in this particular context that the local state performed increasingly as a proactive principal during the reform era. Where the center's administrative tentacles were significantly constricted by measures of fiscal and administrative decentralization, the local bureaucracy filled in to carve out its own sphere of influence. Added was an accelerating trend of omnidirectional opening and marketization, and globalization. Furthermore, ever-growing levels of global–local nexus have also expanded the realm where the local state could perform as a principal with its own strategic and entrepreneurial agenda, often bypassing the central state.[24]

THE CENTER'S EVOLVING PERCEPTIONS
OF THE LOCAL STATE

The central state long viewed the local bureaucracy as its agent, one that acted for and on behalf of Beijing.[25] Given the highly top-down nature of China's political system, this was both the expectation and the reality. In tandem with the deepening of reforms, however, the local state was no longer viewed solely as a faithful agent. In the post-Mao era, Beijing appears to have often faced a dilemma as to whether to assign to the local state a role of a representative. On the one hand, Beijing wanted the local state to take the populace seriously [*yi ren wei ben*] and work for the people's interests [*weiminguan*], thereby enhancing the center's responsive capacity as well as the overall legitimacy of the regime.[26] On the other hand, Beijing was at the same time lukewarm toward making the local state an official representative of the people's interest, because not only was it politically troublesome to establish such a legal procedure, but "representing the people" was also seen as a core responsibility of the center against *corrupt* localities.[27]

During the reform era, Beijing's inclination to view the local state as a principal with its own agenda, interests, and strategic calculation has increased. Interviews in China suggest that local (mainly provincial) interests involve three dimensions in particular: (1) social stability [*shehui wending*]; (2) bureaucratic/organizational accomplishments [*zuzhi yeji*], referring mostly to economic growth; and (3) individual benefits [*geren shouyi*], denoting the advancement of political careers of local leaders. The interconnectedness of all three is problematic, although the third may be more so than the former two. Although tapping directly into the views of central officials in a systematic way is not feasible, we may infer this from some of Beijing's key measures of curtailing the local state's actions that were in contradiction with national or societal interests.

The fiscal contract system [*caizheng baogan zhi*], popularized since the early 1980s, transformed the incentive structure of the local state and resulted in successive revenue imbalances in favor of the local bureaucracy at the expense of the center. The long-term accumulated effects, both economic and political, of the fiscal contract system proved unacceptable to Beijing, which eventually chose to overhaul the tax bases in order to redress the central–local revenue imbalances.[28] Beijing's effort proved successful as the tax-sharing reform tipped the revenue balance in favor of the center. The center's effort continued well into the 2000s, and Beijing's share in the lucrative securities trading tax rose from 50 percent in 1994 to 97 percent in 2003. In 2003, the center's share in the income taxes also increased from 50 to 60 percent. Furthermore, in 2004, Beijing obliged local governments to shoulder 25 percent of the export tax rebates, which were hitherto paid wholly by the center.[29]

Beijing's effort to regulate the local state's zeal for land (mis)appropriation can also be understood in a similar vein. Pressed for more development capital, local governments found an easy solution: appropriating farm land and selling its usage rights to industrial manufacturers and real estate developers. The nationwide fervor for land appropriation led to a drastic reduction of farm land, illegal real estate development, insufficient compensations for the appropriated land, and subsequently widespread popular discontent. Beijing came to view this act as a perverse outcome of the local state becoming increasingly self-interested, assertive, and savvy. The central state, on several occasions, issued circulars and notices to forbid local governments from appropriating farm land beyond a certain percentage of the total land available.[30]

The central state's concern with localities' active pursuit of their own interests without due regard for national or societal interests was voiced on many occasions.[31] Under the system of assessing local cadres' performance mainly on the basis of GDP growth and project financing, local governments were naturally preoccupied with attaining investments by way of establishing various development zones. In 2003, China had over six thousand zones, half of which were illegal (i.e., not officially endorsed by the central or provincial authorities). When accomplishing the target of 1 billion yuan in production value guaranteed a township leader a seat on the county party committee, such fervor was clearly no surprise.[32] As one scholar aptly puts it, "When the regime decided that economic growth was the primary task, the same mobilizational system that had been previously employed for class struggle was used for economic construction."[33]

Beijing's growing concern with local selfishness and assertiveness reached a stage where it was deemed necessary to establish supraprovincial regulatory mechanisms.[34] Four examples are noteworthy in this regard. First, the center's strenuous effort to weaken the local state's capture of local banking authorities is a key case. In the midst of the Asian financial crisis during 1998–1999, the center removed local branches of the state banks from the local party committees' *nomenklatura* (i.e., the list of positions under direct personnel control), thereby significantly weakening the horizontal leverage of the local party committees over these local banks. Additionally, provincial branches of the People's Bank of China were largely abolished, and nine regional [i.e., supra-provincial: *kuasheng daqu*] offices were established, further reducing the room for local capture.[35]

Second, water management has long been a highly sensitive issue in China. As was the case with the Three Gorges Dam project, different provinces, cities, and prefectures had diverse interests, agendas, and preferences, making a single concerted plan by the center virtually impossible to be drawn up.[36] In efforts to better facilitate coordination between the center's preferences and local interests, Beijing introduced a familiar measure—the creation of seven regional commissions for water management [*shuili weiyuanhui*], which were administratively put in charge of the respective jurisdiction of the Yangzi River, Yellow River, Huaihe River, Pearl River, Songhua River, Taihu Lake, and the Haihe River.[37]

Third, the central state sought hard to sustain effective regulation of key functional domains, including taxation, auditing, statistics collection, postal services, national and public security, industrial and commercial management, supervision of securities trading, and implementation of cigarette monopoly. By way of directly and vertically managing the personnel, wages, welfare, and operational scope of these domains through the framework of vertical-line control [*chuizhi guanli*: i.e., not allowing *kuai* or leadership by territorial governments], Beijing strove to maintain tight control over as many as twenty-eight key functional domains (accounting for roughly one-third of all domains under the central ministries, bureaus, and commissions).[38]

Fourth, the central state's effort to centralize the judiciary power of the local state also merits our attention. As in the banking sector, local judiciary and prosecuting authorities have long been captured by local party committees through personnel control and budgetary allocations. Such collusion at the local level expanded room for rampant corruption, bribery, office buying [*maiguan*], and local protectionism, all detrimental to national and societal interests.[39] Since 2002, Beijing has required that all leading officials in the domains of court, procurator, public security, organizational work, and discipline inspection at the county level and above be circulated [*jiaoliu*] among different regions, thereby constricting the room for local collusion and nepotism.[40] More importantly, the much-discussed idea of establishing the system of supra-provincial courts [*kuaqu fayuan*] was finally adopted as a policy at the Fourth Plenum in 2014 of the 18th Central Committee.

THE CENTRAL STATE'S PERCEPTION OF LOCAL
GOVERNMENT BY ADMINISTRATIVE LEVEL

The foregoing discussion treated the central state's perceptions of the local state as if the latter was a single entity represented by the provinces.[41] Although discerning the center's views of different levels of the local bureaucracy is a daunting challenge, we may nevertheless seek to construct some sketches of Beijing's perspective on four tiers of the subnational government—namely, the province, the prefecture/prefecture-level city, the county/county-level city, and the township/town.

Beijing's View of Provinces: High Expectations
with Guarded Suspicion

The central state's view of provinces[42] is largely dualistic in the sense that Beijing regards them as the most indispensable agents for local governance but, at the same time, harbors deep-seated suspicion as to their willful foot-dragging and centrifugal tendencies.[43] Beijing wants the provinces to be effective managers of subprovincial units, but it is simultaneously opposed to allowing them to be independent principals.[44] The central state has intermittently strengthened vertical lines of command so as to consolidate the provinces' leverage over subprovincial units, but Beijing has also sought to prevent the formation of horizontal alliances among the provinces that might be used against the center.[45]

The central state of China—not only the People's Republic but also many of its dynastic predecessors—has always been keen to maintain the total number of province-level units at a manageably low level (as noted in chapter 3). Although the number of provincial units was forty-eight in 1949 and fifty-three in 1953, once the central state's power was firmly consolidated, the total number of the province-level units was reduced back to twenty-nine. During the entire post-1954 period, the center's direct control of the provinces remained unchanged. As of 2014, compared to 1978, the total number of the province-level units increased by only four (Hainan, Chongqing, Hong Kong, and Macau). Calls were frequently made regarding the need to increase the number of provinces to fifty or even ninety, but thus far such changes have not occurred.[46]

Worth noting at this juncture is the practice of assigning provincial leaders to their home provinces: the so-called "native" appointment. The prevalent norms in traditional China—the rule of "avoidance" [*huibi*:

provincial leaders were prohibited from serving in their home provinces lest they work for the interests of their families and relatives]—was generally ignored in the People's Republic.[47] For the period of 1949–1998, more than one-third (35 percent) of all provincial party secretaries and deputy secretaries, governors, and deputy governors were appointed to their home provinces.[48] Although the native ratio had declined during Mao's rule (i.e., 50 percent for the 1950s, 40 percent for the 1960s, and 18 percent at the height of the Cultural Revolution), the figure went back up to 41 percent in 1986.[49] As for the provincial party secretaries alone, the native ratio was 34 percent in 1965, which rose to 41 percent in 1988. A similar upward trend was noted for the mayors of large cities during the 1980s.[50] Despite some oscillations, the native ratio for the top provincial leadership as a whole (i.e., provincial party secretaries, deputy secretaries, governors, and deputy governors) remained well within the range of 40 percent for the three decades (1979–2009) of the post-Mao reform era.[51]

What merits our attention is that a discernible trend has been on the rise since the 1990s; the native ratio for the provincial party secretaries continued to decline due perhaps to Beijing's growing concern with rampant localism and the principalization of the local state. According to one study, the share of provincial party secretaries serving in their home provinces declined from 32 percent in 1999 to 18 percent in 2002.[52] This author's calculation shows that the native ratio for the provincial party secretaries and deputy secretaries declined from 41 and 35 percent in 1992 and 1997, respectively, to 29 percent in 2007 and then 20 percent in 2012. For the same period, however, the native ratio for the governors and deputy governors rose from 38 and 45 percent in 1992 and 1997 to 50 and 48 percent in 2007 and 2012, respectively (see table 4.1).

TABLE 4.1
Native Ratios for Party Secretaries and Governors, 1992–2012

	Party secretaries	Governors	Total
1992	41%	38%	40%
1997	35%	45%	37%
2002	30%	47%	40%
2007	29%	50%	43%
2012	20%	48%	36%

NOTE: Figures are for April in the respective year. The data include deputy party secretaries and deputy governors.

SOURCE: Author's own calculation using the same data set as in note 51.

Tighter control over provincial party leaders—as opposed to governors and deputy governors—suggests that Beijing had ambivalent or dilemmatic perceptions of the provinces as it was concerned with the perils of growing localism on the one hand, and with the acute need for provincial leaders well tuned to specific local conditions on the other. To a certain extent, it may be compared to the well-known mode of governing the ethnic minority regions where "the leaders of the people's government should be chosen by the citizens of the ethnicity exercising regional autonomy," whereas party leaders are usually dispatched from Beijing.[53] In a sense, it can be argued that provincial party leaders were assigned the role of agent, and provincial governors were given a quasi-permission to be a sort of representative.

Beijing's View of the Prefecture-Level City/ Prefecture: Ambiguous Detachment

The center's perception of the prefecture/prefecture-level city is the least clear of all. At least two factors account for such ambiguity. For one, the prefecture had long been a "field administration" [paichu jigou] of the provincial government, and therefore the unit was rarely viewed as separate from the provincial authorities. For another, as noted in detail in chapter 3, the central state remains somewhat ambiguous concerning how to fit this particular tier into the subnational hierarchy, as it is currently caught between the cities-leading-counties [shi lingdao xian] policy implemented for over two decades and the alternative scheme of provinces directly ruling counties.[54] The Constitution formally acknowledges three tiers only (the province, the county, and the township), excluding the prefecture level, although numerous scholarly writings refer to a de facto four-level local administration.

Beijing's biggest concern is twofold. For one, like their imperial predecessors, the leaders in the Zhongnanhai are agonized over the optimal number of county-ruling units [tongxian zhengqu] and the appropriate size of such units. Not only does the number of counties in each province differ considerably, but the size of each county is also vastly different. As Ningxia has only 13 counties and Sichuan has 135 counties (as of 2013), obviously the latter cannot do without intermediate county-ruling units like prefecture-level cities.[55] For another, in contrast with Beijing's initial hope that the the cities-leading-counties scheme would promote economic modernization of the rural counties, prefecture-level cities turned out to be drags and obstacles rather than performing as "growth poles." In order to tame the principal's mentality of the prefecture-level cities, the center introduced the new policy of provinces directly ruling the counties.[56]

Although this new development clearly repudiated the cities-leading-counties scheme, whether the new policy could become popularized even in such large and populous provinces as Sichuan, Shandong, and Henan is uncertain.[57] The way in which the new scheme has been successfully implemented in provinces like Zhejiang, Fujian, and Hainan was clearly related to such province-specific factors as the small size, geographical and topological characteristics, etc.[58] In a nutshell, Beijing's view of the prefectures/prefecture-level cities has of late become generally more negative, placing more political weight on the provinces and the counties. It can be suggested that Beijing, again, faces an intricate dilemma of seeking to maintain the overall number of agents that report directly to the center at a minimum while having to allow the number of subprovincial agents to grow significantly, thereby putting enormous pressure on the provinces.

Beijing's View of the County/County-Level City:
Corrupt Yet Indispensable Mainstay

The center's view of the county is complex as it has the longest history among all subnational units. Like its imperial predecessors, the central state of the People's Republic has been keenly aware of the pivotal position that county-level units occupy in China's system of local governance. The county system has long been stable, even more so than the provincial system.[59] Whether it was a three-, four-, or five-tier system of local governance, the county was always an indispensable layer of China's local administration.[60] The total number of counties was about 1,000 in the Qin dynasty and 1,549 during the Jiaqing Reign of the Qing dynasty. The total number of counties and county-level cities was about 1,927 in 2013, excluding urban districts [shiqu].[61] Given the drastic expansion of China's territory and population, as well as the growth of modern-day governmental functions, the increase in the number of county-level units appears rather minimal.

With Beijing assigning less political weight to the prefecture-level units in recent years, the role of the county/county-level city as its faithful agent has been further highlighted. As one scholar aptly puts it,

"Counties were the units of local governments that actually carried out administration and dealt directly with people."[62] Situated at the nexus of "government control" [*guanzhi*] and "self-governance" [*zizhi*], the county has long constituted the cornerstone of the Chinese body politic.[63] The central state, currently preoccupied with maintaining social stability more than anything else, simply cannot afford to let the counties be the principals playing their own games.

Three aspects seem particularly pertinent in accounting for Beijing's perceptions and intentions regarding the county-level administration. First, located right at the state–society juncture, the counties/county-level cities have long been viewed as the bastion of rampant corruption. Not only was corruption more widespread at the county level (at least in terms of frequency) than elsewhere, but the poor management of counties was also generally perceived as directly affecting the people's view of regime legitimacy.[64] In efforts to boost fiscal capacity and mitigate social discontent at the county level, the central state has sought to reduce excessive fiscal burdens on the county-level administration by way of reinstating direct provincial control of the counties/county-level cities. Although strengthening the county administration meant relative weakening of the township/town governments, whether the provinces-directly-ruling-counties scheme has actually led to Beijing's stronger grip on county-level units remains uncertain.[65]

Second, in order to mold the counties/county-level cities into faithful agents of the center, Beijing devoted special efforts to selecting and training county-level leaders. In the selection of cadres, a notable experiment was undertaken in 2009 in Yunnan, Hebei, and Hunan, to whom the COD specifically requested that appointments of all county-level party secretaries be determined by the provincial party standing committees. The provincial party committees there were asked to inform the COD of personnel changes at the county level on an annual basis.[66] As for cadre training, the Central Party School ran short-term programs designed specifically for county-level party and government heads. Given that nearly 90 percent of the county-level leaders served in only one prefecture throughout their careers, such programs no doubt provided them with broader—i.e., less parochial—perspectives.[67]

Third, whereas Beijing has not implemented the rule of avoidance on a nationwide basis, it has nevertheless paid some attention in recent years to the growing problem of localism in personnel appointments at the county level and above, as well as below.[68] Two distinct measures were employed to cope with the problem. One refers to a partial application of the rule of avoidance. According to the "Tentative Measures for Government Officials" (1993: Article 63) and the "Tentative Measures for Government Officials in Conducting Appointment Avoidance and Work Assignment Avoidance" (1996: Article 2), leading officials at the county level or below and their parents, spouses, and children were not to be assigned to their native places [yuanji], except for ethnic-minority autonomous units.[69] Although the policy framework as such has been there for many years in the form of tentative measures, its implementation appears to have of late become stricter.[70]

The other measure denotes "circulating leaders among different counties, prefectures and cities" [yidi weiguan]. In accordance with the "Regulations Concerning the Circulation of Party and Government Leading Officials" (Article 5), leading cadres at the county level and above were to be assigned to posts in other cities and prefectures for an extended period of time.[71] Given that the county/county-level city was the only subnational unit where both measures [huibi and yidi weigan] were implemented, it provides some clue to the center's view of the county-level units—an indispensable agent that needs constant vigilance and tight supervision lest they should become corrupt principals.

Beijing's View of the Township-Town: Poor and Demoralized "Foot Soldiers"

The central state's view of the township/town is difficult to decipher for two obvious reasons: they are simply too numerous (32,929 in 2013) and located too far away from Beijing. Traditionally, imperial power did not reach this level [guoquan buxiaxian] as the county was its lowest limit.[72] Although the origin of township as a layer of China's local administration dates back to the Western Zhou, it was significantly weakened during the Han and even abolished during the Sui. For most of China's history, townships were regarded as the domain of self-governance largely untouched by government control. The reinstatement of the township as a formal tier of local administration was made only during the late Qing dynasty.[73]

During the People's Republic, the township level had gone through phases of oscillation between government control and self-governance under the schemes of collectivization and de-collectivization. To the central state, the townships/towns were located much too far away, making it necessary to empower the counties to exert tight control over them. In fact, the townships/towns were generally viewed as a domain where power abuse and corruptions were ways of life and cadres were working for the private interests of themselves and county-level superiors.[74] As one scholar aptly describes, the level of trust the people had in the party committees at the township level turned out to be the lowest, compared to those at the county and provincial levels.[75]

As the townships/towns constitute a key arena where state power and societal response closely interacted, the central state was generally more sensitive to and less permissive of perversities at this level. Win–win situations often ensued as the township governments, in close coordination with their county superiors, performed as effective loyal agents of the center.[76] In other cases, they became savvy strategic actors seeking their own parochial interests, particularly under the tight tax-for-fee circumstances. Given that the center's monitoring capacity was disproportionately weaker at this level than above, supervision by the county administration was deemed more important than ever.

The real test is due to take place at this particular level, as noted in chapter 3, since Beijing has been pondering whether the townships/towns should be allowed to hollow out over time. With the nationwide abolition of agricultural taxes in 2006, the township/town government was significantly weakened, with nearly 70 percent of them experiencing budget deficits in 2008. In efforts to make up for the falling tax revenues, township governments became principals by way of seeking to collect illicit fees and misappropriate farm land for sales, inviting fierce criticism and opposition.[77] Despite heated debates on the future of townships and the ongoing experiments since 2005 with organizational streamlining [jingjian jigou], "concurrent assignments" [jiaocha renwu], inter-township mergers [chepin xiangzhen], and "township finance managed by county administration" [xiangcai xianguan], the fate of townships is hanging in the air. In the longer run, the transformation of township governments into field agencies of the county administration or into a sort of self-governing committees is a possibility.[78]

CONCLUDING OBSERVATIONS

In the Maoist era, local governments were expected to be no more than loyal agents of the center. And most of the time, they indeed performed as Beijing's faithful agents, the rhetoric about local diversity and regional variation notwithstanding. During the post-Mao period, thanks to the measures of decentralization and thought liberation, locally specific conditions [*difang teshuxing*] gradually turned themselves into local interests [*difang liyi*], thereby making the local state a savvy and, often, assertive principal with its own agenda and strategic calculus. Views of the local state as a principal seeking its own interests frequently clashed with Beijing's expectations for the local state as an agent in support of national interests and, on some occasions, as a representative in support of societal interests.

The central state's multiple views of the local state are in itself a testimony to the very dilemma that Beijing faces. Beijing's demands for local inputs and initiatives (mostly in the form of innovations and experiments) are not always translated into the tolerance for local discretion and foot-dragging. In fact, such multiple perceptions permeate through the center's views of different tiers of China's subnational administration, although concerns tend to grow bigger as they go down the hierarchy.

As marketization reforms intensify and functional decentralization deepens in China, a wide range of socioeconomic programs—i.e., public services and welfare provision, poverty alleviation, interregional equalization, etc.—may increasingly hinge upon the capacity of subnational administration.[79] These new connections are bound to bring central–local dynamics closer than ever before to key concerns of state-society relations. Under these changing circumstances, where maintaining stability has become the top priority, local governments from the provinces down to the townships may have to carve out their role as representatives of the populace, even without explicit measures of democratization. Down the road, therefore, the three distinct roles of the local state—agents, principals, and representatives—may increasingly overlap and even offset each other, further complicating central-local dynamics.

5

The Center's Instruments
of Local Control

Maintaining stability and ensuring survival are the principal goals of any political regime. China is no exception to this rule whether its rulers were emperors, khans, generalissimos, or general secretaries. History has repeatedly witnessed so many failed states around the world that ended up changing their names or even totally disappearing from the map.[1] Given that, the resilience of China as a unified state is rather impressive. The "restoration" of China as a global player, if not a hegemonic competitor yet, seems all the more remarkable. What, then, has enabled China to avoid the ill fate that had fallen on many socialist dictatorial regimes like the Soviet Union, Yugoslavia, and Czechoslovakia? How did China manage to shield itself from the threats of demise, disintegration, or collapse?[2]

Despite so much forewarning about the possible collapse or even territorial disintegration of the People's Republic, due particularly to the rise of regionalism, provincialism, and localism since the launch of post-Mao reforms and opening, Beijing still seems able to command quite effectively and confidently. It may indeed be that the "reports of China's death have in fact been greatly exaggerated," as John Fitzgerald aptly notes.[3] What made possible this resilient power of Beijing to rule localities? The answer lies in the following two dimensions: (1) the Communist Party leaders' lingering memory of, if not preoccupation with, China's centrifugal traditions; and (2) their adaptive capacity to renovate old institutions and devise new rules to cope with the growing challenges to local governance.

This chapter consists of three sections. The first posits a puzzle as to the nature of the post-Mao era in the context of central–local relations. To paraphrase it, is post-Mao China more akin to the pre-1949 revolutionary period of "localist" governance or to the "suspended centrifugality" of the Maoist era? This study suggests that the decade-long efforts for de-ideologizing central–local relations during the 1980s initially created some room for local discretion and deviation in the 1990s and thereafter. The second section hastens to add detailed discussions of four types of instruments that Beijing has over time devised and refined in order to make up for the shortfalls in its ability to rein in localities. The third section delves into the new challenges that the People's Republic is currently facing in sustaining effective governance.

THE POST-MAO ERA: A REVIVAL OF CENTRIFUGALITY?

The remarkable adaptability of the People's Republic (the Chinese Communist Party in particular) to changing environments and emerging challenges is widely known, especially with regard to its pre-1949 experiences. The revolutionary era (1921–1949) is often remembered as the most ideal and noteworthy period for local governance as it gave birth to the so-called Yan'an tradition—a highly decentralized structure of governance where many policies were decided by county-level authorities, and such distinct styles of local experimentation, two-way communication (i.e., democratic centralism), and the famous tenet of "implementing according to local conditions" [*yindi zhiyi*] were emphasized.[4]

It is equally important to understand that this particular period of extreme hardship was both special and unique. Having to carry out a geographically disconnected revolution in widely scattered areas, Communist leaders simply did not possess the luxury of blind commandism dictated solely from above. Instead, guerrilla-style policy making was necessary for ensuring flexibility, autarky, a united front, and broad-based mass support. To a considerable extent, local autonomy of this era was both an extension of China's centrifugal tradition and an outcome of the special circumstances at the time.

In stark contrast, during Mao's rule (1949–1976), the centrifugal tradition was largely suspended not only because the overall structure of local governance was tightly centralized but also because there was no discernible trend toward local assertiveness vis-à-vis Beijing—not to mention explicit regional defiance. That is, the imperative of modern "state making" made it both important and necessary to introduce and enforce rules and institutions conducive to the consolidation of central dominance in post-revolutionary circumstances. Consequently, during Mao's rule, the commitments to decentralization were mostly formalistic, and Beijing's urge for dominance and pervasive local fears of persecution jointly worked to defeat the revolutionary legacy of *yindi zhiyi*. One crucial lesson from these "unfamiliar" experiences of the Maoist era was that unless the norms of central dominance were sincerely fought against, provincial discretion and regional variation would always be viewed as ideologically faulty and politically unsafe.

The Reform Factor: De-ideologization and Norm Changes

The post-Mao reforms brought about a sea change in the way the central party and government viewed and dealt with localities. The most notable change concerned the weakening of Beijing's omnipresent and omnipotent ideological grips on localities and, as a result, a significant reduction of frantic mass campaigns in the process of policy implementation. To a considerable extent, China's "totalitarian phase of authoritarianism" was over.[5] This crucial change was attributed largely to the post-Mao leadership's painful recognition that its reform platforms were bound to fail without first transforming the prevailing norms of local policy implementation.[6] Hence, the most distinctive aspect of the post-Mao reforms was the regime's persistent efforts for the emancipation of mind [*sixiang jiefang*] in order to redress the excessive ideological control over human relations and economic management in particular.[7]

The reformist leadership's efforts to transform the norms of local governance led to a strong emphasis on the *yindi zhiyi* principle, which was quite reminiscent of the Yan'an tradition.[8] Beijing's re-emphasis on *yindi zhiyi* meant that local discretion and regional variation would be permitted again in implementing central policy in order to take local conditions into account and that the malpractice of imposing blanket policies [*yidaoqie*,一刀切] for all localities was to be stopped. This time, unlike in the Maoist era, it had to go beyond mere rhetoric, and subsequently, single models for the entire nation (e.g., Dazhai and Daqing) were abolished for good.[9]

The post-Mao leadership granted large-scale pardons to many of those stigmatized and persecuted as "rightists" and other "bad elements" during the successive campaigns after 1957.[10] The pardoned included a large number of former local officials who had dared to speak out against Beijing's policies that they had regarded unsuitable for their localities. These measures, along with the reformist leadership's continued efforts to weed out "leftists" and beneficiaries of the Cultural Revolution, mitigated widespread suspicions held by many local cadres and reinforced their trust in the new leadership's vision for the reform.

With the diluting of Beijing's ideological omnipresence came the leadership's meticulous effort to weaken central planning and fiscal centralism. As noted in chapter 2, planned allocation of fiscal and material resources to localities, one of the center's most powerful control instruments, became increasingly irrelevant as the overall extent of marketization—particularly in the domain of material allocation—rose to over 90 percent.[11] The power of the State Planning Commission, once nicknamed the little State Council, in charge of meting out macroplans and micro-quotas, was gradually curtailed and eventually restructured in 2003 as the State Development and Reform Commission. The 11th Five-Year Socioeconomic Plans for 2006–2010 were for the first time designated as "directional guidelines" [guiha, 规划] instead of the usual "operational plans" [jihua, 计划]. The era of centralized state planning, as we have known it, was gradually nearing its end.[12]

Growing inefficacy of the Communist ideology and lax party discipline, as well as increased economic opportunities and fiscal autonomy, produced the joint effect of emboldening localities in post-Mao China. Keenly aware that Beijing was not likely to dampen the overall reform atmosphere just to check on a few noncompliant localities, provinces were often tempted to venture into the hitherto unpermitted realm of policy discretion, foot-dragging, and even willful deviation. Subsequently, various symptoms of local assertiveness and implementation slippage were widely reported in the literature.[13]

Although localities attained a considerably expanded scope of discretion, compared with the Maoist era, the overall balance of power between the center and localities has not uniformly tilted toward the latter. Generally speaking, Beijing is still in command and localities listen to it, though selectively. Two principal variations can be noted in relation to the term "selectively." For one, concerning the issues that the center cares most about, localities mostly tend to comply, although a few with legitimate economic reasons may choose to drag their feet in hopes of obtaining a special exemption.[14] For another, regarding the issues in which some localities have a crucial interest at stake but in which Beijing does not demand uniform compliance, local leaders there may choose to get around central regulations to safeguard their interests. In such a contingency, generally speaking, Beijing will not go after or punish them even if it is aware of such deviations.[15]

Whereas the revolutionary legacy of mass line became largely a rhetoric or formality in the post-Mao era, that of local initiatives and regional variations became more genuine compared with the Maoist period. One crucial difference, though, between the Yan'an period and the post-Mao era lay in the fact that, despite extensive—and genuine—decentralization of the latter, provinces became the principal unit of local policy remake and the overall policy environment was not as favorable to the guerrilla-style policy making at the county level and below as before.[16]

CONTAINING CENTRIFUGAL CHALLENGES: BEIJING'S INSTRUMENTS OF LOCAL CONTROL

The foregoing discussion demonstrated that the Party Center paid genuine attention to certain legacies of the revolutionary era, and as a result, the scope of local discretion was considerably expanded during the post-Mao period. Despite such changes, overall, Beijing is still deemed capable of commanding localities fairly effectively. What enables the center to gather reliable information on local affairs and contain local deviation if necessary? What constitutes the *tentacles* of Beijing that are used to investigate the state of local affairs, prevent excessive local deviation, and punish serious violators? In discussing the center's principal instruments for local control—those for prevention, investigation, rule changing, and suppression—this section looks into the leadership's adaptability and the institutional resemblance between traditional and revolutionary China on the one hand and the reformist China on the other.

Preventive Mechanisms

Beijing inherited from traditional China diverse arrangements and mechanisms for preventing assertive localism and containing provincial defiance. Structurally speaking, above all, a highly stable provincial system [*shengzhi*, 省制] is one such example.[17] During much of Mao's rule, the total number of provincial-level units had been twenty-nine, which rose to thirty-three in the post-Mao era. One cannot help but wonder why there were so few changes to the provincial system over the years. One informed guess is that the rulers of contemporary China, just like their imperial predecessors, are still very much concerned about the centrifugal tendencies of the Chinese body politic. Had it not been for such persistent memories and preoccupations, the People's Republic with a continent-sized territory and the world's largest population would not have so fervently opposed a federal system of local governance.

Because it is so often mentioned, let us briefly reflect on the theme of federalism in contemporary China. As early as July 1922, at the Second National Congress of the Chinese Communist Party (CCP), it was officially announced that "the Chinese Federal Republic [*zhonghua lianbang gongheguo*] was to be formed with three independent nations of Mongolia, Tibet, and Huijiang (Uighur-populated areas)."[18] In his report to the Seventh National Congress of the CCP in 1945, Mao wrote, "All the nationalities within China's boundaries should, on the basis of voluntarism and democracy, organize the Chinese Federation of Democratic Republic (中华民主共和国联邦)." For obvious reasons, this particular passage was not included in the post-1949 editions of the *Selected Works of Mao Zedong*. Furthermore, the 1954 Constitution stressed the primacy of the central government, thereby totally repudiating the need for a federal structure in China. Unlike during the revolutionary era, when forming a united front and maximum winning coalition was a prerequisite for the CCP's survival, in the post-revolutionary phase there was simply no room for federalism or other institutional arrangements that might weaken or challenge the insurmountable authority of the Center.[19]

In efforts to rein in regionalism and localism, the imperial throne often manipulated provincial boundaries. In traditional China, what is generally referred to as the principle of "jagged teeth of a dog" [*quanya xiangru*, 犬牙相入] was utilized. That is, instead of employing natural environments like rivers, mountains, and lakes as the points of demarcation [*shanchuan xingbian*, 山川形便], Chinese emperors occasionally relied on imposing artificial boundaries and man-made borders between localities. The hoped-for gains of such an act were to prevent the rise of localism embedded in common dialects, cultures, and customs cultivated over long periods of time. One recent example was placing Shandong—a province geographically and culturally more akin to

North China [*huabei*] and for long a stronghold of Communism—together with the provinces in East China [*huadong*], traditionally more friendly toward the Kuomintang forces, in the same great administrative region (1949–1954).[20] Technological advances in transportation and communication have, however, rendered this particular tactic much less relevant today.

An additional tool concerns the establishment of special administrative areas designed specifically for the management of ethnic minorities. Although the Ming and the Qing had special bureaucracies to deal with non-Han minorities, the Republic of China [*minguo*] set up two "regions" [*difang*] for the management of Mongolia and Xinjiang. In the People's Republic, full-scale restructuring took place, by which a total of five province-level ethnic minority regions (Tibet, Xinjiang, Inner Mongolia, Ningxia, and Guangxi) were established in 1953. As of 2012, there were twenty-nine such prefectures [*zizhizhou*], 117 counties [*zizhixian*], five urban ethnic minority districts [*chengshi minzuqu*], and over fifteen hundred ethnic minority townships [*minzuxiang*], jointly accounting for 65 percent of China's land mass and 75 percent of all ethnic minority populations.[21]

More important is, of course, the personnel system through which the center has sought to wield formidable influence over localities.[22] Because much has already been discussed on the *nomenklature* control run by the Central Organization Department of the CCP, we focus here on one key feature—the popular practice of assigning provincial leaders to their home provinces. In stark contrast with traditional China, the rule of avoidance [*huibi*, 回避] was largely ignored in the People's Republic.[23]

Two reasons account for this contrast. For one, because the Communist regime emphasized the tenet of implementing according to local conditions at least on a rhetorical level, natives were naturally deemed better tuned to local conditions and therefore more suitable for promoting local development. For another, residues of centrifugal localism (as shown with the Gao Gang Incident in the early the 1950s), it was thought, could be effectively fought against with some doses of Communist discipline, along with occasional rectification campaigns.[24] As detailed in chapter 4, the native ratio in the provincial leadership continued to rise nationwide after the Cultural Revolution and throughout the reform era, and stabilized in the range of 40 percent for much of the 2000s.[25] Most interesting is the fact that in the last twenty years, the native ratio became much higher for the governors than for the provincial party secretaries as the figures for the former were 38 and 48 percent in

1992 and 2012, respectively, while the comparable figures for the latter were 41 and 20 percent, respectively.[26]

The CCP has also strictly prohibited the provinces and cities from organizing themselves laterally for collective action against Beijing. In efforts to avoid the charges of "divisive factionalism" [*paixing*], localities chose to engage mostly in dyadic bargaining with the central government, thereby more often than not tipping the power balance in the center's favor. Although numerous interprovincial associations and intercity networks sprang up during the post-Mao reform era, often under Beijing's initiatives, they were almost always economic in their primary functions, short of constituting political pressure groups.[27]

Above all, the weakening of ideological mechanisms left the most profound impact on the center's capacity for local governance. The demise of the totalitarian system—although China still is an authoritarian one—has flung open the door for more local discretion and provincial assertiveness. In the absence of self-policing norms of compliance, Beijing had to bring in other varieties of control instruments.

Investigative Instruments

Information on local affairs is a valued commodity regardless of time and space. It is particularly so for a continent-sized nation like China with a huge population to manage. For effective local governance, therefore, the central government needs a wide range of channels and networks to be well informed of local performance and to better facilitate central–local communication. Some of these instruments originated in imperial China, including intricate formal document systems and personal investigative visits by emperors and high-level officials. Others have their roots in the Yan'an and Maoist years, such as the dispatch of cadre work teams, convening specialized meetings of lower-level officials at higher levels, conducting statistical surveys, etc.[28]

Top-level directives issued by the Party Center, called *zhongfa* [中发], have held a unique status in central–local communicative processes. At the same time, due to these documents' heavy use of highly "formalized wording" [*tifa*, 提法], dissemination generally has entailed considerable variations and distortions at local levels.[29] In efforts to reduce the degree of excessive local variation and willful distortion, Beijing typically has relied on editorials in *People's Daily* and *Red Flag* to relay the spirit of the center's policy and to highlight the core contents that are to be implemented at local levels. Beijing has also utilized local branches of the New China News Agency to provide special information to central party and government elite through its *Internal Reference* [*neibu cankao*] materials.[30]

Fabricating performance statistics and over- or underreporting has long been a silent weapon of local officials vis-à-vis the center. By 1995, Beijing dictated that all provincial-level governments should be penalized if they violated the Statistics Law [*tongjifa*] promulgated in 1983. More importantly, the State Statistical Bureau sought to consolidate its own vertical control by shouldering personnel appointments and budgetary responsibilities in such a way that interference by the provincial authorities could be minimized. As of 2009, statistical compilation was listed as one of twenty-eight domains for which Beijing's vertical-line control [*chuizhi guanli*] was to be implemented, with little intervention by regional authorities.[31]

Despite Beijing's strenuous efforts, inflated or deflated reporting has been prevalent about the provincial and local GDP, total grain output, per capita income, the inflation rate, and average birth rate. For instance, it was widely publicized in 2012 that the sum of the provinces' GDP surpassed China's total GDP by a margin of 11 percent.[32] Down the road, however, China's system of administrative monitoring and supervision, if properly managed with new technologies, may offer Beijing a distinct edge over defiant localities.

The center has not relied solely on the formal document and informational systems, as the national leadership was so keenly aware of their inherent limitations and loopholes. Just as the Qianlong Emperor of the Qing dynasty journeyed out of the Forbidden City six times to carry out grand inspection tours during his reign, Mao Zedong, Deng Xiaoping, Jiang Zemin, Hu Jintao, and Xi Jinping, as well as members of the Politburo Standing Committee, went on frequent personal inspection [*kaocha*, 考察] trips to gain a better understanding of local affairs and to provide on-site instructions for important—often controversial—policy issues.[33] As a matter of fact, the overall frequency of personal inspection trips by top leaders considerably increased in recent years due both to the improvement in transportation and a pressing desire to oversee local implementation of economic reforms.[34]

In traditional China, the emperors dispatched trusted high-level envoys [*qinchai*, 钦差] or eunuchs on their behalf to check on local affairs in different corners of the nation. Similarly, from the days of the Jiangxi Soviet and the Yan'an Base Areas, the CCP Party Center frequently utilized ad hoc work teams and investigative units to "squat at a point" [*dundian*, 蹲点] or to tour a province or a region to get valuable local information.[35] These practices of dispatching top-down investigators are quite analogous to the traditional system of sending "royal inspectors" [*yushi*] regularly to provinces and counties.[36]

The CCP's Discipline Inspection Commission [*jiwei*] merits our attention in this regard. Because much had already been written on this crucial supervisory system, the discussion here focuses primarily on the central–local dimension.[37] As table 5.1 illustrates, the pattern and nature of organizational leadership over the local discipline inspection commissions changed frequently, reflecting Beijing's oscillating preferences and priorities over time. At least eight reversals have been made since 1950 as to whether the vertical line authorities or the horizontal territorial governments would control the local discipline inspection commissions. Since 2004, when the dual leadership over the local discipline inspection commissions was finally broken, the appointments and assessments of provincial discipline inspection commissioners and deputy-commissioners have been made solely by the Central Discipline Inspection Commission, thereby limiting the possibility of interference by the provincial Party committees. Now, local discipline inspection commissions are able to investigate members of the corresponding local Party committees without authorization from the latter's leaders.[38]

The "central inspection groups" [*zhongyang xunshizu*], established in August 2003 and legally mandated in July 2009, are but the most recent addition to a series of Beijing's efforts by Beijing to rein in errant regional and local authorities. The fact that these groups consist mainly of high-level (i.e., provincial-level or above) retired officials who are near or above seventy years old and have no connections with the particular provinces or sectors under investigation is illustrative of how the Party Center strives to disconnect the guardians from the guarded. Members of these groups (a total of twenty groups in 2013) are selected by the Party Center and report only to the Central Inspection Leadership Small Group in Beijing. This reminds us of traditional China's imperial inspectors [*qinchai dachen*] or the "inspector-generals with embroidered clothes" [*jinyiwei*] of the Ming dynasty. The chair of each of these inspection groups may serve as such only once, thereby making it more difficult for this person to develop a relationship of collusion with provincial leaders.[39]

In present-day China, of course, news media, online tip-offs, investigative journalism, public opinions, petitions, and other sources of

TABLE 5.1
Changing Leadership Over Local Units of Discipline Inspection

Year	Unit of concern	Nature of leadership
1950	Local discipline inspection commissions	Horizontal (regional) leadership
1955	Local supervisory commissions (*jianwei*)	Vertical (central) leadership and horizontal guidance
1956	Local supervisory commissions	Horizontal (regional) leadership
1963	Local supervisory commissions	Vertical (central) leadership and horizontal guidance
1969	Discipline inspection commissions abolished	–
1980	Discipline inspection commissions revived	Dual leadership with a focus on horizontal (regional) leadership
1982	Local discipline inspection commissions	Dual leadership (no specification)
1983	Local discipline inspection commissions	Vertical leadership and horizontal guidance
1991	Local discipline inspection commissions	Dual leadership (no specification)
1996	Central inspection groups (*xunshizu*) set up	–
2003	*Xunshizu* becoming permanent	Dual leadership (no specification)
2004	Local discipline inspection commissions	Vertical leadership only

SOURCES: Yang Lihong, "Jianguo yilai zhongyang jijian lingdao tizhi de bianqe yu fazhan" [The changes and developments of the central discipline inspection leadership system since 1949], *Lingnan xuekan*, no. 4 (2004): 58–61; Guo Yong, "The Evolvement of the Chinese Communist Party Discipline Inspection Commission in the Reform Era," *China Review* 12, no. 1 (2012): 1–24; and Xuezhi Guo, "Controlling Corruption in the Party: China's Central Discipline Inspection Commission," *China Quarterly*, no. 219 (August 2014): 610–11.

information on local affairs are becoming increasingly important, further complementing the informational shortfalls on the part of the Center.[40] As the speedy advances in transportation and communications technologies in recent years make it both necessary and imperative for the Center to be adaptive and innovative, interesting linkages between traditional, revolutionary, and contemporary China are discernible in Beijing's constant search for means to ensure effective local governance.

The People's Republic as a unitary system denotes that, structurally, more power is allowed for the central government at the expense of local autonomy and diversity. Furthermore, as a unitary authoritarian regime, the central government can and does prevail over localities by way of changing the rules of the game at will. The Constitution, the Organization Law [*zuzhifa*], and Party Regulations stipulate that the local authorities are subject to "unified central control" [*zhongyang tongyi lingdao*]. Whenever it is deemed necessary, therefore, Beijing has the authority to introduce new rules to tip the balance of power in its favor.

The 1994 tax-sharing reform is a key case in point.[41] In the face of growing fiscal imbalances with localities, Beijing suddenly changed its mind by abolishing the fiscal contract system and adopting the tax-sharing reform despite the earlier commitment to the status quo at least until 1995. The changed rule dictated that the consolidated industrial-commercial tax was to be divided into the business tax as a local income, and the product circulation tax as a part of the value-added tax to be shared between Beijing and localities, thereby enabling the center to bite into a more voluminous and stable tax than any other. *Guangming Daily*, for instance, made it clear that "those who argue 'localities have their own measures to block central policy' [*shangyou zhengce xiayou duice*] will be severely criticized . . . [and] according to the discipline of our Party, lower-level organizations must obey the orders of their superior organizations."[42]

Beijing has changed key rules of the game whenever it found levels of local interference to be excessive. The center's strategy to cope with growing localism has included the mode of establishing supra-provincial mechanisms, thereby reducing the institutional room for provincial interference.[43] In the midst of the Asian financial crisis during 1998–1999, for instance, the Party Center removed local branches of the state banks from the local party committees' *nomenklatura* (i.e., the list of positions under direct personnel control), thereby significantly weakening the horizontal leverage of the local party committees over these local branches. Additionally, Beijing set up nine supra-provincial [*kuashengqu*] offices of the People's Bank of China in order to constrict the room for interference by the provincial party committees (see table 5.2 for details).[44]

Yet another strategy of Beijing has entailed the adoption of vertical-line control [*chuizhi guanli*]. Since the early 1990s, Beijing has sought

TABLE 5.2

The Post-1998 Structure of the People's Bank of China

Nature of relationship	Number	Administrative level	Scope
Directly controlled branches (*zhishu fenhang*)	9[a]	Deputy-provincial level	Supra-provincial
Directly controlled business sections (*yingye guanlibu*)	2[b]	Bureau level	Provincial
Key branches in separately planned cities (*zhongxin zhihang*)	5[c]	Deputy-bureau level	City-wide
Key branches in provinces where directly controlled branches are not located	20[d]	Deputy-bureau level	Provincial

NOTES: (a) These nine refer to two centrally administered municipalities of Tianjin and Shanghai, plus seven cities representing the seven macroregions—Shenyang, Jinan, Nanjing, Guangzhou, Wuhan, Chengdu, and Xi'an; (b) Beijing and Chongqing; (c) The five separately planned cities of Shenzhen, Dalian, Qingdao, Ningbo, and Xiamen; (d) Twenty provinces where the first two (a & b) items are not applicable.

SOURCES: Li Ruichang, *Zhengfujian wangluo zhili* [Intergovernmental networked governance] (Shanghai: Fudan daxue chunbanshe, 2012), 105, 108; and the author's interviews in Beijing in October 2014.

hard to sustain effective levels of control over key functional domains. By way of directly managing the personnel, wages, welfare, and operational scope through the framework of vertical-line control, Beijing has been seeking to maintain tight control and supervision over as many as twenty-eight key domains (accounting for roughly one-third of all domains under the central ministries, bureaus, and commissions) such as taxation, banking, insurances, auditing, industrial and commercial management, statistics collection, postal services, national and public security, and the implementation of a cigarette monopoly.[45] Although considerable variations exist among these sectors in terms of actual degrees of exclusive control, Beijing has nevertheless managed to get a grip on key sectors despite the successive measures of decentralization over the years.[46]

Tools of Suppression

What if all these preventive and deterrent mechanisms discussed above should fail? The ultimate solution would rest with deploying physical force at the center's disposal. The menu for Beijing's choices varies with the scale and impact of possible anticenter actions that may take the form of local subversion, societal resistance, or both. If they were to take place in small geographical areas, Beijing would find it relatively easy to contain them by utilizing a small civilian force under the Ministry of Public Security. Violent protests on a larger scale, though limited in geographical scope, were more often suppressed by the People's Armed Police (PAP) under the dual command of the State Council (by way of the Ministry of Public Security) and the Central Military Commission. According to a source, collective protests involving more than a thousand people (i.e., "large" collective protests) were generally dealt with by PAP, which normally has at least a divisional force stationed in each province-level government.[47]

The People's Liberation Army (PLA) constitutes the last resort for guaranteeing regime survival in the face of extraordinarily large (i.e., involving more than five thousand people) and violent antigovernment acts. Article 22 of the National Defense Law passed in 1997 stipulates, "The standing army, when necessary, may assist in maintaining order in accordance with the law." The 2004 edition of China's *Defense White Paper*, unlike the three earlier editions of 1998, 2000, and 2002, specifically lists "cracking down on criminal activities of all sorts and maintaining public order and social stability" as among the PLA's primary functions.[48] More importantly, the PLA is now required to perform so-called "diverse duties" [*duoyanghua renwu*], which include maintaining political stability in addition to fighting epidemics, combating natural disasters, and contributing to economic development. Under the broad rubric of "national defense mobilization" [*guofang dongyuan*], all military, semi-military, and civilian security forces can be deployed not only for combatant situations but also for non-war emergencies such as containing large-scale social disorder.[49]

If the PLA is indeed the last bastion for ensuring regime survival, how does Beijing make sure that the PLA has virtually no chances for local collusion against the central government? First, the PLA's highest subnational command consists of seven regional headquarters [*dajunqu*, 大军区], whereas their civilian counterparts have been situated one level down at the provinces. This purposive "mismatch"—just like the supra-provincial mechanisms for economic management noted earlier—reduces the chance for local collusion against Beijing. It can be speculated that the decision not to restore the great administrative regions at the beginning of the post-Mao reform era might be related to the leadership's concern with local–military collusions at the supra-provincial level.[50]

Second, from the days of the Jiangxi Soviet in the late 1920s, the non-central governments have been specifically prohibited from taking part in executing military-related policies.[51] Even so, were provincial governments to team up with the provincial-level military districts, it would pose at best a slight threat since leaders of the provincial military districts possess little control over the PLA's main force units.[52]

Third, while regional military commanders and political commissars served in one locality for as long as ten years or more during the Maoist era, since the early 1990s, especially after the PLA's involvement in the Tiananmen suppression in 1989, they now serve at one place for three years on average to reduce the chances of collusion. This is quite reminiscent of the rule of "fixed-term rotation" [*luntiao*, 轮调] for high-level local–military officials in traditional China. The average tenure for the viceroys during the Qing dynasty was, for instance, three years.[53]

Fourth, Beijing conventionally stations a large number of PLA and PAP forces in ethnic regions where anti-Beijing separatist movements have been active—most notably the Tibetan and Xinjiang regions. This is also reminiscent, in reverse, of the Yuan and Qing imperial courts dispatching and stationing loyal Mongol and Tartar garrisons at key strategic points to the northwest of Beijing to keep the Han populace under control.[54] Given the familiar dilemma that confronts the rulers of contemporary China, the degree of institutional resemblance is by no means surprising.

The center's conscious efforts to rein in any possibility of local–military collusion highlight the presence of real centrifugal dangers lurking in the background and the Chinese leaders' perceptions of this ominous potential. Given that the movement of any PLA troops larger than a battalion, even for the purpose of conducting a routine drill, must be authorized beforehand in writing by the Central Military Commission,[55] Beijing's preoccupation with military insubordination or local–military collusion is as real as its iron-fisted control over local military forces.

CHALLENGES FOR AUTHORITARIAN RESILIENCE

China's success with economic development since the early 1980s is undoubtedly daunting. Yet, to this author, its record of regime maintenance and social management for the past three decades deserves much credit. In spite of so many internal challenges, the People's Republic has shown a surprising level of resilience. And that durability has thus far rested very much upon the Communist Party and its leaders' adaptive strategies for survival, among which reining in localities has been an indispensable part.[56] It should be noted, however, that what worked well in the past does not automatically guarantee a continuous success in the future, just as the organizational principles of the Yan'an era proved difficult to implement during much of the People's Republic. Worse yet, new problems are constantly generated to pose a grave challenge to the People's Republic's chance of survival in the long run.

Aside from the much strengthened voices of local actors, multiple sources of instability have of late emerged to distract Beijing's attention and resources. They include increasingly turbulent conditions in some ethnic minority regions (Xinjiang and Tibet in particular); growing institutional decay at the grass-roots level, caused in large part by the weakened ideological control and the strong comeback of local clans; the nationwide spread of "collective public security incidents" [*quntixing shijian*, 群体性事件]; and the rise of unofficial religious sects and criminal organizations.[57] Furthermore, with the advances in telecommunications technologies—the Internet, mobile phones, and social network services (SNS) in particular—organizing a large-scale anticenter act has become easier and less costly, posing an unprecedented threat to resilient authoritarianism.[58] Any combination of these sources of instability could be quite lethal.

Despite such uncertainties, the future of the People's Republic as a resilient authoritarian state is pretty much an open-ended question. China's intermittent—yet successful—adaptation of traditional and revolutionary legacies, the CCP's persistent efforts to learn from the debacle of the Soviet Union, and Beijing's adept passing of the buck for many policy failures to local governments, as well as the central government's conscious reflections on its own mismanagement during the severe acute respiratory syndrome (SARS) crisis in 2003, offer ample room for a relatively optimistic projection, at least in the short run.

6

Determinants of Local Discretion
in Implementation

Exploring Policy-Contingent Variations

Implementation is such a complex interactive dynamics that the extent of discretion actually permitted for local governments is determined by a wide array of factors. Elite-centered studies, many of which flourished in the 1970s and 1980s, generally focus on factional ties and patron–client relations between the center and localities.[1] Their main argument is that the stronger the intergovernmental clientelistic/factional ties, the more room for local discretion (either for early adoption/advocacy or for foot-dragging/defiance) because such paternalistic ties more often than not have the effect of ensuring protection and therefore of mitigating the fears of persecution at times of political uncertainty.

In this imagery, local governments are depicted mostly as faithful agents who carried out their administrative duties on behalf of the central state (or part of it). Whereas this agent imagery often leaves an impression that the local bureaucracy was totally helpless, in reality, local officials were rather savvy strategic actors who often strove to maximize their own interests by pretending to accommodate the center's demands or by fabricating local performance. When the local bureaucracy eventually complied with Beijing's demands, it did so not because it necessarily preferred such an outcome, but because it had no other choices under the totalitarian reign of the Maoist period or under authoritarian control of the post-Mao era. More recent scholarship has therefore focused much on the institutional—i.e., personnel-related—control over localities.[2]

What can be termed as "local/societal explanations," on the other hand, focus on whether localities inherently have high stakes over a specific policy and therefore are likely to stand up against the center if their preferences differ significantly. That is, the higher the stakes for a locality as a whole, the more likely it is to behave proactively and assertively either in support or defiance of the central policy.[3] In contrast with the agent imagery described above, this alternative image—representative (or as bridges or corridors)—presupposes that on some occasions local governments did operate in a bottom-up fashion to articulate and represent views and interests of the populace to the central state.[4]

Despite the common sense that demonstrating allegiance to the Party Center was more advantageous to one's political career, some provincial leaders were courageous enough to push for local interests. It is not entirely clear why they chose to make a case for locally specific interests even at the risk of being stigmatized as parochial or counter-revolutionary.[5] Apparently, they went beyond the calculus of personal interests and fought for some *missions* of their own—i.e., safeguarding the people's livelihood by way of policy experimentation, innovation, or foot-dragging.[6] In most cases, provincial leaders' actions were reactive in that they were intended to redress a central policy that did not take into account particular local conditions. Overall, the cases where local governments represented locally specific interests against the preferences of the Party Center were neither common nor always successful.

In the post-Mao era, in tandem with the rise of a proactive entrepreneurial local state, a new imagery of principal—often dubbed as "local dukes" [*difang zhuhou*]—has emerged.[7] This imagery presupposes that the local state has its own distinct agenda, interest, strategic calculus, and risk assessment, all independent of the center.[8] The post-Mao local state, therefore, does not merely reacts to central policy but also proactively initiates plans and schemes designed specifically to promote its own interests that may not be in line with the interests of the center or the society. After thirty-some years of systemic reform, the overall extent of local discretion in implementation has reached a stage where the central state often has to adopt drastic measures of recentralization.[9]

If the center has a high stake over a policy but localities don't, Beijing will push hard for its implementation, and localities are most likely to comply. If the policy at hand does not affect local interests too much, there is no reason to stand against the center by risking the careers of local leaders. If both the center and localities have similarly high stakes, under the norms of post-Mao decentralization, neither is likely to back off easily. The center, then, would resort to a wide range of control instruments and punitive actions, whereas localities might rely on their patronage networks or other evasive tactics. Methodologically, it is virtually impossible to come up with pertinent information on every province's clandestine networks with the center. Even if a province does have some known linkages with Beijing, it is uncertain if it would utilize them every time it faced some difficulties.[10] Therefore, from a methodological viewpoint, central–local patronage networks are not actually that helpful in constructing a nationwide picture of implementation.

Assuming that all other things (i.e., local assertiveness, patronage networks, and societal demands) are similar among the provinces, the level of local discretion actually permitted for implementation is likely to vary with different *types* of policy.[11] That is, once we step outside of actor-based perspectives, what type of policy it is may to a considerable extent determine the level of local discretion actually allowed for implementation. In typifying different policy issues, the following three categories seem analytically useful: (1) policy scope, (2) policy nature, and (3) levels of urgency.

Policy scope refers to the number of local targets in which central policy is to be implemented. With this yardstick, any policy can be categorized as either encompassing or selective. The former denotes a policy to be applied indiscriminately to all or most local units, whereas the latter refers to a policy with a limited number of local targets. A crucial ramification of this distinction is that the broader the scope of implementation (i.e., if a policy is more encompassing than selective), the more likely is the level of local discretion to be restricted because Beijing generally prefers to pose itself as a "fair" center and to push for a standardized mode so as to facilitate easier monitoring of local compliance.[12]

Policy nature refers to functional characteristics as to whether a policy is mainly geared toward resource allocation or toward governance. The former—termed here as resource policy—is concerned mainly with the allocation of tangible resources such as budgets, grants, investment, materials, development projects, etc. The latter—termed here as governance policy—is of political, ideological and/or administrative nature without involving direct allocation of fiscal or material resources between the central and local government units. Governance policy includes personnel management, political campaigns, organizational restructuring, stability maintenance, etc. A key implication here is that governance policy generally allows low levels of local discretion because the implementation of nonresource policy is more often guided by political/ideological considerations and therefore likely to demand higher levels of compliance. Resource policy, on the other hand, is more susceptible to bargaining and negotiation and therefore more likely to offer room for local discretion.[13]

Policy can also be categorized by the degree of urgency involved. The degree of urgency refers to the central policy makers' perception and recognition as to how swiftly the policy at hand must be implemented. The crucial implication of this factor is that the more urgent the need for a policy is deemed, the harder the center will push for its swift implementation and therefore the less room for local discretion.[14]

Table 6.1 utilizes the three dimensions of policy type to illustrate two extreme contingencies and the extent of local discretion expected of each. If a policy is encompassing (i.e., to be executed in most or all local units), governance geared (i.e., involving no direct allocation of tangible resources), and urgent (i.e., requiring immediate implementation), the room for local strategic maneuvering and discretion is the most limited. Suppressing *Falungong* and containing SARS are good examples of this extreme contingency. On the other hand, if a policy is selective (i.e., with only a few local targets), resource geared (i.e., involving the allocation of financial and material resources), and nonurgent, it is likely to allow more room for local discretion in the process of implementation. The Sanxia Dam project and many region-specific development schemes belong to the latter contingency.[15]

TABLE 6.1
Extent of Local Discretion by Policy Type: Two Extremes

Policy scope	Policy nature	Urgency	Local discretion	Total time taken
Encompassing	Governance	Urgent	Low	Short
Selective	Resource	Non-urgent	High	Long

All three dimensions are of ordinal scale on a continuum, and most policies of the post-Mao era fall somewhere between the two extremes shown in table 6.1.[16] As measuring the extent of local discretion in the implementation of every policy in every province is impossible, this study bases its appraisal on six different types of policy from the post-Mao era: (1) the policy of taking Hainan out of Guangdong to make it a province-level unit in 1988, (2) the household responsibility system [*jiating lianchan chengbao zerenzhi*] reform of 1979–1984, (3) the tax-sharing reform [*fenshuizhi*] in 1994, (4) the Revive the Northeast [*zhenxing dongbei*] scheme since 2004, (5) the stability maintenance [*weiwen*] policy since the mid-2000s, and (6) the provinces-directly-ruling-counties [*sheng zhiguan xian*] policy since 2009. Key features of these six policies are laid out in table 6.2.

If the aforementioned framework as to the impact of policy type on local discretion is applied here, the room for local discretion in each of the six policies would be as shown in the far-right column in table 6.2. That is, theoretically speaking, the stability maintenance policy (abbreviated as WW) would allow the least room, and the "Revive the Northeast" scheme (abbreviated as ZXDB), the most room, with the Guangdong/Hainan policy (HN-GD), the household responsibility reform (HRS), the tax-sharing reform (FSZ), and the provinces-directly-ruling counties policy (SGX), placed somewhere in the middle.[17]

TABLE 6.2
Characteristics of the Six Case Policies

	Policy scope	Policy nature	Urgency	Expected local discretion
ZXDB	Selective	Resource	Non-urgent	High
SGX	Encompassing	Resource	Non-urgent	Medium
HN-GD	Selective	Governance	Urgent	Low/medium
FSZ	Encompassing	Resource	Urgent	Low/medium
HRS	Encompassing	Governance	Non-urgent	Low/medium
WW	Encompassing	Governance	Urgent	Low

NOTE: ZXDB denotes the "Revive the Northeast" scheme; SGX denotes the provinces-directly-ruling-counties policy; HN-GD refers to taking Hainan out of Guangdong to make it a province-level unit; FSZ points to the tax-sharing reform; HRS refers to the household responsibility reform; and WW refers to the stability maintenance policy. Not all different types of policy have actually existing examples. For instance, although an example of selective-resource-urgent policy is "Aiding the regions in Sichuan affected by the earthquake," an example of selective-governance-non-urgent policy is difficult to come up with.

SELECTIVE-RESOURCE POLICY:
THE CASE OF REGIONAL DEVELOPMENT

Like the coastal development strategy of the 1980s and 1990s, the "Develop the West" [*xibu dakaifa*] program initiated in the late 1990s and the "Raise the Central Region" [*zhongbu jueqi*] scheme officially pronounced in late 2005, the "Revive the Northeast" scheme, decided in late 2003 and formally launched in 2004, was a selective-resource policy. The "Revive the Northeast" scheme is used here as a case of selective-resource policy, which theoretically allowed ample room for central–provincial bargaining and local discretion.[18]

Beijing's Political Agenda Meeting the Northeast's Economic Motive

Coastal provinces had benefited the most from Beijing's preferential policies and opening reforms in the 1980s. By the mid-1990s, the perils of regional disparities became noticeable, and it was in this particular context that Jiang Zemin announced the "Develop the West" program in 1999 in order to herald a key change to China's regional development strategy.[19] After succeeding Jiang as the General Secretary of the Chinese Communist Party in 2002, Hu Jintao came up with a "centrally coordinated regional development strategy" [*tongchou xietiao quyu fazhan zhanlue*]. Subsequently, while continuing with the "Develop the West" scheme, the Hu-Wen leadership put forward its own signature regional development project catered to the Northeast as China's "fourth engine."[20]

The decline of the Northeast, formerly dubbed as "China's eldest son" and the "cradle of China's industry," was long deemed a disgrace on Chinese socialism. In fact, the Northeast had been the showcase for all the problems—most notably the plummeted productivity and high levels of urban unemployment—embedded in the state-run economy, providing fertile soil for widespread social discontent and collective protests. It is not surprising that Jilin was home to the sect of *Falungong*, and moreover, half of the local petitioners heading to Beijing allegedly came from the Northeast in the early 2000s.[21]

Naturally, Beijing wished to devise a scheme for the troubled region in order to prevent it from being a drag on the national economy, as well as to maintain social stability there. Provincial initiatives and local activism played a crucial role in making the "Revive the Northeast" scheme possible as, since the mid-1990s, provincial officials of the Northeast actively called for more support from the center. Explicit demands for Beijing's preferential policy, voiced by the Northeastern Group of the 15th Central Committee at the Third Plenum in late 1998, were a notable example.[22] Yet the "Revive the Northeast" scheme had to wait for five more years before coming into being as different opinions were available at the time regarding whether Beijing's support should precede the region's own efforts toward restructuring. Additionally, because the "Develop the West" program was Jiang Zemin's signature project, it was only after Jiang stepped down that Hu could launch his own priority scheme for the Northeast.[23]

Provincial Initiatives and Central Auspices

As Beijing's political agenda (i.e., reducing social discontent in the Northeast and preventing it from being a drag on the national economy) matched well with the region's economic motives, central–provincial differences were easy to settle. The center was of the position that the three provinces should focus mainly on restructuring state-owned enterprises, rationalizing their industrial structure, and establishing a workable welfare system instead of merely asking for Beijing's support.[24] The preferences of the provinces were hardly different. In December 2003, before the Office for Reviving the Northeast [*Zhenxing dongbei bangongshi*] was established, the development and reform commissions of all three provinces submitted plans for one hundred key projects to the National Development and Reform Commission.[25] All the provisional targets stipulated in these plans by the three provinces were subsequently approved by the State Council Office for Reviving the Northeast.[26]

In contrast with the "Develop the West" project, the "Revive the Northeast" scheme was a typical case of "provision of policy only" [*zhigei zhengce bugei qian*]. That is, Beijing focused mainly on formulating preferential policies for attracting foreign direct investment in the Northeast, but not on offering direct financial support.[27] Coordination and negotiation went fairly smooth in designating priority sectors for the Northeast scheme as the region was dying to get preferential policies. Beijing designated six key sectors for the region as a whole: equipment manufacturing, petrochemical industry, shipbuilding, automobile manufacturing, agricultural processing, and pharmaceuticals. The center's support for these sectors largely took the form of exempting selected enterprises in the region from paying consumption-related value added taxes and of allowing the regional firms in these sectors to shorten the depreciation period for fixed assets by a maximum of 40 percent.[28]

Of the six priority sectors, Heilongjiang got four (equipment manufacturing, petrochemical industry, agricultural processing, and pharmaceuticals), Liaoning attained five (equipment manufacturing, petrochemical industry, shipbuilding, agricultural processing, and pharmaceuticals), and Jilin had four (petrochemical industry, automobile manufacturing, agricultural processing, and pharmaceuticals).[29] Although there certainly was some overlap (i.e., all three went for petrochemical industry, agricultural processing, and pharmaceuticals), because the provinces were supposed to look for funding on their own mainly from overseas, bargaining with Beijing was rather simple as they only had to agree on the overall framework. Interestingly, the agricultural tax was abolished in the Northeast in 2004, nearly two years earlier than the rest of the country.[30]

Although Beijing's support for the "Revive the Northeast" scheme was mainly in the form of policy provision, the center nevertheless offered some financial resources for infrastructure development in the region. The most noteworthy project was the construction of express railways linking Harbin with Dalian [*dongbiandao tiedao*], for which not only provincial funds but also central resources were jointly deployed. The central government also utilized funds from selling bonds in financing the building of infrastructure and industrial upgrading in the Northeast.[31]

The "Revive the Northeast" scheme was a typical selective-resource policy, and therefore ample room was available for central–local bargaining and local discretion. Because the target date for its completion was set at some time no earlier than 2020, the level of urgency involved was also very low, allowing more room for flexibility. Although Beijing was not really in the position to provide sufficient resources—as it was at the same time preoccupied with the West, the Central Region, Pudong, Binhai, and the Pan Pearl River Delta—the provision of special policies was sufficient enough to satisfy the Northeast region long in hunger for central support.

SELECTIVE-GOVERNANCE POLICY:
MAKING HAINAN A PROVINCIAL UNIT

On April 13, 1988, the State Council officially designated Hainan as a province-level unit. It was the first case where a new provincial-level unit was created effectively since 1952. Given Beijing's propensity to keep the number of provincial units at a minimum—as noted in chapter 3 in this volume—it was a surprising decision to many. Particularly because the Hainanese had long been known for their desire to establish a province of its own, independent from Guangdong, the announcement was indeed taken as a significant change.[32]

Hainan's longing for a provincial status matched perfectly with the reformist leadership's design to make it a special economic zone for tourism and investment.[33] Initially, the scheme was a part of Beijing's plan for accelerating the development of Guangdong's economy, which was in turn an integral part of China's coastal development strategy. As early as 1980, the State Council permitted Hainan to utilize the same set of preferential policies accorded to Shenzhen and Zhuhai. And in 1983, the State Council and the Central Committee jointly granted a de facto special economic zone status to Hainan. Soon after, Beijing began to think in terms of separating Hainan from Guangdong.[34]

The center's plan to upgrade the island's administrative rank faltered in the midst of Guangdong's staunch opposition as well as of the infamous car-smuggling scandal in Hainan in 1985.[35] After a brief hiatus, the central leadership again committed itself to a scheme of developing Hainan's economy. In late 1986 and early 1987, Zhao Ziyang, then premier, sent investigative teams to Hainan. The reports by the investigative teams included a strong recommendation that Hainan be administratively upgraded to a provincial status with privileges as a special economic zone. The recommendation was soon approved by Zhao, Hu Yaobang, and finally by Deng Xiaoping. The news about Hainan becoming a provincial-level unit was first revealed by Zhao on June 12, 1987, and ten months later, it was announced officially by the State Council.[36]

The scheme of "taking Hainan out of Guangdong to make it a province" was a selective-governance policy with some resource implications. It is not totally clear whether much room was available for the discretion of local governments. In designating Hainan as a province-level unit, Beijing did not really provide material resources—except for the provision of special policies—but it was clearly eager to proceed quickly so as to produce visible results as soon as possible. That is, the level of urgency involved was fairly high, thereby constricting the room for local discretion in the implementation of a governance policy.

ENCOMPASSING-RESOURCE POLICY (I): THE TAX-SHARING REFORM

Unlike the "Revive the Northeast" scheme, which was a selective-resource policy, the tax-sharing reform was an encompassing-resource policy. The implication is, of course, that the level of discretion allowed for local implementers would be more limited in the latter case. With a series of fiscal devolution during the 1980s, Beijing opened a Pandora's box full of local perversities. On two occasions, the center tried in vain to induce provincial compliance in changing the dominant system from that of overall revenue sharing to one of specific revenue sharing, first in 1980 and again in 1985. By the late 1980s, the decline of central control became apparent in the fiscal dimension where, despite some readjustment measures and austerity programs, Beijing successively failed to increase its share of budgetary revenues.[37]

Because provinces were willing to give up the profits from locally owned enterprises so long as they could get a larger chunk of more voluminous industrial-commercial taxes [*gongshangshui*], the overall revenue sharing system was sustained during 1985–1987 despite Beijing's preference for changing it.[38] Given that Beijing did not wish to spoil the reform atmosphere by imposing too much politically, local diversities in the mode of sharing revenues with the center were once again permitted in 1988, thereby rendering standardized central control more difficult.[39] In 1990, the Seventh Plenum of the Thirteenth Central Committee again decided to leave the fiscal contract system unchanged during the entire period of the 8th Five-Year Plan (1991–1995).

Propellants of the Tax-Sharing Reform

The share of central revenues in gross national product (GNP), which fell from 57 percent in 1981 to 33 percent in 1993, was indicative of how unsuccessful Beijing was in increasing the size of revenues at its disposal. Extra-budgetary funds (EBFs) increased nine times, from renminbi (RMB) 34.7 billion in 1978 to 324 billion in 1991, while the total budgetary revenues only doubled. EBFs as a percentage of budgetary revenues grew from 31 in 1978 to 95 in 1991.[40] Under the circumstances where Beijing failed to expand its revenues but had to shoulder increasing responsibilities (administrative expenditures, defense spending, price subsidies and enterprise deficit subsidies, payments for bonds, etc.), budget deficits became successive. In stark contrast, local governments reaped seven-year surpluses during 1981–1990.[41]

According to the 1993 budget report, China recorded a deficit of RMB 89.9 billion, of which 38.5 billion was financed by domestic debts, 30.9 billion by foreign debts, and the rest, 20.5 billion, remained unfinanced.[42] Given that tax revenues accounted for more than 80 percent of all budgetary revenues, readjusting the ways in which tax revenues were distributed between different levels of governments was the most appealing option. At the Third Plenum of the 14th Central Committee in November 1993, despite its earlier commitment to the status quo at least until 1995, Beijing announced an immediate abolition of the financial contract system and the nationwide adoption of the tax-sharing system, signifying a high level of urgency involved. These changes were immediately enacted as a national law [yusanfa] at the second plenary session of the Eighth National People's Congress in March 1994.

Provincial Responses to the Tax-Sharing Reform

One key component of the reform was the division of the consolidated industrial-commercial tax into the business tax [yingyeshui] as a local income, and the product circulation tax [shangpin liutongshui] as a part of the value-added tax to be a shared income. Because the provinces' preference for the system of overall revenue sharing lay in getting a large share of the consolidated industrial-commercial tax—more voluminous and stable than any other single tax category—the change was undoubtedly a hard blow to the provinces.[43] It was an encompassing policy as the uniform tax rate of 33 percent was imposed on all domestic enterprises, as opposed to four different tax rates prior to 1994.[44] Furthermore, the power to grant tax reductions and exemptions was recentralized back to the State Council for the value-added tax and business tax. All consumption taxes levied on the sales of tobacco products and liquor were to go to the center, and 75 percent of the value-added taxes levied on the production and circulation of these two products would also be retained by the center.[45]

Provincial responses to the tax-sharing reform as an urgent, encompassing resource policy were initially mixed, as views of some

TABLE 6.3
Number of Votes for Four NPC Decisions

Issues	Vote yes	Vote no	Abstain	Invalid
Budgetary Law	2,110	337	225	49
Budget for 1994	2,403	178	129	11
National Economic Development Plan for 1994	2,584	60	56	21
Government Work Report	2,655	23	25	18

SOURCE: *Ming Pao*, March 23, 1994.

coastal provinces were highly negative. They regarded the reform as "robbing the rich to help the poor" [*jiefu jipin*] and "implementing egalitarianism" [*gao pingjunzhuyi*]. Many provincial delegates to the second session of the Eighth National People's Congress, held in March 1994, demanded that the new policy should avoid the malpractice of standardization.[46] Some inland provinces heavily dependent on the taxes levied on tobacco and liquor products—Yunnan and Guizhou in particular— were also critical.[47]

Negative views held by many provinces were manifested in the number of votes against the legislation of the Budgetary Law at the National People's Congress in March 1994. According to table 6.3, among the four key issues subjected to voting, the first two budget-related ones got many more "no" votes and abstention than the other two. With regard to the Budgetary Law in particular, more than a quarter of the delegates either voted against it or abstained, demonstrating pervasive local discontents.

Inducing Local Compliance

The implementation of the 1994 tax-sharing reform was starkly different from Beijing's earlier attempts. The urgent and encompassing nature of the policy made the implementation swift, standardized, and nationwide, allowing little room for provincial foot-dragging. At the National Financial Work Conference in December 1993, Finance Minister Liu Zhongli stressed that the provinces must implement the reform without arbitrary changes.[48] *Guangming Daily* made it clear that "those who argue 'localities have their own measures to block central policy' [*shangyou zhengce xiayou duice*] will be severely criticized."[49] The Ministry of Finance even sent down work teams to oversee local implementation in Shanghai, Jiangsu, Shandong, Tianjin, Hebei, Henan,

Heilongjiang, Shaanxi, and Sichuan.[50] Official documents did not specify any concrete figures, but references were frequently made to the effect that Beijing's share in the budgetary revenues should be raised to 50 percent in the short run and 65 percent in the long run.[51]

Although the encompassing aspect of the reform was conducive to reducing the room for local foot-dragging, the resource-related dimension of the policy allowed some pre-coordination and bargaining between Beijing and the provinces. As is typical of the post-Mao mode of policy implementation, the tax-sharing reform had already been tested in four province-level units and five "central economic cities" since 1992. In pushing the reform forward, the center deployed two measures to mitigate provincial discontents. For one, Beijing made a pledge that if the provincial revenues for 1994 should drop below the 1993 baseline, the balance would be paid in cash. For another, Beijing introduced a transitional arrangement that the preexisting provincial decisions on tax reductions and exemptions for enterprises with low profitability would be honored through 1995.[52]

The nationwide implementation of the tax-sharing reform took less than a year, pointing to a swift pace of local compliance.[53] In retrospect, the center's will prevailed as Beijing's share in budgetary revenue rose from 22 percent in 1993 to an annual average of 52 percent during 1994–2002.[54] Although some incremental adjustments were made to coordinate differing provincial interests, one thing was clear: If a high level of urgency dictated the center's firm commitment, Beijing was sufficiently able to enforce new rules and induce full local compliance.[55]

ENCOMPASSING-RESOURCE POLICY (II): THE PROVINCES-DIRECTLY-RULING-COUNTIES POLICY

Another case of encompassing-resource policy under consideration here is the provinces-directly-ruling-counties [sheng zhiguan xian] reform of the 2000s.[56] As discussed in chapter 3, this was in significant part a measure of correcting the problems associated with the cities-ruling-counties policy implemented nationwide since the mid-1980s. That is, although prefecture-level cities were put in charge of ruling counties and county-level cities for twenty-some years, their overall performance was deemed far less ideal than Beijing's expectations in terms of actively assisting those county-level units to develop fast. Instead, the prefecture-level cities kept milking cash out of counties and county-level cities and impeded their economic growth.[57] Hence, the provinces-directly-ruling-counties reform was introduced specifically to put the counties—initially their budgets and finances—back into direct control by the provinces.

The processes where both the cities-ruling-counties policy and the provinces-directly-ruling-counties scheme were implemented appear analogous in that what had begun as a limited local experimentation was gradually expanded to become a nationwide reform. In the former case, the "Jiangsu experiment" in 1982 was diffused to Liaoning, Guangdong, and other provinces. By 1991, 170 prefecture-level cities, comprising 89 percent of all prefecture-level cities in China, ruled 696 counties. By 2006, 316 prefecture-level cities (95 percent of 333 prefecture-level units) directly ruled counties and county-level cities.[58]

In the latter case, too, the policy began in 2002 as a small pilot program in Zhejiang, with the specific purposes of weakening prefecture-level cities and putting counties back under provincial control. Hainan, Fujian, and Hubei soon followed suit. By 2006, the scope of implementation expanded significantly as Central Document No. 1 [2006] stipulated that "localities with proper endowments [*jubei tiaojian de difang*] *may* set up experimental sites for the scheme." In 2009, it became something more than an experiment as Central Document No. 1 [2009] stated that "provinces with proper conditions should be *encouraged* [emphasis added] to promote the 'provinces-directly-ruling-counties' policy." By mid-2009, it became clear that the policy was to be carried out nationwide except for ethnic minority regions, and even the target date for completion was set for the end of 2012.[59]

Whereas a quarter of China's counties were under direct control by the provincial authorities in 2007, the ratio went up to 50.2 percent of all counties in twenty-two provinces (excluding the centrally administered municipalities and ethnic minority regions) by 2009.[60] Worth noting at this juncture, however, is the fact that, as of 2014, neither was the original target (i.e., completing the nationwide adoption of the scheme by the end of 2012) accomplished, nor does the process of the nationwide implementation appear as smooth as planned (see table 6.4).[61]

The proposed scheme became an encompassing (i.e., nationwide) policy by 2009; nevertheless, it remained largely a resource policy as it allowed direct provincial control over county finances in most cases.[62] The resource aspect of the policy produced some room for local discretion, interlocal conflicts, and central–local bargaining, thereby impeding swift nationwide implementation. Because Beijing has never clarified what those "proper conditions" mean, a considerable degree

TABLE 6.4
Implementation of the Provinces-Directly-Ruling-Counties Scheme (2013)

Full adoption (100 percent)	Fujian, Hainan, Hubei, Jilin, Jiangsu, Zhejiang, Anhui, Jiangxi, Guangxi, Gansu (10)
Near-full adoption (80~90 percent)	Hunan (1)
Mid-range adoption (50–80 percent)	Shanxi, Guizhou (2)
Low-level adoption (10–49 percent)	Hebei, Sichuan, Liaonin, Qinghai, Guangdong, Shandong, Shaanxi, Ningxia (8)
Non-Implementation (0–9 percent)	Henan, Heilongjiang, Yunnan (3)
Exempted[a]	Neimenggu, Xizang, Xinjiang (3)

NOTE: (a) This refers to ethnic minority regions. It is not clear why Ningxia and Guangxi did not get this status in contrast with the remaining three.

SOURCES: Anhui, http://vip.chinalawinfo.com/newlaw2002/slc/slc.asp?gid=17084651; Fujian, http://www.srd.yn.gov.cn/ynrdcwh/1013091113344434176/20111110/231378.html; Gansu, http://gsrb.gansudaily.com.cn/system/2011/01/12/011852062.shtml; Guangdong, http://finance.people.com.cn/GB/70846/18011931.html; Guangxi, http://www.legaldaily.com.cn/index/content/2011-03/25/content_2544421.htm?node=20908; Guizhou, http://www.gzgov.gov.cn/zwgk/show.aspx?id=22fa67c2-08d0-4c9e-bf85-076a814b3dfb; Hainan, http://www.hainan.gov.cn/data/news/2010/07/106992/; Hebei, http://code.fabao365.com/law_65022_1.html; Heilongjiang, http://www.hljorg.gov.cn/page/Article.aspx?NewsId=e157c305-0821-48c0-b0be-26788fb30d06; Henan, http://news.xinhuanet.com/local/2011-06/30/c_121605551.htm; Hubei, http://www.ecz.gov.cn/wzlm/zwdt/bmgzdt/czxj/19956.htm; Hunan, http://www.hnczt.gov.cn/zt/szgx/Index.html; Jiangsu, http://www.chinareform.org.cn/area/inshore/Forward/201010/t20101014_46763.htm; Jiangxi, http://www.srd.yn.gov.cn/ynrdcwh/1013091113344434176/20111110/231378.html; Jilin, http://finance.sina.com.cn/g/20050627/21411729752.shtml; Liaoning, http://www.china.com.cn/guoqing/gbbg/2012-12/05/content_27314813.htm; Neimenggu, http://www.nmg.chinanews.com/show.asp?id=1034; Ningxia, http://news.xinhuanet.com/politics/2009-12/16/content_12655853.htm; Qinghai, http://www.chinalawedu.com/news/1200/22016/22019/22073/2007/5/lio2113545122570021254-0.htm; Shaanxi, http://www.shaanxi.gov.cn/0/103/4901.htm; Shandong, http://www.mof.gov.cn/pub/mof/xinwenlianbo/shandongcaizhengxinxilianbo/200910/t20091015_218283.html; Shanxi, http://kq.xiaoyi.gov.cn/?thread-1195-1.html; Sichuan, http://sc.sina.com.cn/news/m/2013-12-28/0702165323.html; Yunnan, http://www.srd.yn.gov.cn/ynrdcwh/1013091113344434176/20111110/231378.html; Zhejiang, http://wenku.baidu.com/link?url=N5P5Qh9DpoNzFkiAigHbgaJl1heMWuH7g0-Z5ad8clGZOt98aoyGWnKRPW8QrRdL5B8m9IL9tEZN8jFoLgx8xs5rrbMXZB1I9C9bsEsj3k_.

of discretion was permitted to localities in interpreting these conditions either to adopt the new policy fast or to drag their feet over it.[63] Consequently, many prefecture-level cities—to be most adversely affected by the proposed change—were not so willing or eager to follow the central directives in relinquishing power and authority to the county-level units under their jurisdiction. In the case of Henan, for instance, nine out of the ten experimental counties experienced serious difficulties as their prefecture-level superiors did not wish to transfer key approval authority for license issuing, etc.[64]

The weakening and eventual cancellation of the prefecture level as an intermediate tier of the subnational administration was an agonizing issue for the center. Although the provinces-directly-ruling-counties policy was successfully carried out in Zhejiang, Fujian, and Hainan with a small number of counties, the same could not be said of others, because a single province was then forced to administer over eighty county-level units.[65] This dilemma must have put some constraints on Beijing's original plans to accelerate the completion of the policy, thereby slowing down the entire process of nationwide popularization. The center's stance, as of 2012, was one of "coordinated gradualism" [*shitiao jianjin*].[66] The lack of consensus on the urgency of the reform at hand also generated further impetus for local foot-dragging.

ENCOMPASSING-GOVERNANCE POLICY (I): THE HOUSEHOLD RESPONSIBILITY REFORM

The household responsibility reform of the early 1980s was similar to the 1994 tax-sharing reform in that they both required nationwide implementation—i.e., encompassing in scope. The former, however, differed from the latter in that the household responsibility reform did not have direct resource bearings on central–provincial relations. That is, although the household responsibility reform entailed crucial economic dimensions, these were mostly confined to micro-interactions between peasants and grass-roots authorities. Their overall impact on central–provincial dynamics was more political/institutional and even ideological than economic. Although the household responsibility reform was by no means a routine task because of the sheer magnitude of institutional remolding in almost every corner of the nation, the issue of urgency had to be interpreted somewhat differently from that of demanding immediate one-shot compliance.

The household responsibility reform—defined as the nationwide adoption of *baochan daohu* [household production quota] and *baogan daohu* [household contract with fixed levies] during 1979–1983—was designed to cope with the problems of collective farming such as lax labor discipline, prevalent free-riders' symptoms, and egalitarian redistribution. The household responsibility reform went through three distinct stages.[67] The first was the pre-1980 period, during which not only the Party Center was "strongly opposed" [*buxu*] to it, but provincial and local authorities also forbade the practice except for the so-called "special cases" [*chuwai*] in accordance with the Fourth Plenum decisions.[68] Except for Anhui (as well as Guizhou and Gansu), where roughly 10 percent of the production teams were already under the household production quota in 1979, the rate of implementation elsewhere was very low.[69]

During the second stage of 1980–1981, Beijing displayed some flexibility and permissiveness [*yunxu*] toward the new systems. Central Document No. 75, issued on September 25, 1980, designated "poor and backward regions" [*pinkun luohou diqu*] and "production units dependent on state subsidies" [*sankaodui*] as areas permitted for *baochan daohu* and *baogan daohu*.[70] By August 1981, the center's position on household farming became more relaxed; it was even regarded as a "good" way of relieving poverty and enhancing productivity without tainting the collective nature of the socialist economy.[71]

The third stage began with an official blessing written into Central Document No. 1, issued on January 1, 1982. The document formally endorsed both *baochan daohu* and *baogan daohu* as systems of the socialist economy. Subsequently, both (then popularly called *shuangbao*) became the key policy to pursue on a full scale. From January 1982 through December 1983 (when the nationwide implementation rate reached 98.3 percent), the process of inducing provincial compliance took more than two full years.

The Provincial Calculus: Strategic Opportunism and Local Conditions

Available data on the provincial-level implementation suggests that many were highly opportunistic and cautious toward the controversial policy until they became pretty certain about the center's preference (see table 6.5). In June 1981 (i.e., before Beijing officially displayed its preference for household farming), the level of provincial compliance was relatively low, with an average rate of 37.9 percent. Once Beijing's preference was fixed by January 1982, most provinces hurried to adopt the household responsibility reform on a full scale. Within a year, the extent of nationwide implementation rose to 80.6 percent, with more than fifteen provinces reaching the 90 percent bar. Noteworthy is the standard deviation value, which actually increased by 2.2 percent compared to that of June 1981. That is, despite the significantly enhanced compliance rate, a few provinces were successfully dragging their feet.

Because the problems of collective farming were so widely recognized for so long, unless the center's preference did not differ, many provinces were willing and eager to adopt the system of household

TABLE 6.5
Provincial Implementation of Household Farming (%)

Province	June 1981	December 1982
Anhui	69.3	95.0
Fujian	33.1	91.0
Gansu	72.2	99.0
Guangdong	41.8	91.8
Guangxi	35.7	96.3
Guizhou	95.0	99.7
Hebei	36.4	96.0
Heilongjiang	0.7	12.0
Henan	33.2	93.1
Hubei	n/a	75.3
Hunan	11.2	93.0
Jiangxi	n/a	94.1
Jilin	4.0	30.0
Liaoning	6.4	31.8
Neimenggu	40.1	90.0
Ningxia	51.6	n/a
Qinghai	n/a	92.0
Shaanxi	n/a	90.0
Shandong	38.2	82.8
Shanxi	58.4	95.0
Sichuan	n/a	89.2
Xinjiang	33.3	82.5
Xizang	39.2	n/a
Yunnan	35.5	91.7

NOTES: $n=17$ (provinces with data for both time points)
mean   37.9   80.6
s.d.   25.2   27.4
SOURCE: Chung, *Central Control and Local Discretion in China*, 67.

farming. If the new policy could bring about enhanced productivity and increased income, there would be little lost on the part of the provincial authorities. Furthermore, household-based experiments of the 1960s provided some assurance about the workability of the new system.[72]

The same could not be said of a few "resisters": Heilongjiang, Jilin, and Liaoning. The average compliance rate for these three provinces was only 26.9 percent in December 1982. Even in December 1983, the rate stood at 92.1 percent, still lower than the national average by 6.2 percent.[73] The common factor for these Northeast provinces was a complex relationship between the size of land available to individual households, the average size of a production team, and the specific type of mechanization pursued there. Unlike elsewhere in China, the Northeast provinces had an exceptionally large plot of land for each household, which was not susceptible to manual labor or even small machinery-based mechanization.[74]

Inducing Provincial Compliance

Securing provincial compliance was not as easy as it seemed. One fundamental obstacle was Beijing's pronounced principle of implementing according to local conditions. Having stressed the imperative of *yindi zhiyi* so strongly since the late 1970s, the center could not easily dismiss the locally specific interests of the Northeast provinces. Particularly when a provincial leader stood up to safeguard provincial interests on the basis of *yindi zhiyi*, Beijing had to find a persuasive way to justify administrative imposition. Heilongjiang, for instance, highlighted the unique characteristics of the province as follows: "Our province has one outstanding difference from the rest of the country: our province is a region of modernized large-scale agriculture . . . with a mechanization level of 60 percent. . . . This indicates the advanced level of our production forces. Therefore, the implementation of the household responsibility systems should proceed in accordance with these local characteristics."[75]

Even after Central Document No. 1 [1982] was issued, Heilongjiang was still of the position that the scope of household-based farming was to be confined only to poor teams (accounting for 15 percent of all teams there) with low levels of mechanization and that the pace of implementation should be gradual in accordance with the *yindi zhiyi* principle.[76] Liaoning's and Jilin's positions differed little from that of Heilongjiang throughout 1982–1983.[77]

Over time, Beijing came to identify the pace of local compliance with the legitimacy of the policy, thereby raising the level of urgency for the reform. Soon, Beijing put political pressure on the noncomplying provinces, starting in the second half of 1982. In July, Premier Zhao Ziyang visited Liaoning and called for an immediate popularization of the household responsibility reform in the Northeast. In August, Hu Yaobang went to Heilongjiang, where he criticized the sluggish pace of decollectivization there.[78] In October, Du Runsheng of the Rural Development Research Center issued a stern warning: "In carrying out the household responsibility reform, we have to continue liberating our ideology and relax control. . . . A few regions are still unwilling to act on the demands of the masses by refusing to change the 'one big bowl' situation."[79]

Beijing's pressure reached its apex with the speech by Wan Li, vice-premier in charge of agriculture at the National Agricultural Secretaries Conference in November. Wan remarked: "Comparatively speaking, the household responsibility reform has not been successful in all corners of our countryside. In fact, there exists certain 'passivity' in many areas and, in some areas, such passivity is of a very bad sort. . . . The implementation of *baogan daohu* has not been very smooth due to the obstruction on the part of some leading cadres."[80]

Heilongjiang and its first party secretary, Yang Yichen, did not succumb to the pressure from Beijing. One day after the publication of Wan's speech, Yang delivered his own at the Prefecture, County and City Party Secretaries' Work Conference: "In determining which responsibility system to implement, we have to value the opinions of the masses that will eventually choose a system on the basis of their *local conditions*."[81]

The center drew the last card: personnel reshuffle. In February 1983, Yang Yichen was transferred to Beijing as the supreme people's procurator-general. Given that his transfer had already been decided in December 1982, Yang's speech was apparently the last expression of his firm stance on the household responsibility reform. With Yang's departure, Heilongjiang's pace of implementation skyrocketed within two months, from 12 percent in December 1982 to 73 percent in February 1983. Because Yang's successor, Li Li'an, was known to be sympathetic to the decollectivization reform, Heilongjiang's household responsibility reform took off thereafter.[82]

In sum, despite the encompassing-governance nature of the household responsibility reform, protracted debates and the lack of Beijing's clear commitment—up until January 1982—led to extensive provincial variations in the initial stage. Once the center's stance became clearly known, opportunism and wait-and-see attitudes quickly disappeared, highlighting the very characteristic of the encompassing-governance policy. In inducing compliance of the resisting provinces with high stakes on large-scale mechanization, the center adopted political imposition rather than bargaining. As Beijing was somewhat torn between swift implementation and considerations of the *yindi zhiyi* principle, the level of urgency became lower than other reforms such as the tax-sharing scheme.

ENCOMPASSING-GOVERNANCE POLICY (II):
THE CASE OF SOCIAL STABILITY MAINTENANCE

As Deng Xiaoping's famous dictum that "China cannot afford chaos" [*Zhongguo bu neng ruan*] demonstrates, instability is viewed as the most perilous impediment to China's development.[83] Frequent references to stability in official documents make one wonder about the real extent of instability in China today. Collective public security incidents [*quntixing zhian shijian*: abbreviated as *quntixing shijian*, or "collective protests"] are popularly regarded as a good indicator of social instability.[84] According to a widely subscribed definition, collective protests denote incidents whereby a group of five or more people gathers to parade illegally, surround government offices, attack government officials, disrupt public transportations, fast or commit suicide in public, etc.[85]

By 2003, the extent of social instability was already quite alarming as collective protests occurred in 257 (99.2 percent) of 259 prefecture-level cities and in 792 counties (53 percent of all counties).[86] Although some Chinese analysts contended that the frequency of collective protests had stabilized since 2006, as table 6.6 demonstrates, collective protests have actually occurred more frequently.[87] If the data for 2010 in table 6.6 are credible, that means an average of sixteen protests took place in each of the 31 province-level units per day. According to a 2010 study, the number of large-scale collective protests involving more than five hundred people has also been on the rise.[88]

In short, collective protests became a crucial source of instability in China (perhaps that is why Beijing has not made public the official data on collective protests since 2006). As expected, the government authorities came up with a wide array of measures to prevent, monitor, and contain them in recent years. Apparently, however, not only has the overall frequency continued to increase, but more importantly, a trend of regional spread also emerged. Given the encompassing-governance nature of the stability maintenance [*weiwen*] policy with a high level of urgency, how did this happen?

The Nationwide Diffusion of Instability

In efforts to eradicate the root cause of collective protests, Beijing adopted several measures, including the nationwide abolition of the agricultural tax in 2005. Because nearly two-thirds (65.1 percent) of rural

TABLE 6.6

Number of Collective Protests, Select Years

Year	Frequency	Participants (per 1,000 people)
1993	8,909	n/a
1994	10,000	730
1998	25,000	1,390
2003	58,000	3,070
2004	74,000	3,760
2005	87,000	n/a
2006	90,000+[a]	n/a
2008	127,467	12,176
2010	183,000	n/a

NOTE: (a) Data cited in Yu Jianrong's presentation at the 6th Beijing Forum held at Peking University on November 7, 2009.

SOURCES: Chen Jinsheng, *Quntixing shijian yanjiu baogao* [A research report on collective incidents] (Beijing: Qunzhong chubanshe, 2004), 62, 170; Mu Muying, "Zhou Yongkang chengren guanbi minfan" [Zhou Yongkang admits that popular protests were caused by officials], *Zhengming-Dongxiang* [Contend-trend magazine], February 2009, 10; Hu Lianhe et al., *Dangdai zhongguo shehui wending wenti* [Problems of social stability in contemporary China] (Beijing: Hongqi chubanshe, 2009), 60; Jae Ho Chung, "Managing Political Crises in China: The Case of Collective Protests," in *China's Crisis Management*, ed. Jae Ho Chung (London: Routledge, 2011), 29; and "180,000 Protests in 2010," *Bloomberg News*, March 6, 2011.

collective protests were caused by local governments' misappropriation of peasant land, Beijing issued stern warnings against forced evacuation and undercompensation.[89] Beijing also enacted laws and regulations against collective protests, including a "law governing public security in the People's Republic of China" in 2005 and a "statute on regulating mass activities" in 2006, which required the organizers of any activity involving more than a thousand people to apply for official approval by public security departments at least twenty days in advance. Violators were to be charged with fines of RMB 100,000 to 300,000. On August 30, 2007, the National People's Congress passed yet another "law on coping with accidental incidents" [*zhonghua renmin gongheguo tufa shijian yingduifa*].[90]

Contrary to popular belief, collective protests took place in both poor and rich regions. A report compiled in 2000 by the Macroeconomic Research Institute of the now-defunct State Planning Commission identified three regions as most susceptible to collective protests: (1) old industrial bases along the Third Front—Hunan, Sichuan, Chongqing, and Hubei; (2) provinces heavily endowed with state-owned enterprises—

TABLE 6.7

Regional Distribution of Collective Protests

2000 report	2006 study	2010 study	2012 report
Heilongjiang, Hubei, Hunan, Jiangsu, Jilin, Liaoning, Sichuan, Zhejiang	Anhui, Guangdong, Henan, Hubei, Hunan, Jiangsu, Shaanxi, Shanxi, Shandong, Sichuan	Anhui, Hainan, Henan, Hubei, Hunan, Jiangsu, Shaanxi, Shandong, Sichuan, Yunnan	Fujian, Guangdong, Guangxi, Henan, Hunan, Jiangsu, Shaanxi, Shanxi, Sichuan, Zhejiang

SOURCES: Chung, Lai, and Xia, "Mounting Challenges to Governance in China," 21; Tong and Lei, "Large-Scale Mass Incidents in China," 24; and "Erlingyaoer nian quntixing shijian yanjiu baogao" [The 2012 study report on collective protests], 2.

Liaoning, Jilin, and Heilongjiang; and (3) provinces with advanced rural economies like Jiangsu and Zhejiang.[91] According to studies done in 2006 and 2010, wealthy provinces like Guangdong, Jiangsu, and Shandong were among high-risk areas for collective protests, along with poor ones like Henan, Hunan, and Shaanxi.[92] The most recent report, compiled in 2012 by *Legal Daily* [*Fazhi ribao*], revealed that the regions south of the Yellow River were more vulnerable to collective protests and that the top three provinces on the list were Guangdong, Sichuan, and Henan.[93]

Table 6.7 lists a total of nineteen provinces as areas vulnerable to collective protests over a period of eleven years. With the five ethnic minority regions and four centrally administered municipalities excluded, 81.8 percent of the provinces (eighteen out of twenty-two) proved susceptible to collective protests. Both rich provinces like Guangdong, Zhejiang, and Jiangsu and poor ones like Shaanxi, Hunan, and Sichuan are listed. Furthermore, all three macroregions—the eastern, central, and western—are fairly evenly represented.[94] Sichuan (western), Hunan (central), and Jiangsu (eastern) were the three provinces listed as the most consistently vulnerable to collective protests for the entire period under consideration.

Accounting for Mediocre Outcomes

Why has the impact of Beijing's effort been so mediocre despite the governance-encompassing nature of the *weiwen* policy? At least five factors may account for this puzzling outcome. First, unlike the tax-sharing or even the household responsibility reform, the *weiwen* policy touched upon so many diverse aspects of human life (ranging from simple bursts of anger, property rights, and environmental protection to official corruption and rights consciousness) that it went way beyond the boundary of control by any single local government. More often, local governments faced a dilemma between preemptive containment (i.e., seeking a quick resolution by using or threatening the use of physical force at the risk of escalation) and "soft" handling (i.e., relying on persuasion and negotiation at the risk of increased demands).[95]

Second, in contrast with the tax-sharing and the household responsibility reforms, the *weiwen* policy lacked a specific timetable for completion as it was designed to cope with the everyday aspect of social control. From the local government perspective, therefore, the whole policy became a routine task unless a large-scale protest took place demanding immediate attention and quick containment. In most cases, numerous small-scale protests just became statistics. Beijing's eventual realization that "absolute stability" [*juedui wending*]—i.e., zero protest—proved an impossibility was an additional factor.[96]

Third, the increased frequency of collective protests may as well have been an outcome of local governments' heightened alertness. That is, Beijing's push made local governments more sensitive to symptoms of social disorder than they would otherwise have been, thereby facilitating a better collection of statistics on collective protests. Furthermore, collective protests were more often subsumed under a broad category of "accidental incidents" [*tufa shijian*], insinuating that they were mostly beyond prevention and complete control. Additionally, Beijing often found some utility in allowing collective protests as a channel of letting public discontents out so long as they remained peaceful and limited in scale.[97]

Fourth, the factor of issue transformation was also at work. As the *weiwen* policy was routinized over a long span of time, a linkage was created with a resource dimension. That is, local governments wanted more budgets to be allocated to the task of stability maintenance. From the province down to the county level, public security-related agencies were newly established (e.g., the Commission for Comprehensive Management of Public Security and the Stability Preservation Office) or preexisting ones were reinforced.[98] Additionally, roadside patrol and twenty-four hour surveillance were introduced, and community police control [*shequ jingwu*] and police offices [*jingwushi*] were newly established in many rural areas.[99] Since 2006, both peasants and urban residents have been encouraged to register as voluntary information officers [*zhiyuan xinxiguan*], to whom the county's or city's stability preservation office offered payments. As the term "*weiwen* budget" suggests, the governance-related and urgent aspects of the stability maintenance policy were gradually diluted over the years.[100]

Fifth, the center repeatedly underscored that local government response—or the lack thereof—was the primary cause of many collective protests. By attributing wrongdoings on the part of local governments to a key source of instability, Beijing passed the buck and carved out some space for its own maneuvering. The "leadership responsibility system" [*lingdao zerenzhi*] is a good example in point, by which local leaders were directly held responsible for collective protests that transpired within their jurisdictions [*shui guanxia shui fuze*].[101]

Although the *weiwen* policy became more of a routine matter, once something of grave political importance took place, the atmosphere would become totally different. *Falungong* and SARS offer two most notable cases in this regard. As the *qigong*-based religious sect equipped with a nationwide hierarchy of its own—which is illegal for nongovernment organizations in China—organized antigovernment protests all over the nation, it was deemed a menace to the regime. Subsequently, Beijing opted for fierce struggles against it by mobilizing all localities to eradicate the "evil sect." Large-scale protests were contained within a few months, and after very tight suppression for a year or so, *Falungong* ceased to be a political entity in China. As soon as its urgency was recognized by Beijing in implementing the *weiwen* measure as an encompassing-governance policy, the Chinese government proved fairly effective in inducing local compliance within a short period of time.[102]

The SARS case is illuminating, with its utmost urgency involved in the midst of a deadly pandemic at hand. Whereas both Beijing and localities remained lukewarm in coping with the new strain of pneumonia from November 2002 through March 2003, once the death tolls rose steeply in and outside China, the case was no longer a routine *weiwen* issue. With the dismissal of the Minister of Health (Zhang Wenkang) in April 2003, SARS control became a highly sensitive political issue as well as a public health concern. The dismissal was accompanied by the firing of 120 local officials for their initial negligence and mishandling of the problem. Soon, nationwide total mobilization was harnessed—i.e., the issue became an encompassing-governance-urgent policy—to contain the pandemic as soon as possible. And the Chinese central government managed to get a hold of the deadly disease within two months.[103]

In this chapter, an issue-variant framework has been presented to see if policy characteristics are likely to have a differential impact on the extent of local discretion in implementation. The foregoing analysis of the six cases suggests that the actual amount of local discretion—indicated by the overall time taken for nationwide completion of the respective policy—is fairly consistent with the theoretically posited level of discretion (table 6.2). According to table 6.8, the theoretical predictions and empirical findings well matched in the case of the "Revive the Northeast" scheme as the provinces exercised the highest level of discretion in carrying out the program as a non-urgent selective-resource policy with a very long time frame for completion. In the case of the provinces-directly-ruling-counties policy, too, empirical findings were congruous with the theoretical prediction because at least a medium level of local discretion was permitted for this non-urgent encompassing-resource policy.

The framework predicted that the level of local discretion would be similar for the household responsibility and the tax-sharing reforms, as well as the policy of taking Hainan out of Guangdong. In real settings, however, the discretionary level for the household responsibility reform turned out to be higher than that for the tax-sharing scheme. Although decollectivation was an encompassing-governance policy, the sheer magnitude of institutional transformation that came with the task required a longer time frame, as well as an acute need for flexible implementation. In contrast, even if the tax-sharing reform was a resource-contingent

TABLE 6.8
Expected and Actual Levels of Local Discretion

Rank	Expected level	Actual level	Total time taken
1	ZXDB	ZXDB	20 years or more[a]
2	SGX	SGX	5 years or more[a]
3	HN-GD/FSZ/HRS	HRS	2+ years
4	WW	WW (FLG)	1 year or so
5	–	FSZ/HN-GD	Less than a year
6	–	WW (SARS)	A few months

NOTE: ZXDB denotes the "Revive the Northeast" scheme; SGX refers to the provinces-directly-ruling-counties policy; FSZ means the tax-assignment reform; HRS refers to the household responsibility reform; HN-GD refers to taking Hainan out of Guangdong to make it a province-level unit; and WW (FLG) and WW (SARS) refer to the stability maintenance policy regarding *Falungong* and the SARS.
   (a) This refers to a policy whose implementation is still in progress.

policy, the degree of urgency involved dictated a specific date of completion (i.e., a shorter time frame for implementation), constricting the room for local foot-dragging. The degree of urgency—i.e., Beijing's will to make Hainan a showcase for Taiwan—also weighed in heavily in the case of "making Hainan a province out of Guangdong."

Interesting is the case of stability maintenance policy. Although it is by definition an encompassing-governance policy (i.e., the predicted level of local discretion would be very low), it is generally not time specific and is therefore likely to be deemed a routine matter at local levels. Once it became a particular event-driven task that required immediate attention, control, and containment, a specific timetable was issued and fast execution pursued, thereby leaving little room for local foot-dragging. Certainly, the deadly SARS case allowed far less local discretion than the *Falungong* case, where the complex issues of religious freedom, political persecution, and intergovernmental buck passing were interwoven.[104]

In efforts to gauge the central–local balance of power in policy implementation, this study suggests that we need to go beyond the convention of looking only at clientelistic ties and/or interest congruence between the central and local governments. Policy characteristics and their variant impact on local discretion are also a useful analytical perspective to explore. The degree of urgency—as deemed by Beijing—seems to delineate a macro-boundary of local discretion as it provides a specific time frame for completion. If the degree of urgency is similar, then, the two remaining characteristics—resource involvement and target scope—come into play, either separately or jointly. The target scope generally determines the extent of policy standardization (i.e., the more encompassing, the more standardized, and the less discretionary), and the policy nature (governance- or resource-related) adjusts the room for central–local bargaining as opposed to Beijing's outright imposition (the more resource related, the more discretionary).

7

The Political Economy of Vertical Support
and Horizontal Networks

Whereas the preceding chapters examined mostly vertical dynamics of decentralization/recentralization, administrative hierarchy, imposition, autonomy, compliance, discretion, and contention between the central and local governments, this one explores horizontal-lateral dimensions of coordination, competition, exchanges, and cooperation among regions and localities. In China, where the inertia of geographically fragmented economic management (i.e., local protectionism) remains strong due mainly to the constraints imposed by the transitional reforms, developing a unified national market and fostering horizontal cooperative linkages and lateral exchange networks, thereby reducing the room for local autarky and compartmentalization, are deemed necessary but prove difficult.[1]

In the early phase of post-Mao reforms, symptoms of local protectionism and relational contracting were prevalent throughout China. The legacy of shortage economy and high uncertainties surrounding the system transition led to widespread hoarding of key resources, raw materials, consumer goods, etc., for local production and consumption rather than for the national market and interprovincial trade. Consequently, markets were highly territorialized; local protectionism, reinforced; and the room for interregional trade and horizontal exchanges, reduced.[2]

Despite the adoption of extensive measures of decentralization, interregional horizontal linkages could not be fully harnessed because the nationwide market mechanism was not yet fully established to replace Beijing's omnipresent plan control. In order for horizontal networks to take root and become effective, both the structure and thinking of local autarky had to be tackled first, for which initially some doses of central intervention and, later, market-based exchanges were crucial.[3] If the ongoing trend toward marketization is any practical guide, horizontal linkages and lateral networks are bound to constitute a crucial factor in central–local relations in contemporary China.[4]

Because China has already entered a stage of seeking sustainable and equitable growth starting in the early 2000s, mitigating regional disparities became a key priority of the regime. Although the center's intermittent provision of vertical support—along with the tenet of local self-reliance—was the principal remedy for regional disparities during Mao's China, more options became available during the reform era. Beijing's resource capacity was most adversely affected by the decentralization reform in the 1980s, so it was not really in a position to offer much support for poor and underdeveloped regions.[5] Even during the 1990s, bridging regional disparities was not a top priority, although Beijing showed growing interest in "regionally coordinated economic development" [quyu jingji xietiao fazhan].[6] It was only in the 2000s that the center came up with specific policy and resource support for the underdeveloped regions, demonstrated by such platforms as the "Develop the West," "The Rise of the Middle Region," and "Revive the Northeast" projects.[7]

Missing in most of the scholarly discussions of China's local development is the fact that interregional lateral networks and linkages have always been on Beijing's menu of choices. This chapter seeks to fill the void first by examining the type of policy instruments available to the center in coping with regional disparities from 1949 to the present day. Then, it assesses the relative importance of Beijing's vertical resource and policy support during different periods, as well as the evolving roles of vertically induced and voluntarily formed horizontal networks. The crux of the argument here is that, whereas Beijing's policy support and vertically induced horizontal networks were important in the early phases of the reform era, the center's resource support and voluntarily formed lateral linkages have become increasingly crucial in recent years.

VERTICAL AND HORIZONTAL OPTIONS:
THEORETICAL DISCUSSION

In dealing with regional disparities, the central government generally has four types of options at its disposal: (1) vertical resource support, (2) vertical policy support, (3) vertically induced horizontal support networks, and (4) voluntarily formed horizontal linkages.[8]

Vertical resource support refers to a Keynesian remedy of the central government by way of allocating financial and material resources to needy localities. In the case of China, this particular policy alternative includes budgetary grants [*yusuan buzhu*], fiscal transfer [*zhuanyi zhifu*], investment [*touzi*], funds [*jijin*], subsidies [*butie*], and loans [*daikuan*] as well as "relief by giving employment" [*yigong daizhen*].[9] Effective execution of vertical resource support presupposes a strong central government capable of commanding and redistributing sufficient financial and material resources on the basis of solid administrative and informational capacities. Vertical resource support is most commonly utilized due to its administrative convenience and its ability to offer immediate fixing effects.[10]

The central government may resort to vertical policy support by way of devising preferential policies specifically targeted at localities with development potentials or needy localities. If vertical resource support is designed to equalize local outputs (e.g., incomes, grain consumption, social welfare, education, etc.) by providing grants, loans, funds, and subsidies, vertical policy support generally goes beyond a first-aid approach by seeking to shape the environment for local economic development. Vertical policy support denotes the provision of locality- or industry-specific privileges and/or preferential treatment such as tax incentives and location priorities.[11] The provision of targeted policy support is a significant resource-saving measure because the center only has to improve economic environments of certain local units by bestowing on them favorable policy frameworks instead of directly offering financial and material support. Not all recipients of such preferential policies prove successful, however.[12]

The central government may choose to promote interregional networks. Such networks involve trilateral interactions in that the center issues administrative orders to "mobilize" better-off regions to provide support for backward ones. In this framework, the center performs as an imposing mediator while localities are made to interact directly with each other. This, too, is a resource-saving measure from the center's viewpoint because, instead of offering financial and material support or locality-specific preferential policies, the center only has to forge horizontal cooperative networks in which the material input is to come from the better-off regions. Horizontal networks so established are plagued with incentive problems that cause team shirking and free riding as the better-off regions generally seek to save resources for their own development and, consequently, provide only token donations simply not to offend the center. Forging horizontal networks with sufficiently high levels of interdependence and information symmetry, therefore, is a daunting challenge for a continent-sized nation like China.[13]

The final option refers to voluntarily formed linkages for inter-regional cooperation. Although the former three alternatives presuppose a proactive center, this one points to a passive role by the central government. In a sense, this particular alternative is similar to a neo-classical laissez-faire prescription in that localities and enterprises seek cooperative partners voluntarily on the basis of mutual benefit and reciprocity.[14] An outstanding difference, however, is that the main player in this framework is local government, and therefore the problem of information insufficiency may arise. That is, local governments generally lack sufficient information on firms and products outside their territorial jurisdictions. Hence, in order for this option to succeed, concerted efforts to bring down local protectionist barriers and to forge comprehensive information networks must be made.[15]

Table 7.1 compares the four options in terms of their respective characteristics. Theoretically speaking, if the center's fiscal capacity is strong, vertical resource support is most likely and effective. As the center's resource capacity decreases, it might resort to vertical policy support and vertically formed horizontal networks. Growing levels of decentralization and marketization, however, may weaken the role of the center and instead strengthen the role of local governments, paving the way for voluntarily formed horizontal linkages. The larger the number of local targets to support and the weaker the central government's capacity to intervene fiscally and/or administratively, assuming the presence of market forces, the more likely are mutually beneficial horizontal linkages to become important.

Figure 7.1 illustrates four contingencies related to the center's resource capacity and the level of marketization. The Chinese case since the 1st Five-Year Plan (1953–1956) seems to point to a dynamic process in which Beijing's dominant policy choices have evolved counterclockwise

TABLE 7.1
Comparing Vertical and Horizontal Alternatives

	(I) Vertical resource support	(II) Vertical policy support	(III) Vertically induced horizontal linkages	(IV) Voluntarily formed horizontal linkages
Structure of relationship	Bilateral (central–local)	Bilateral (central–local)	Trilateral (central–local–local)	Bilateral (local–local)
Origin of relationship	Center initiated	Center initiated	Center initiated	Locally initiated
Incentive structure	Center's political incentives (legitimacy)	Center's resource-saving incentives	Center's resource-saving incentives and asymmetrical local incentives	Symmetrical local incentives
Number of targets	Small/medium	Small/medium	Medium/large	Large
Control instruments	Fiscal	(De)regulatory	Administrative	Informational
Policy choices	Grants, funds, investments, loans, subsidies	Special policy, locationing privilege, tax incentives	Cadre exchange, administrative pairing, collective support	Trade, investment, personnel exchanges

	Center's resource capacity	
	Strong	Weak
High	I and IV	II, III, and IV
Level of marketization		
Low	I (Principal)	II and III

FIGURE 7.1 Environments conducive to the four alternatives.

from the bottom left. That is to say, Beijing's principal options have shifted from an almost exclusive reliance on vertical resource support in the Maoist era to the utilization of vertical policy support and vertically induced horizontal networks during the 1980s and 1990s, and gradually to a mixture of all four options during the 2000s and beyond, with the relative importance of voluntarily formed horizontal networks and vertical resource support growing since the mid-2000s.[16]

REGIONAL DISPARITIES AND POLICY OPTIONS IN MAO'S CHINA

The Mao era (1949–1976) displayed a strong egalitarian commitment in that the central government continued to allocate a lion's share of grants and investment to the backward inland regions in an effort to mitigate regional disparities. In the 1st Five-Year Plan period of 1953–1956, only 37 percent of total state capital investment went to the coastal region while 68 percent of 694 industrial projects were allotted to the inland region.[17] From the mid-1960s, after the Sino-Soviet rift, the regime's changing national security imperative led to a massive transfer of key industrial facilities to the hinterland, the Third Front. During the 3rd and 4th Five-Year Plan periods (1966–1975), 65 percent and 53 percent, respectively, of total state capital investment went to the inland region.[18]

During Mao's rule, the central government relied predominantly on the option of vertical resource support. Above all, Beijing's capacity to extract and allocate fiscal and material resources under the highly centralized system of vertical plan control made this option feasible. The chronic problems of resource insufficiency and information asymmetry were tackled by the self-reliance tenet of the Maoist developmental strategy, under which every locality was supposed to rely on its own resources and to minimize horizontal liaison with other localities or overseas entities.[19]

The prevalence of local autarchy and plan control along the lines of vertical functional bureaucracies [xitong] obstructed horizontal coordination and cooperation. Although there were some horizontal networks even during the Maoist period, they were either confined to a few sectors—most notably, materials allocation—or largely limited to intraprovincial, rather than interregional, exchanges.[20] In the absence of interregional networks for trade and horizontal exchanges, the fragmentation of the market and local autarchy were reinforced. For instance, grain outflows across the provinces as a percentage of total grain production declined from 6 percent during the 1950s to about 1 percent in the late 1970s. Provincial per capita agricultural and industrial outputs also became highly correlated (from –0.16 in 1957 to 0.75 in 1980), demonstrating that the very basis for interprovincial trade was sharply reduced.[21] Under such circumstances, only the center remained capable of transferring resources across regional barriers.

Assessments vary as to how successful Beijing was in mitigating regional disparities under Mao's rule. During that era, the system of local governance was sufficiently—if not overly—politicized so that ideology (i.e., egalitarianism) effectively imposed such super-ordinate goals as achieving "co-prosperity" among different regions. The system of economic management was also highly centralized so that Beijing was nearly omnipotent in extracting revenues, allocating resources, and setting regional development priorities. The problem, however, was that China's economy was so backward that the central government often lacked the necessary resources to undo the disparities. Even when Beijing induced individual provinces and municipalities to donate and contribute to the cause of even development, they were simply too poor to produce meaningful impact.[22] For instance, despite Beijing's prioritized investment in the hinterland, the share of the inland region in China's total gross value of industrial output (GVIO) rose by only 1.8 percent during 1965–1975.[23]

EVOLUTION OF VERTICAL SUPPORT
IN THE REFORM ERA

As the regime's perceptions of its security significantly improved in the post-Mao reform period, the central government came to pursue regional development strategies starkly different from those of the Third Front era. That is, Beijing adopted a strategy of supporting the well-endowed coastal region first, at the expense of the rest of the country, thereby widening—rather than mitigating—regional disparities. Table 7.2 illustrates that, chiefly through target policies, the coastal region took the lion's share among the areas opened up for preferential foreign economic relations during the 1980s. Arrangements included tax incentives to attract foreign investment, preferential rates for foreign exchange retention, higher approval ceilings for foreign direct investment, and selective sectoral deregulation. As a result, 87 percent of all foreign investment committed during 1985–1995 went to the coastal region.[24]

The regionally biased strategy of the post-Mao era induced a heavy toll in terms of regional disparities, with their levels rising well above that of the pre-reform era.[25] More troublesome was the fact that Beijing found its capacity to extract and allocate fiscal resources to be constantly dwindling during the first decade of the reform period.[26] State revenues as a share of gross national product (GNP) declined from 30 percent in

TABLE 7.2

State-Designated Special Zones and Tax Privileges (1995)

Designation	Number	Tax rates (%)
Special economic zones (C: 1979, 1988)	5	15
Coastal open cities (C: ~1984)	14	24
Coastal open areas (C: 1988)	260	24
Bonded zones (C: ~1992)	13	0
Economic and technological development zones (C & I: ~1984)	30	10–15
New and hi-tech industrial development zones (C & I: ~1991)	52	15
Tourism and leisure zones (C & I: ~1992)	11	24
Riverine open cities (I: ~1992)	6	24
Border-region open cities (I: ~1992)	13	24

NOTE: (C) stands for all coastal locations; (I) refers to all inland locations; and (C & I) denotes mixed locations.

SOURCES: "Cujin diqu jingji xietiao fazhan yanjiu" [Study on the promotion of regionally co-ordinated development], *Jingji yanjiu cankao*, no. 914/915 (July 25, 1996): 33–34; Li Haijian, *Zouxiang pinghengshi kaifang* [Toward a balanced opening] (Beijing: Shehuikexue wenxuan chubanshe, 1999), 166, 186–90; and Tang Renwu and Ma Ji, eds., *Zhongguo jingji gaige 30nian—duiwaikaifang juan* [Thirty years of China's economic reform—Volume on external opening] (Chongqing: Chongqing daxue chubanshe, 2008), 47–79, 275–79.

1978 to 11 percent in 1995, and Beijing's share in total government expenditure also dwindled from 54.3 percent in 1980 to 29.2 percent in 1995.[27] Beijing's weakened fiscal capacity is further demonstrated by its sharply reduced share of budgetary investment: Whereas 78 percent of the basic construction investment [jiben jianshe touzi] came from the state budget in 1978, that figure dropped to 9 percent in 1998.[28]

Under these circumstances, relying solely on the center's vertical resource support to mitigate regional disparities became not only burdensome but also unsustainable. In addition to such indispensable government expenditures as operating expenses and national defense spending, Beijing had to pay huge sums of "subsidies for loss-making state enterprises" [qiyie kuishun butie] and "price adjustment subsidies" [jiage butie]. Consequently, the rate of increase in Beijing's subsidies for ethnic minority regions declined from 10 percent to 5 percent in 1988, and was eventually canceled in 1993.[29]

The central government found its capacity rapidly deteriorating in the domain of materials allocation as well. According to a 1991 survey, only 13 percent of industrial production was directly regulated by the State Planning Commission. Whereas 97 percent of national retail prices, 94 percent of agricultural product prices, and 100 percent of industrial production materials prices were set by Beijing in 1979, by 1993, the comparable figures dropped to 5, 10, and 15 percent, respectively. In 1993, only twelve production materials were directly controlled by the State Planning Commission, whereas the figure was 256 in 1979. Furthermore, the adoption of a "domestic trade agency system" [neimao dailizhi] permitted individual firms to have expanded power in materials allocation, further reducing the room for state control.[30]

By the early 1990s, it became clear that the expected trickle-down effect of the coastal development strategy was not happening, and instead, regional disparities were widening. With its capacity for vertical resource support decimated, Beijing then opted for vertical policy support by granting preferential policies to the inland region. Initially, in January 1991, Beijing permitted all province-level units to retain the same portion of foreign currency earnings, which had the effect of abrogating the privilege previously reserved only for the coastal provinces.[31] The scope of opening was also expanded in 1992 to include the Yangzi Region and seventeen border cities and counties in Heilongjiang, Inner Mongolia, Yunnan, Guangxi, Xinjiang, and Tibet, as well as another seventeen inland cities designated as "open cities" with preferential policies.[32]

With Beijing's power in the provision of fiscal and material resources reduced, the center increasingly resorted to the option of vertical policy support. Table 7.3 on the regional distribution of national-level development zones in the last thirty years is illustrative of Beijing's changing priorities. For the period of 1984–1999 (i.e., prior to the announcement of the "Develop the West" scheme), China's regional development priority was still largely the coastal east, accounting for 85 percent of all national-level developments zones established. From 2000 through 2014, however, Beijing's priority shifted as 61 percent (95 out of 157) of the national-level development zones established during that period were located in the inland central and western regions.

Even as the central government's fiscal power—particularly after the tax-sharing reform in 1994—steadily increased, its reliance on vertical policy support did not stop. As Beijing's fiscal support was spread thinly

TABLE 7.3
Distribution of National-Level Development Zones, 1984–2014

Year	East	Central	West	Annual total	Cumulative total
1984	10	0	0	10	10
1985	1	0	0	1	11
1986	2	0	0	2	13
1987	0	0	0	0	13
1988	1	0	0	0	14
1989–1991	0	0	0	0	14
1992	6	0	0	0	20
1993	7	3	1	11	31
1994	1	0	1	2	33
1995–1999	0	0	0	0	33
2000	0	6	6	12	45
2001	1	1	2	4	49
2002	1	0	1	2	51
2003–2005	0	0	0	0	51
2006	0	1	1	2	53
2007–2008	0	0	0	0	53
2009	2	0	0	2	55
2010	27	21	10	58	113
2011	5	8	3	16	129
2012	6	4	3	13	142
2013	16	14	9	39	181
2014	4	4	1	9	190
Total	90	62	38	190	

SOURCES: National Development and Reform Commission, *Zhongguo kaifaqu shenhe gongbao mulu* [List of China's development zones] (2006); the official website of the Ministry of Commerce at http://www.mofcom.gov .cn/xglj/kaifaqu.shtml; http://www.ndrc.gov.cn/2cfb/zcfbgg/2007gonggao/W020070406535176330304.pdf; and http://zh.wikipedia.org and http://baike.baidu.com (searched with *guojiaji jingji jishu kaifaqu* as the keyword).

TABLE 7.4

Regional Distribution of National-Level Development Zones

	East	Central	West	Total	Cumulative total
1984–1985	11	0	0	11	11
1986–1990	3	0	0	3	14
1991–1995	14	3	2	19	33
1996–2000	0	6	6	12	45
2001–2005	2	1	3	6	51
2006–2010	29	22	11	62	113
2011–2014	31	30	16	77	190
Total	90 (47%)	62 (33%)	38 (20%)	190	

SOURCES: National Development and Reform Commission, *Zhongguo kaifaqu shenhe gongbao mulu* [List of China's development zones] (2006); the official website of the Ministry of Commerce at http://www.mofcom.gov.cn/xglj/kaifaqu.shtml; http://www.ndrc.gov.cn/zcfb/zcfbgg/2007gonggao/W020070406535176330304.pdf; and http://zh.wikipedia.org and http://baike.baidu.com (searched with *guojiaji jingji jishu kaifaqu* as the keyword).

TABLE 7.5

Regional Distribution of National-Level New Zones (2014)

Year established	Location	Province	Region
1992	Pudong	Shanghai	Coastal
2001	Binhai	Tianjin	Coastal
2010	Liangjiang	Chongqing	Inland
2011	Zhoushan	Zhejiang	Coastal
2012	Lanzhou	Gansu	Inland
2012	Nansha	Guangdong	Coastal
2014	Xixian	Shaanxi	Inland
2014	Guian	Guizhou	Inland

SOURCE: Cao Yun, *Guijiaji xinqu bijiao yanjiu* [Comparative study of national-level new zones] (Beijing: Shehuikexue chubanshe, 2014), 2–8.

over several macroregions (the West, the Central Belt, the Northeast, and new special zones like Pudong and Binhai), it also made good use of vertical policy support as a supplement. As table 7.4 shows, the center actually increased the overall number of national-level development zones rather significantly after 2005 by designating a large number of development zones in the central and western regions.[33]

Another notable characteristic is that, as of 2014, the total number of national-level development zones granted to the coastal region (ninety) was nearly the same as that to the inland region (one hundred). Beijing's conscious design for "equitable" growth is also demonstrated by the "equal" coastal-inland distribution of national-level new zones [*guojiaji xinqu*] for development (see table 7.5).

THE RISE OF HORIZONTAL NETWORKS IN THE
REFORM ERA

As the share of fiscal and material resources at Beijing's disposal continued to dwindle in the 1980s, the center adopted the alternative of forging
horizontal support networks to mitigate regional disparities. Horizontal
support networks were a key resource-saving measure on the part of
Beijing as they obligated the wealthy coastal region to donate portions
of their surplus revenues and other resources to assist the backward inland region. In the process of cultivating horizontal networks, it was
hoped, some spirit of interregional cooperation would be generated,
thereby offsetting pervasive local-protectionist sentiments.[34]

This particular alternative includes two categories of Beijing-induced
horizontal networks. One refers to a donor-recipient type that has
specific donors and target recipients, both of which are designated by the
central government. The other category denotes intra- and interregional
cooperative networks designated and endorsed by Beijing for the exchange of raw materials, products, investment, information, technologies, and human resources without specifying the donors or recipients.

Donor-Recipient Networks

The donor-recipient category can be subdivided into collective and dyadic formats. The collective type refers to nationwide networks in which
multiple donors are designated to provide support for one or more target recipients. Key examples include aiding the Tibet Autonomous Region, supporting the localities in Sichuan and Hubei affected by the
Three Gorges Dam project, and assisting the areas in Sichuan affected
by the 2008 earthquake. In the case of assisting Tibet, in 1994, Beijing
ordered that all twenty-nine province-level units come up with at least
one investment project to help the autonomous region, particularly in
the area of infrastructure construction. All complied within two months,
and investments ranging from RMB 39 million to 60 million were pledged
by Guangdong, Shandong, Shanghai, Jiangsu, and Zhejiang. Poor provinces like Qinghai, Jiangxi, Anhui, Gansu, and Inner Mongolia were also
"asked" to contribute RMB 3 million to 6 million to the cause.[35]

As for the case of the Three Gorges Dam project, in 1993, Beijing
"requested" that better-off coastal provinces donate a portion of their
surplus revenues to support the relocation of dam-related refugees from

Hubei and Sichuan. Shandong, for instance, was designated specifically to assist the relocation work in Sichuan's Zhong County and Hubei's Yichang County. Subsequently, it offered at least RMB 20 million for the construction of a cement factory in Zhong County, where it also trained seventeen township- and village-level cadres and provided jobs for a total of 414 refugees. Qingdao (a deputy-provincial city in Shandong) was given the responsibility to support Yichang County for the period of 1995–2015. Similarly, Liaoning was "requested" to assist Hubei's Xingshan County.[36]

With regard to assisting Sichuan's Wenchuan prefecture damaged by the 2008 earthquake, the central government came up with the scheme of "each province supporting one county in Wenchuan" [yi-sheng bang yizhongzhaixian]. Nineteen coastal and central provinces (except for Hainan) were called on to offer assistance to eighteen counties in Wenchuan.[37] The minimum level of financial support was set by Beijing at no less than 1 percent of the previous year's income of each province. Areas of support included housing and hospital construction, educational support, road construction, and building agricultural infrastructure.[38]

One noteworthy linkage concerns Beijing's transfers and exchanges of cadres, through which several hundred cadres from Beijing and other provinces were sent to remote inland regions to work in economic management, finance, foreign trade, and tourism. The most crucial targets of this policy were Tibet and Xinjiang. The "cadre work in support of Tibet" [yuanzang ganbu gongzuo] began in 1995 with a transfer of 621 cadres, who came from the central government, thirteen province-level units, and seventeen centrally owned state enterprises. Transfers have been made every three years since then, amounting to a total of six transfers by 2010. In 2010, 775 cadres from seventeen province-level units were transferred to work in Tibet, accounting for 78 percent of all cadres transferred there that year.[39]

The "cadre work in support of Xinjiang" [yuanjiang ganbu gongzuo] started in 1997 with a transfer of two hundred cadres from the central government and eight province-level units; these have occurred every three years since 2002 (although probably more frequently and irregularly before that). They amounted to a total of seven transfers by 2011, when 2,792 cadres from nineteen province-level units were transferred there, accounting for 86 percent of the cadres transferred that year.[40] The transfer of an average of 997 cadres in each dispatch was not an insignificant measure. At least four coastal provinces were engaged in exchanges and training of government personnel with Xinjiang. In 2012 alone, Shanghai, Zhejiang, Jiangsu, and Shandong sent officials to and trained cadres from Xinjiang.[41]

In contrast, the dyadic type of the donor-recipient category refers to horizontal relationships in which one province (or a subprovincial unit) was directly paired with [jie duizi] another to provide a wide range of assistance and support. The first of such networks was designated by Beijing in 1979 when Central Document No. 52 dictated that Gansu be paired with Tianjin, Inner Mongolia with Beijing, Qinghai with Shandong, Xinjiang and Guangxi with Jiangsu, and Yunnan and Ningxia with Shanghai. It was hoped that rich coastal partners would actively help their backward inland counterparts with economic development and opening. The coastal partners so designated were obliged to offer a wide range of support, including making investments there, providing connections with foreign businesses, utilizing surplus labor in the inland provinces, donating poverty-alleviation funds, etc.[42]

Dyadic support networks were also formed for poverty alleviation [fupin] under the 8–7 Plan [baqi jihua] promulgated in 1996. According to the scheme, thirteen developed provinces were to provide support and investment for ten poor provinces in the hinterland. For the period of 1996–1999, the donors together offered financial and material support worth RMB 1 billion over twenty-six hundred projects, in addition to the actually committed investment of RMB 4 billion.[43]

Dyadic pairing was used in the exchange and training of local cadres as well. Two examples are illustrative. Fujian sent a total of twenty-one cadres [yuanning ganbu] to nine counties in Ningxia in July 2012, bringing the total to eight dispatches since the 1990s. Similarly, Hebei and Guizhou agreed to exchange ten cadres each between the former's Quju County and the latter's Yupin County in 2012, although they cross-served for just three months at that point. The exchange became an annual one thereafter.[44]

Shanghai and Yunnan were designated in 1997 by Beijing as a dyadic pair. The two provinces set up "leadership small groups for paired support and coordination" [bangfu xiezuo lingdao xiaozu] and carried out cooperation in ten sectors, including industrial production, agriculture, education, tourism, etc. For the period of 1996–2005, Shanghai provided support worth RMB 711 million spread across 2,577 projects.[45] Similarly, Fujian provided RMB 665 million in grants for poverty alleviation and other relief missions in Ningxia for the period of 1996–2011.

Also, Fujian's firm-level investment in Ningxia amounted to a total of RMB 36.9 billion for the same period.[46]

Intra- and Interregional Cooperative Networks

The other category of vertically induced horizontal linkages denotes numerous intra- and interregional cooperative networks promoted by Beijing, but without designated donors or recipients. In fact, these networks were neither new nor the product solely of the reform era. Interregional cooperative networks in the domain of materials supply dated back to the 1950s, when state-directed exchanges of scarce resources and compensation trade within the boundary of each great administrative region were widespread. The importance of intra- and interregional exchange was further highlighted during the Cultural Revolution decade, culminating in 1975, when the State Material Resources Bureau established the Intraregional Cooperation Office [*xiezuo bangongshi*]. Thereafter, under the Office's direction, similar units were duplicated at all province-level governments.[47]

The State Council continued fostering intra- and interregional cooperation in the reform era. Key outcomes included the Shanghai Economic Zone [*Shanghai jingjiqu*; established in 1982], the Northeast Economic Region [*Dongbei jingjiqu*; 1983], the Three Gorges Economic Development Zone [*Sanxia diqu jingji kaifaqu*; 1986], and the Yellow River Economic Cooperation Zone [*Huanghe jingji xiezuoqu*; 1986], all established by the State Council. Their specific functions were, respectively: (1) to coordinate the supply of silk and cotton in the cases of the Shanghai Economic Zone and the Yellow River Economic Cooperation Zone, (2) to promote the development and coordinate the transportation of coal and petroleum in the Northeast Economic Region, and (3) to develop the backward areas near the Three Gorges.[48]

A brief discussion is due at this juncture on a key example: the evolution of the Shanghai Economic Zone into the Association of Sixteen Cities in the Yangzi River Delta Region [*Changjiang sanjiaozhou diqu 16chengshi jingji xietiaohui*]. The Shanghai Economic Zone, designated by the State Council in October 1982, started out with ten cities and fifty-five counties under Shanghai and Jiangsu. As the 14th Party Congress in 1992 adopted a measure of developing the Yangzi Delta region, the zone was expanded to include fourteen deputy-provincial and prefecture-level cities in Jiangsu, Zhejiang, and Shanghai (including Nanjing, Ningbo, Wuxi, Yangzhou, and Zhoushan). By 2004, the number of large cities in the zone reached sixteen. And in 2010, the National Commission on Development and Reform added Anhui to the network so as to facilitate lateral cooperation between the three coastal provinces and Anhui.[49]

The State Council's latest efforts—particularly after the announcement in 2000 of the "Develop the West" scheme—include the Guanzhong-Tianshui Economic Zone, linking Shaanxi and Gansu (approved by the State Council in 2009), the Cheng-Yu Economic Zone connecting Chongqing with Sichuan (approved in 2011), and the Zhongyuan Economic Zone linking Henan, Shandong, Anhui, Hebei, and Shanxi (approved in 2012).[50] These schemes were a mixture of the center's vertical policy support and vertically induced horizontal cooperative networks. To a considerable extent, these are Beijing's efforts to minimize the impact of local protectionism and administrative boundaries.[51]

Incentive Problems in Vertically Induced Horizontal Networks

Vertically induced networks have been plagued with incentive problems. When confronted with a group task of supporting the poor, individual units were generally inclined to pass the buck and free-ride. As incentives to save scarce resources for their own development overshadowed the causes of even development, coastal donors often sought to offer token donations, simply not to offend Beijing.[52] The center's will and capacity to monitor every donor's contribution closely over an extensive period proved problematic as well. If Beijing appeared lax in checking the extent to which the pledged support actually came through, coastal donors were apt to say much but do little. No ministerial or higher organization was put in charge of supervising the tasks related to horizontal cooperation. The highest central unit involved was just a bureau-level organization [*guotu diqusi* under the State Planning Commission, later renamed *diqu jingji fazhansi* in the 1998 streamlining]; this was a definite drawback.[53]

The different perceptions that the center and the provincial donors held with regard to regional disparities were yet another factor. Whereas Beijing generally associated regional disparities with its regime legitimacy, coastal provinces viewed the issue in much less political terms. Although a call from the center for interregional cooperation and even development might have appealed to some coastal donors, the marginal effectiveness of Beijing's imposition declined in proportion to the overall duration of the campaign. Unless specific incentives were provided for the donors, vertically induced interregional networks only produced token donations with little genuine achievement. Although interregional support networks were typically compared to "brotherhood," as the saying went, "brothers, too, had to settle accounts" [*xiongdi zhijian ye yao suanzhang*].[54]

Compared with collective support networks, in dyadic pairs, team shirking was not so much of a problem. Yet there were also problems of incentives with dyadic networks; coastal donors were still inclined to save scarce resources for their own development unless they found specific motives to support inland partners.[55] Because many of the pairs designated by Beijing lacked reasonable levels of interdependence (i.e., room for interprovincial trade and/or resource exchanges), the problem of information asymmetry (i.e., uncertainties as to what to cooperate on) was rather severe.[56] The less than ideal nature of the vertically induced dyadic networks announced in 1979 was acknowledged in 1996 when Beijing revamped interprovincial dyadic networks in an effort to better utilize comparative advantages and geographical proximity.[57]

Overall assessments of the vertically induced interregional cooperative networks appear to have been less than positive. As these networks focused more on fulfilling the interests of the State Council—i.e., producing more energy resources and facilitating a coordinated and stable supply of cotton and silk for Shanghai, Jiangsu, and Zhejiang, which jointly accounted for a lion's share of Beijing's revenues—the extent to which specific local interests were genuinely accommodated in these vertical arrangements was questionable. Additionally, local protectionism and "duke economies" [*zhuhou jingji*, i.e., territorially fragmented economies] also accounted for this less than ideal outcome. Because self-maximizing actors would retain hidden information as to how much they could actually contribute, ceteris paribus, coastal provinces naturally preferred to say much but do little and to act alone, rather than collectively, unless absolutely necessary due to Beijing's political push.[58]

FROM IMPOSITION TO HORIZONTAL RECIPROCITY

With the level of marketization rising in China, an increasing number of horizontal linkages and networks were established largely on a *voluntary* basis (the far right column in table 7.1). Alternatively, lateral connections formerly set up by the center came to have some elements of voluntary exchange based on reciprocity.[59] Initially, some of these linkages were voluntarily formed among inland localities as self-help networks instead of merely waiting for Beijing's preferential policies or for donations from the coastal region.[60] Principal examples included the Regional Economic Coordination Association of Southwest China, the Regional Association of Northwest China, the Shanxi-Gansu-Sichuan Economic Cooperative Region, the Yunnan-Guangxi-Guizhou Economic Cooperative Zone, and the Hubei-Henan-Sichuan-Shaanxi Cooperative Region.[61]

What is noteworthy is that some of these linkages adopted a collective bargaining approach vis-à-vis Beijing. On at least two occasions in 1988 and 1990, the Regional Association of Northwest China [*Xibei 5shengqu jingji jishu xiezuo lianxihui*] proposed to the Party Center that special zones be established in Gansu, Qinghai, and Ningxia. The Regional Economic Coordination Association of Southwest China [*Xinan 5shengqu jingji xietiaohui*] also requested in 1990 that Beijing take appropriate measures to improve the region's economic environment, including that of raising the region's foreign exchange retention rate from 25 percent to at least 80 percent. In 1991, all provinces (except for the SEZs) were permitted to retain the same proportion of foreign exchange earnings regardless of geographical location.[62] A few years later, in 1994, the party chiefs of Shaanxi, Gansu, Qinghai, Ningxia, and Xinjiang held a "summit meeting" where they demanded more preferential policies from Beijing.[63] Then, in 1996, the State Council raised the inland region's FDI approval ceiling to US$30 million, on a level with the coastal region. A number of measures granted in the "Develop the West" scheme in 1999–2000 also amounted to a fulfillment of earlier requests by those networks among the inland provinces.[64]

Although many voluntary networks were formed among inland localities, some were established between inland and coastal provinces. Key examples were the Yellow River Economic Cooperative Association, the Mid-China Economic Cooperative Zone [*Zhongyuang jingji hezuoqu*], and the Nanjing Association for Regional Economic Coordination [*Nanjing quyu jingji xietiaohui*]. Formed in 1988 among six inland provinces (Henan, Shanxi, Shaanxi, Ningxia, Gansu, and Qinghai) and a coastal province (Shandong), the Yellow River Economic Cooperation Zone [*Huanghe jingji xiezuoqu*; hereafter YECA] was based on reciprocity. For the inland partners, Shandong provided a gateway to ports and overseas business linkages as well as a guaranteed seat at the annual Qingdao Trade Fair. The inland partners, on the other hand, offered Shandong a stable supply of cheap labor and raw materials. For all seven participants, YECA provided a valuable source of information on market, labor, trade, and investment. During 1988–1995, over fourteen thousand cooperative projects were signed among the YECA partners, with mutual borrowings and investments reaching RMB 4.6 billion and material exchanges totaling RMB 18.2 billion. YECA's success was further attested by the institutionalization of annual meetings where deputy-governors and bureau chiefs took part, and by the addition of two new members, Inner Mongolia and Xinjiang, in 1990 and 1992, respectively.[65]

Two additional examples are noteworthy. One refers to the institutionalization of high-level local officials' meetings. They include "Deputy-Governors Meeting for Cooperation and Development in the Yangzi River Delta Region" [*changjiang sanjiaodiqu hezuo yu fazhan lianxi huiyi*] among Shanghai, Jiangsu, Zhejiang, and Anhui; "Governors' Meeting for the Development of Four Northeast Provinces" [*dongbei sishengqu hezuo xingzhengshouzhang lianxi huiyi*; inclusive of Neimenggu]; and the "Pan-Pearl River Delta 9+2 Framework" [*Fan Zhusanjiao 9+2 quyu hezuo jiagou*] among Guangdong plus nine inland provinces, which includes the Governors' Networking Conferences.[66] These high-level meetings were beneficial not only in devising coordinated development plans for the macroregion as a whole but also for bargaining collectively with Beijing when necessary.

Another notable example is the China East–West Cooperation, Investment, and Trade Fair [*zhongguo dongxibu hezuo yu touzi maoyi qiatanhui*; commonly abbreviated as *Xiqiahui*]. *Xiqiahui* began in 1997 among Jiangsu, Shanghai, Tianjin, and Shaanxi with the initiative of the Special Zone Office of the State Council. Soon after, *Xiqiahui* became an annual event that continuously expanded in size over the next sixteen years. As table 7.6 demonstrates, *Xiqiahui* grew not only in the number of provincial organizers and firms participating but also in the number of projects signed and investments committed between the eastern and western regions. Although it was first initiated by Beijing, its success can be attributed largely to the convergence of mutual interests and voluntary incentives between firms of the eastern and western provinces.[67]

A key—though often neglected—factor in the growth of voluntarily formed horizontal networks needs to be mentioned. Sources indicate that during 1981–1995, interprovincial coefficients of industrial isomorphism (i.e., the degree of similarity in industrial structures among the

TABLE 7.6

The Expansion of *Xiqiahui*, 1997–2014

Year	Number of provincial participants	Number of firms participating	Number of projects	Total investment (100 million yuan)
1997	4	n/a	305	36.4
1998	6	3,000	433	78.6
1999	8	6,200	n/a	n/a
2000	22	7,000	752	315.4
2001	25	n/a	1,049	368.8
2002	27	8,000	831	357.0
2003	27	n/a	1,040	590.0
2004	26	10,000	1,039	1,062.8
2005	26	10,000+	1,055	765.6
2006	28	n/a	1,155	1,257.4
2007	31	n/a	1,166	1,718.6
2008	31	n/a	n/a	n/a
2009	31	n/a	n/a	3,955.7
2010	31	n/a	n/a	4,980.7
2011	31	n/a	n/a	5,714.0
2012	31	n/a	n/a	7,138.6
2013	31	100,000+	12,168	7951.9
2014	31	300,000	12,350	8956.6

SOURCES: Zaixian xiqiahui at http://www.onlinews.gov.cn; *Chengshi jingji daobao* [City economic herald], April 7, 2011; "Xiqiahui shunli bimu" [The Xiqiahui concludes with a success] at *Xibuwang* [The Western Network] at http://news.cnwest.com/content/2013-04/09/content_8920925.htm; and http://news.xinhuanet.com/house/xa/2014_05_23/c_1110830084.htm.

TABLE 7.7

Industrial Isomorphism Indicators

Year	Shanghai-Zhejiang	Shanghai-Jiangsu	Zhejiang-Jiangsu
1988	0.86	0.92	0.97
2000	0.74	0.86	0.91
2009	0.65	0.79	0.88

NOTE: The coefficient varies between 0 and 1; 1 refers to the state where two or more regions had exactly the same industrial structures.

SOURCE: Miao Jianjun, *Chengshiqun liyi chongtu de lilun yu shizheng yanjiu* [Theoretical and empirical study of interest conflict between city groups] (Beijing: Jingji guanli chubanshe, 2014), 168.

provinces) declined only marginally from 0.91 in 1981 to 0.86 in 1995.[68] During the 2000s, however, as the national market was being further unified, the level of specialization at the provincial level has been rising rather significantly. As table 7.7 demonstrates, even among Jiangsu, Zhejiang, and Shanghai, the coefficients of industrial isomorphism have been declining (i.e., expanding the room for interprovincial trade and reciprocity).

The voluntary search for cooperative partners beyond provincial boundaries was not limited to multimember networks. Several provinces formed dyadic partnerships based on reciprocity and voluntarism. Examples include Guangdong's investment in Yunnan's power plants, a union created in the interest of ensuring a stable supply of electricity to Guangdong's manufacturing industries. Tianjin and Hebei established extensive cooperative networks in as many as fourteen hundred projects, with Tianjin's investment in Hebei exceeding RMB 100 million. Shandong's investment in Xinjiang's cotton industry and Xinjiang's guaranteed supply of textile materials for Shandong's garment industry constituted another key case of voluntary cooperation based on reciprocal incentives.[69] Shandong and Sichuan also agreed on exchanges of both cadres and scholars in science and technology for the period of 2010–2014.[70] Since 2012, Guangdong (Zhaoqing) and Guangxi (Wuzhou) have jointly sought to establish a "special cooperative experimental zone" [yuegui hezuo tebie shiyanqu] as a bridge that could lead to China–Southeast Asian cooperation.[71]

Many horizontal networks have been operating at subprovincial levels as well. The Pan-Bohai Economic Cooperation Zone [Huan Bohai jingji xiezuoqu], established in 1987, encompassed twenty-two prefecture-level cities in Shandong, Liaoning, Tianjin, Hebei, and Shanxi. The Huai-hai Economic Zone [Huaihai jingjiqu] was set up by sixteen prefectures and cities of Jiangsu, Henan, Shandong, and Anhui. Fourteen coastal open cities [yanhai kaifang chengshi] and fifteen deputy-provincial cities [fu shengji shi] also formed a wide range of networks for information exchange, market sharing, and collective bargaining with Beijing.[72] With the further intensification of decentralization and marketization, participant units in these voluntarily formed networks came to include county-level cities, townships, and enterprises.[73]

One additional factor in the expansion of voluntarily formed horizontal networks was the nationwide fervor for "interlocal diplomacy" that began in the early 1990s. By the mid-1990s, all provinces and over a hundred prefecture-level cities had already established "liaison offices" [lianluo bangongshi or zhuwai banshichu] in Shenzhen, where the firms owned by outside localities accounted for one-third of all firms in the city.[74] As of 1995, over 280 liaison offices had been set up in Qingdao by other localities. Inland localities maintained these offices in the coastal region in order to obtain access to key economic information and overseas markets and capital. Henan, as of 1993, had set up all of its seven liaison offices in Shanghai, Guangzhou, Tianjin, Shenzhen,

TABLE 7.8
Liaison Offices of Select Provinces (2009)

Sending units	Bureau level	Deputy-bureau level	Department level	Total
		Receiving units		
Guangdong	Beijing, Shanghai		Chengdu, Xi'an, Lanzhou, Urumqi, Qingdao, Nanjing, Hangzhou	9
Guangxi	Beijing, Guangzhou	Shanghai, Guiyang		4
Chongqing	Beijing, Shanghai, Guangzhou	Shenzhen, Hainan, Chengdu		6
Sichuan	Beijing	Shanghai, Shenzhen Guangzhou, Urumqi, Chongqing, Shenyang, Fuzhou, Hangzhou, Kunming, Wuhan		11
Tibet	Beijing, Shanghai, Chengdu, Xi'an, Ge'ermu			5
Shaanxi	Beijing, Shanghai,	Wuhan, Guangzhou, Urumqi		5
Xinjiang	Beijing	Shanghai, Xi'an, Guangzhou		4
Beijing		Shanghai		1
Tianjin	Beijing, Shanghai, Guangzhou	Shenyang, Fuzhou, Xi'an, Chengdu, Jinan, Urumqi		9

Hebei	Beijing	Tianjin, Shanghai, Guangzhou	Shenzhen	5
Shanxi	Beijing	Tianjin, Shanghai, Guangzhou, Nanjing, Shenyang	Shenzhen, Zhuhai, Hainan, Urumqi	10
Liaoning	Beijing, Shanghai, Shenzhen	Beijing, Shanghai, Guangzhou	Tianjin, Xi'an, Wuhan, Shenzhen, Chengdu	8
Shanghai		Wuhan, Guangzhou, Chongqing, Xi'an, Taiyuan, Shenzhen, Harbin, Qinhuangdao		8
Jiangsu	Beijing, Shanghai, Shenzhen	Taiyuan, Lanzhou		5
Zhejiang	Beijing, Shanghai, Fuzhou, Hainan	Tianjin, Taiyuan, Shenzhen, Zhuhai, Chengdu, Chongqing, Shenyang		11
Fujian	Beijing	Shanghai, Guangzhou, Shenzhen		4
Shandong	Beijing, Shanghai	Tianjin, Shenyang, Guangzhou, Shenzhen, Chongqing, Xi'an, Fuzhou, Hainan	Urumqi, Harbin	12
Hubei	Beijing	Shanghai		2

SOURCE: He Linzhou, *Difang zhengfu zhuwai banshichu zhineng yanjiu* [Study of liaison offices of the local government] (master's thesis, Nankai University, 2009), 21–22.

Shandong, and Xiamen.[75] As of 2009, all thirty-one province-level governments currently maintain liaison offices in other localities, and table 7.8 demonstrates the magnitude and scope of such horizontal liaison.

"BRINGING THE CENTER BACK IN": THE RETURN OF VERTICAL RESOURCE SUPPORT

Although horizontal networks—both vertically induced and voluntarily formed—emerged as a significant modus operandi of interregional cooperation in the reform era, problems remain. Official statements do make occasional references to the importance of horizontal cooperation and interregional networks, but the center rarely assigns these operations a top priority. Even though horizontal cooperative networks formed among inland localities might have somewhat enhanced their collective bargaining potentials vis-à-vis Beijing, cooperation among the weak and poor tended to have limitations. Here, too, the benefits of cooperation were more often than not unevenly distributed.

It is thus suggested that although horizontal linkages no doubt became important as market reforms deepened, they alone cannot resolve the complex problem of regional disparities. That is, "bringing the center back in" might become inevitable at some point. Because vertical policy support was bound to have diminishing returns as the overall area under special policies increased, vertical resource support might still be a necessary—at least supplementary—measure (the upper-left cell in figure 7.1), particularly given that the center's fiscal power has been significantly reinforced following the 1994 tax-sharing reform.[76]

Under the transitional arrangements of the 1994 tax-sharing reform, Beijing was to reimburse portions of the tax incomes received if the province's revenue fell below the level prior to 1994. Such tax reimbursements [shuishou fanhuan] constituted the lion's share of Beijing's total fiscal transfers [caizheng zhuanyi zhifu] to the provinces during the 1990s. Because tax reimbursements were made on the basis of the 1993 baseline figures, coastal provinces with higher baseline figures benefited more than their inland counterparts. As the center's fiscal strength continued to expand in the 2000s by increasing the overall tax collection and passing the buck in paying for expenditures to localities, the proportion of tax reimbursement in the center's total fiscal transfer to localities fell from 72 percent in the mid-1990s to 43 percent in

2006. Between 1994 and 2006, of Beijing's fiscal transfer, the share for the central region rose sharply, from 15 to 47 percent; that for the western region increased even more, from 12 to 53 percent, clearly demonstrating the positive impact of a fiscally re-empowered center on the needy regions.[77]

Table 7.9 illustrates Beijing's enhanced fiscal power for the period of 1994–2011, as well as its changing priorities in fiscal transfers. Three points are worth mentioning here. First, Beijing's fiscal transfers expanded nearly seventy times (from 46 billion yuan in 1994 to 3.2 trillion yuan in 2011) during these seventeen years. Second, these figures represented 29 percent of China's total expenditures as well as 66 percent of local budgetary incomes for the same period.[78] Third, whereas the respective share of "lump-sum transfers" [cailixing: equivalent of block grants] and "earmarked transfers" [zhuanxiang: equivalent of functional grants] in total fiscal transfer was 22 and 78 percent in 1994, respectively, those for 2006 and 2011 were 52 and 54 percent as opposed to 48 and 46 percent, respectively. These figures point to Beijing's changing capabilities and willingness to distribute the benefits of fiscal transfer to needy regions rather than providing general welfare outlays for the entire nation.[79]

Long-term successes of horizontal cooperative networks are highly contingent upon Beijing's continuous efforts to raise the level of provincial specialization and to lower interprovincial market barriers, thereby weakening local protectionist sentiments. Some data suggest that the

TABLE 7.9

Compositional Changes in Beijing's Fiscal Transfer (RMB 100 million)

	1994	2006	2011
Financial portion	99.4 (22%)	4732.0 (52%)	17336.8 (54%)
General category	n/a	1,529.9	n/a
Ethnic regions	n/a	155.6	n/a
Wage adjustment	n/a	1,723.6	n/a
Tax-for-fees reform	n/a	751.3	n/a
Support for poor counties	n/a	234.6	n/a
Functional portion	361.4 (78%)	4411.6 (48%)	14905.2 (46%)
Supporting agriculture	n/a	551.5	n/a
Supporting education	n/a	168.0	n/a
Medicine and hygiene	n/a	113.8	n/a
Social welfare	n/a	1,666.8	n/a

SOURCE: "Guowuyuan guanyu guifan caizheng zhuanyi zhifu qingkuang de baogao" [State council report on the situation regarding the changes to fiscal transfer] (June 27, 2007), http://www.gov.cn/zxft/ft98/content_903353.htm.

levels of regional specialization and interprovincial trade have been gradually increasing.[80] In China, the center alone can tackle the symptoms of local protectionism—i.e., "duplicate construction," local rivalries, "miniaturization," and duke economies—and widen the basis for comparative advantage and interprovincial trade.

Beijing can also make contributions by establishing nationwide information networks on the basis of which interregional cooperative linkages can better survive. In order for horizontal cooperative networks—whether vertically imposed or voluntarily formed—to sustain themselves, the central government must seek to generate extensive information networks that can offer a clearly defined basis of mutual incentives and reciprocity. If the size of the key participant in these horizontal cooperative linkages is reduced to the level of a firm, informational requirements may get larger because the individual firm's boundary of attention is likely to be fairly limited. In dealing with this problem, Beijing must devise ways to share its ever-expanding information and statistical networks with localities and firms in different regions.

However important it may be, the center's vertical intervention may often prove unsuccessful, as Beijing is generally likely to value a political logic (i.e., sustaining a political status quo and seeking administrative convenience) more than an economic rationale, often overlooking the centrality of reciprocal incentives for cooperation.[81] Hence, vertical control and horizontal cooperation may often clash with each other. In a continent-sized nation like China, therefore, fostering (or reviving) natural economic territories may be an effective option for supplementing hierarchical coordination and breaking administrative boundaries in an increasingly marketized system.

8

Conclusion

The foregoing discussions have delved into the spatial, temporal, functional, hierarchical, and horizontal factors that were conducive in different ways to the prevalence of centrifugal forces in China in both traditional and modern times. The evolution of the center's instruments of local governance has also been examined in detail. As for the post-Mao era in particular, the overall impact of the system reforms on central–local balances of power was neither straightforward nor uniform. That is, although subnational governments generally obtained a significantly expanded scope of discretion in the making and implementation of policy, especially compared with the Maoist era, the balance between Beijing and the localities did not predominantly tilt toward the latter. Not only do assessments vary for different time periods, but issue areas also constituted a key variable in determining the room for local discretion and regional diversity.

The preceding chapters have also substantiated the proposition that the leaders of the People's Republic, just like their imperial predecessors, were highly preoccupied, if not obsessed, with centrifugal forces against central control. Although the People's Republic is deemed fairly young for a state—particularly given that the average life expectancy for a Chinese dynasty was about two hundred years—and full of moving energy, that does not necessarily mean that it is totally immune or invulnerable to the possibility of implosion or collapse, of which centrifugal forces have always constituted a key ingredient throughout Chinese history.

The traditional three-pronged challenge for the emperors of Chinese dynasties—foreign aggression, the rise of alternative military forces, and peasant rebellions—poses different problems to the People's Republic today. With China's "rapid" rise on a global scale, already to a so-called G-2 status with the capacity for minimum nuclear deterrence, it is hardly conceivable that any country would even contemplate invading or waging a total war with China. As noted in detail in chapter 5, the emergence of alternative military forces is nearly unthinkable in the context of the People's Republic today. Therefore, of the three types of threats, the only one that most closely resembles the fatal recipe of implosion or collapse is the frequent occurrence of collective protests in different corners of China.[1] Yet, even concerning this factor, except for those protests in support of Tibetan independence and the separation of Xinjiang, principal targets have mostly been local (i.e., by and large subprovincial) governments, and the central government has generally been perceived as a potential ally or at least a neutral umpire.

Table 8.1 illustrates that the level of the Chinese public's political trust in government officials tended to decline along the administrative hierarchy. That is to say, the lower the administrative level of a government, the less political trust it commanded among the Chinese people. Although these figures are adapted from three different series of surveys, at least an overall trend is clearly discernible: the Chinese people posited more trust in the central government than all the other levels of local government. These figures may, therefore, constitute a key piece of evidence against the imminent likelihood of large-scale anticenter protests.[2] As a matter of fact, these figures render support for the basis of further cooperation between Beijing and the provinces in reining in subprovincial governments deemed to be plagued with pervasive corruption, lax discipline, institutional decay, and moral hazard.[3]

How long is this state of affairs likely to last? Or, conversely, what would happen if the level of trust posited in the central government should significantly worsen in the coming years? What would be the contributing factors to such an ominous reversal? These questions are important because, in the mid- to long run, the marginal space under Beijing's tight control is likely to decrease in proportion with the overall duration of the systemic reform. In retrospect, at the end of each cycle of decentralization and recentralization, a set of structures and interests

TABLE 8.1
The Chinese Public's Political Trust in Different Levels of Government (%)

Years	Trust level	Central	Provincial	City	County	Township
1999–2001[a]	Very high	53.5	42.4	n/a	25.7	16.1
	Very low	1.4	2.1	n/a	3.7	11.0
2003–2005[b]	Very high	70.5	45.1	30.5	17.8	12.4
	Very low	0.6	1.2	3.3	11.5	26.5
2008[a]	Very high	44.6	24.3	n/a	17.1	n/a
	Very low	3.6	5.7	n/a	8.2	n/a
2010[c]	High	75.5	66.4	58.7		n/a
2014[c]	High	78.5	65.6	58.9		n/a

SOURCES: (a) Li Lianjiang, "Chaxu zhengfu xinren" [Political trust in different levels of government], *Ershiyi shiji* (The twenty-first century), no. 131 (June 2012): 109–110; (b) Hu Rong, "Nongmin shangfang yu zhengzhi xinren de liushi" [Peasant petitions and the loss of political trust], *Shehuixue yanjiu* [Sociological research], no. 3 (2007): 39–55; (c) Bruce J. Dickson, "Public Goods and Government Support Survey," 2010 and 2014. I thank Bruce for sharing these data.

emerged largely in favor of local incentives and discretion. That is, if the tenure of the reform should be further elongated, the scope of local discretion at t+2 would certainly become at least a bit wider than that at t+1, all other things being equal.[4] The crux of the matter, then, is whether the empowered local administration would be capable of handling and managing a wide range of public policy issues that the society cherishes and cares about.

CENTRAL–LOCAL DYNAMICS MEET STATE–SOCIETY RELATIONS

Further deepening of marketization and ownership diversification in China may well interact with decentralization reforms in ways that we have not been able to foresee. That is, as the reforms of marketization and privatization further intensify, a wide range of socioeconomic programs—e.g., welfare provision, poverty alleviation, interregional equalization, etc.—may become increasingly bottom heavy in their resource and informational requirements. This unforeseen linkage may put central–local dynamics much closer to the crucial concerns of state–society relations in today's China.[5] This is, of course, not to suggest that certain political logic has totally replaced the dominant economic logic of the system. Rather, the economic logic has become increasingly mixed with the political logic to produce tensions and conflicts among the center, localities, and social communities in the process of systemic reforms.[6]

One most notable anomaly in China today is that regions and local units with greater responsibilities and needs tend to have weaker financial and material power. On average, poor, western, and inland regions had much smaller budgetary bases and received far fewer foreign direct investment projects. Even with the belated granting of highly preferential policies, they still found competing with the advanced, eastern, and coastal regions to be a tough challenge. Although some changes have currently been on the way, as noted in chapter 7, Beijing's "fiscal transfer payments" [caizheng zhuanyi zhifu], thus far, have not been as sufficiently geared toward the poor, western, and inland regions as one would expect.[7] Furthermore, the nationwide abolition of the agricultural tax totally diluted the township-level finance so that educational and public health expenditures had to be paid mostly by the counties. Worse yet, many counties were in heavy debt and did not have sufficient tax revenues for effective delivery of key public services.[8]

Institutional decay and loss of control at the subcounty and grassroots levels are also issues of growing concern. The fast-expanding influence of local clans over the basic-level party and state units, particularly in the rural areas, as well as the infiltration of bad elements into the grass-roots apparatus, poses a crucial question of governance. Is the center's capacity to rule stretching down effectively to the subcounty and grass-roots levels so that key societal demands are met satisfactorily?[9] The queer paradox here is that the swift success of Beijing's tax-sharing reforms led to the provinces' excessive milking of subprovincial governments, which in turn resulted in heavy arbitrary levies on the peasants and the misappropriation of farmland without proper compensation. Subsequently, peasant outbursts were translated into an increased frequency of collective protests all over the country, highlighting a growing interconnectedness between central-local dynamics and state–society relations.[10]

Turbulent and often violent situations in some ethnic minorities regions—Xinjiang and Tibet in particular—continue to haunt the center and its leadership irrespective of whether they actually pose a grave threat to the regime itself. The core problem is as much between the authoritarian unitary state and parts of the Chinese society with specific geographical foci as between the Han and the ethnic minorities.[11] Furthermore, the growth of "invisible economies" [*yinxing jingji*] and massive capital flight that are well beyond state taxation and regulation, the prevalence of cross-border smuggling, pervasive corruption, the breakdown of the *hukou* and *danwei* systems, and widening regional and rural–urban disparities provide ample room for a complex entwinement of central–local dynamics with state–society relations.[12]

The growing difficulties with local governance, the rise of subnational actors in many key domains, and the subsequent manifestation of centrifugal tendencies push us back to the very question posed in the beginning of this volume: Despite its continental size and multiple ethnicities, why has China consistently held on to the unitary system? Some regard China of the reform era as having adopted a sort of "behavioral federalism," "fiscal federalism," or "federalism, Chinese style."[13] Yet, federalism in its genuine sense must entail specific arrangements for dual sovereignty and power sharing safeguarded by the Constitution that explicitly forbids the center from arbitrarily altering the provisions so stipulated. In that respect, such modifiers as "Chinese style," "fiscal," and "behavioral" do not give full credit to the fundamental changes that a genuine federal system may bring to China.[14]

Let us push the envelope a bit further here. When localities were strongly tempted to venture into the hitherto prohibited realm of policy discretion, their frame of reference in making such daring moves generally focused on the means of personnel control in Beijing's hand. What would happen if the logic of China's electoral experiments should expand to the point where the central party's exclusive *nomenklatura* power gets significantly weakened? Under the circumstances where at least subnational leaders are selected via popular elections, what kind of connections are to be established between the CCP's power to rule, on the one hand, and central–local relations on the other?[15] As long as the central party/government remains the "center" of power and policy making, as is true in many unitary systems, will antinomies of decentralization be bound to stay with it?[16] Whether, in the long run, the political reform on the state–society front will eventually spill over to the realm of central–local relations in ways that we have not foreseen remains to be seen.

The future is unequivocally God's domain, almost always defying human predictions except for some fortuitous coincidences. Social sciences are way too poorly equipped even to lay out key parameters of an immediate future. Nearly a decade ago, on the basis of collaborative scholarly endeavors, this author took a shot at delineating the boundary of China's near- to mid-term future.[17] In doing so, a total of eight scenarios were posited, and from today's vantage point, three (the Yugoslavian, Indonesian, and Latin American models) are already off the list and another three (the Indian, Soviet, and French models) have only low possibilities. The remaining two—a strong authoritarian but advanced market-based China and a democratic but hegemonic-realist China—still remain to be substantiated.[18] Although both scenarios presuppose a very strong China economically and militarily, the former is more status quo oriented, whereas the latter refers to a revisionist strategic competitor. As far as my own judgment is concerned, the jury is still out on these two remaining scenarios and their subcategorical contingencies, because for both of them, stable central–local relations are crucial, if not indispensable (i.e., not replicating the experiences of Yugoslavia, the Soviet Union, or Indonesia).[19]

In delineating the trajectory of China's uncertain future as it relates to the centrifugal challenge, the following set of questions seems pertinent: (1) What does a strong China mean domestically or internally? (2) What should we make of a democratic China in the context of central–local relations? And (3) how durable is a strong democratic (or even federal) China going to be? Although answers to these questions are bound to be in the realm of speculations or informed guesses at best, they are nevertheless important and worth exploring.

A Strong China

At least for the foreseeable future, the rise of a strong China appears to be predestined, although the pace of its ascendancy may vary depending on a wide range of internal and external factors. Irrespective of so many theories on "bubble/crash/disintegration/collapse," China is likely to become stronger than before, both economically and militarily.[20] The fact of the matter is that many of the problems that China now faces were also found in the United States and many other countries during their ascent toward the status of great powers. But, too often, we fail to apply the same yardstick. At the end of the day, it may not be simply economic or military competitiveness per se, but, as we have seen in the case of the Soviet Union, it will come down to the issue of internal cohesion or local governance capacity.[21] Will the People's Republic of China, with global military projection capabilities and potent international economic influence, be able to effectively regulate and contain centrifugal forces embedded in its physical size and regional diversity?

A Democratic China

All too often, the future of China gets "unfairly" discounted due to the "nondemocratic" nature of its political system. Yet, it seems that the "democratic bias" in such assessments is grossly overlooked: neither the Roman Empire nor the Tang dynasty was democratic, but both rose to the top and were sustained for an elongated period of time. Are democratic structures and processes necessarily more conducive to effective local governance? Some refer to India as a rising "democratic" giant for the future, but, of course, such forecasts await empirical substantiation in due time.[22] The case of India (and Indonesia to a certain extent) constitutes a crucial countercase in terms of democracies with weak capacity for local governance. Although it is widely known that key innovations originate from the free thinking characteristic of a democratic system, there is no guarantee that durable stability always goes hand in hand with democracy. Furthermore, what specific variant of democracy will best suit China's needs for local governance is also a big open-ended question. Of course, a federalist possibility can be presented, but then again, will China be able to survive a genuinely federal structure?[23]

A Durable China

The United States has proved fairly durable as it has thus far survived nearly 240 years. If we define the Nixon Shock (i.e., President Richard Nixon's announcement to relinquish the dollar–gold pegging principle in 1971) as a watershed that heralded a beginning of America's decline, Washington has still endured forty-some more years and is still counting. Whereas America's—relative—decline is attributed to so many diverse domestic and external problems, federal–local relations do not seem to occupy a top place on the list. May the same appraisal be applicable to the Chinese case? Or is it simply for the fact that China is now only sixty-some years old—equivalent to the United States in the 1840s? Will the People's Republic continue to be adaptive enough to last as long as its imperial predecessors like the Ming and the Qing?

For a durable China to materialize, the Chinese central leadership will have to continue with their reflections on traditional and revolutionary legacies and on key lessons from the debacle of the Soviet Union. Undoubtedly, what matters most is how the central state is going to cope with different tiers of local governments now equipped with new roles, specific interests, and strategic calculus.[24] Whether the much-discussed ideas of better delineating central–local responsibilities and implementing legal reforms can be indeed carried out is a real litmus test for the center's adaptability in the long run.

A Chinese China

The People's Republic today is no longer a totalitarian system in the sense that it stopped indoctrinating the people's thinking. Yet, China still is an authoritarian regime in the sense that it seeks to monitor, police, and regulate the populace's behavior. In the mid to long run, however, Communist or socialist ingredients that remain today will become increasingly diluted, gradually giving way to a neo-traditional return of many familiar problems of local governance.[25] It is this author's assessment that, down the road, the People's Republic's future challenge of local governance will not be so different in nature from the difficulties that traditional China repeatedly faced for so long. In the longer run, therefore, the emerging Chinese empire is likely to have centrifugal forces that are strong enough to stand up against the center, which will in turn resort to many of the traditional means of local control in addition to modern, innovative ones. Hence, history continues, with cumulative memories and institutional evolution.

Notes

1. CHINA AS A CENTRIFUGAL EMPIRE: SIZE, DIVERSITY, AND LOCAL GOVERNANCE

1. The *loci classicus* are Joseph LaPalombara, "Penetration: A Crisis of Government," in *Crises and Sequences in Political Development*, ed. Leonard Binder et al. (Princeton: Princeton University Press, 1971), 205–32; and Charles Tilly, *The Formation of National States in Europe* (Princeton: Princeton University Press, 1975).

2. See Samuel Humes, *Local Governance and National Power: A Worldwide Comparison of Tradition and Change in Local Government* (Herdfordshire UK: Harvester Wheatsheaf, 1991).

3. These 2013 figures are from the entries by country in *Encyclopedia Britannica*, http://www.britannica.com.

4. Alberto Alesina and Enrico Spolaore, *The Size of Nations* (Cambridge, Mass.: MIT Press, 2003).

5. A similar outlier in this regard is Indonesia with the world's fourth-largest population, where the formal federal structure was very short-lived (i.e., only during 1949–1950).

6. The concept of federalism is interpreted here in its strictest sense as it is often used more as a metaphor for lax central control in some areas. See, for instance, Evan A. Feigenbaum and Damien Ma, "Federalism, Chinese Style," *Foreign Affairs* 93, no. 3 (May–June 2014).

7. For the concept of diseconomies of scale, see "The Optimal Size of Countries—Posner," *The Becker-Posner Blog*, December 3, 2012, http://www .becker-posner-blog.com/2012/12/the-optimal-size-of-countries-posner.html (accessed on February 25, 2014).

8. See Zhang Xiaolin, *Wendinglun* [Theory of stability] (Beijing: Zhongyangwenxian chubanshe, 2004), 14. See also Jae Ho Chung, "Assessing the Odds

against the Mandate of Heaven: Do Numbers on Popular Protest Really Matter?" in *Charting China's Future: Political, Social and International Dimensions*, ed. Jae Ho Chung (Lanham, Md.: Rowman & Littlefield, 2006), 107–28.

9. See Paul C. Light, *Thickening Government: Federal Hierarchy and the Diffusion of Accountability* (Washington, D.C.: The Brookings Institution, 1995). Of course, the prestige and reputation that come with bureaucratic thickening provide a very important motivation for modern states to expand. See Jonathan Mercer, *Reputation and International Politics* (Ithaca: Cornell University Press, 2010), 14–43.

10. See Amy Chua, *Day of Empire: How Hyperpowers Rise to Global Dominance—and Why They Fall* (New York: Anchor, 2009); and Greg Woolf, *Rome: An Empire's Story* (Oxford: Oxford University Press, 2012), chap. 17.

11. See Sewelyn Bialer, *The Soviet Paradox: External Expansion, Internal Decline* (New York: Knopf, 1986).

12. The long list of Chinese publications on the Soviet debacle is illustrative of the preoccupations that the leaders in Beijing have with the imperative of local control. See Ding Weiling et al., *Sulian dongou jubian qishilu* [Revelations from the major changes in the Soviet Union and Eastern Europe] (Changchun: Jilin renmin chubanshe, 1992); Wei Zehuan, *Sugong xingshuai toushi* [Looking into the rise and fall of Soviet communism] (Guangzhou: Guangdong renmin chubanshe, 1998); Lu Nanquan, *Sulian xingwang shilun* [History of the rise and fall of the Soviet Union] (Beijing: Renmin chubanshe, 2002); and Feng Shaolei, ed., *Sulian jieti de yuanyin ji sikao* [Thoughts on the dissolution of the Soviet Union] (Beijing: Shishi chubanshe, 2013).

13. Zhang Liang, *The Tiananmen Papers*, trans. Perry Link, Andrew Nathan, and Orville Schell (New York: Public Affairs, 2002).

14. See *Renmin ribao* [People's daily], February 21, 2014; Kor Kian Beng, "End Is Nigh for Ex-Security Czar," *Straits Times*, February 26, 2014, http://news.asiaone.com/news/asia/end-nigh-ex-security-czar; Michael Forsythe, Chris Buckley, and Jonathan Ansfield, "Severing a Family's Ties, China's President Signals a Change," *New York Times*, April 19, 2014; "Zhou's Power Base: Interactive Graphic," Caixin Online, http://english.caixin.com/2014-07-29/100710458 .html (accessed on August 5, 2012); "Meiti mingming dangnei yuan sandabangpai" [The media names three intra-party factions], *Jinghua Shibao* [Beijing times], January 4, 2015, originally accessed at http://energy.people.com.cn/n /2015/0104/c71661_26317825.html; and Keira Lu Huang, "Falling Down: The Disgrace of Ling Jihua Is a Drama Years in the Making," *South China Morning Post*, July 22, 2015.

15. For China's overall threat perception—both domestic and external—see Jae Ho Chung, ed., *China's Crisis Management* (London: Routledge, 2011). Also see "Xi Jinping to Lead National Security Commission," *Xinhua*, January 24, 2014, http://news.xinhuanet.com/english/china/2014-01/24/c_133071876.htm.

16. See chapter 3 for more detailed discussions on these cyclical changes.

17. Zheng Lin, *Difang zhengfu diwei—Caili peizhi wenti yanjiu* [The place of local government—A study of allocating fiscal powers] (Beijing: Renmin fayuan chubanshe, 2008), 189–92; and Wu Licai, "Xiangzhen gaige" [Reforms of

townships], in *Difang de fuxing* [The re-rise of localities], ed. Yang Xuedong and Lai Hairong (Beijing: Shehuikexue wenxian chubanshe, 2009), 229–47.

18. Gabe Collins and Andrew Erickson, "Dissecting China's Economy: 15 Chinese Provinces and Municipalities Could By Themselves Qualify as Top-50 Global Economies," *China SignPost*, no. 19 (January 23, 2011).

19. Matt Schiavenza, "China Only Has One Time Zone—and That's a Problem," *Atlantic*, November 5, 2013, http://www.theatlantic.com/china/archive /2013/11/china-only-has-one-time-zone-and-thats-a-problem/281136/.

20. There are at least seven broad language groups in Chinese, and one most popular group [*guan—Putonghua*] is even divided into more than forty dialect groups. See S. Robert Ramsey, *The Languages of China* (Princeton: Princeton University Press, 1989). For the 2004 survey results, see "Greater Numbers Speak Mandarin," *China Daily*, December 26, 2004.

21. Jiaotong fazhan yanjiuyuan, "Zai nongcun de daolu" [Roads in the countryside] (2005), originally accessed at http://dev.catsic.com/gzdt-show.asp ?column_id=8&column_cat_id=11&fileName=gzdt.

22. See, for instance, Ciqi Mei and Margaret Pearson, "Killing a Chicken to Scare the Monkeys? Deterrence Failure and Local Defiance in China," *China Journal*, no. 72 (2014): 75–97; and Tucker Van Aken and Orion A. Lewis, "The Political Economy of Noncompliance in China: The Case of Industrial Energy Policy," *Journal of Contemporary China* 24, no. 95 (2015): 798–822.

23. China's land area currently amounts to 9.6 million square kilometers, whereas that of the Roman Empire was about 6.5 million. The Roman Empire ruled about 100 million people, roughly one-fifth of the world population at the time. China currently has a population that is roughly an equivalent (22 percent).

24. For this connection between policy type and local discretion, see Jae Ho Chung, "Studies of Central–Provincial Relations in the People's Republic of China: A Mid-Term Appraisal," *China Quarterly*, no. 142 (June 1995): 487–508. For more details, see chapter 6 of this book.

25. Jae Ho Chung, "The Evolving Hierarchy of China's Local Administration: Tradition and Change," in *China's Local Administration: Traditions and Changes in the Sub-national Hierarchy*, eds. Jae Ho Chung and Tao-Chiu Lam (London: Routledge, 2010), 1–13.

26. Central documents and administrative supervision are key instruments for connecting these intermediate units with the center and with the lower-level units. Studies on interactions between intermediate-level units are rare, however. For exceptions, see Maria Edin, "State Capacity and Local Agent Control in China: CCP Cadre Management from a Township Perspective," *China Quarterly*, no. 173 (March 2003): 35–52; and Gunter Schubert and Anna L. Ahler, "County and Township Cadres as a Strategic Group: 'Building a New Socialist Countryside' in Three Provinces," *China Journal*, no. 67 (January 2012): 67–86.

27. Although this was pointed out earlier, not much research has been done on this increasingly crucial dimension. See Jae Ho Chung, "Vertical Support, Horizontal Linkages, and Regional Disparities in China: Typology, Incentive Structure, and Operational Logic," *Issues and Studies* 37, no. 4 (July–August 2001): 121–46.

28. In the long run, these dynamics are bound to have crucial ramifications for the "fragmented" nature of China's authoritarian system.

29. See, for instance, Robert H. Bates, Avner Grief, Margaret Levi, Jean-Laurent Rosenthal, and Barry R. Weingast, *Analytic Narratives* (Princeton: Princeton University Press, 1998).

30. "Yi lishi wei jingjian xiqu zhiguo lizheng zhihui" [Use history as a mirror to absorb wisdom for statecraft], *Xinhuawang*, November 15, 2014, originally accessed at http://news.xinhuanet.com/politics/2014_11/15/c_1113259641.htm.

31. Fieldwork in China over many trips was indispensable. Equally important was the Universities Service Center for China Studies [Zhongguo yanjiu daxue fuwu zhongxin] in Hong Kong, whose collections were the most valuable archival resource for this research.

32. A. P. Tant, "The Politics of Official Statistics," *Government and Opposition* 30, no. 2 (Spring 1995): 254–66; and Tim Harford, "A Head for Figures," *Financial Times Magazine*, November 17–18, 2007.

2. CHINA GOES LOCAL (AGAIN): ASSESSING POST-MAO DECENTRALIZATION

1. Frederick Wakeman Jr., *The Fall of Imperial China* (New York: Free Press, 1975); and James E. Sheridan, *China in Disintegration* (New York: Free Press, 1975). See also Jae Ho Chung, "Assessing the Odds Against the Mandate of Heaven: Do the Numbers (on Instability) Really Matter?" in *Charting China's Future: Political, Social and International Dimensions*, ed. Jae Ho Chung (Lanham, Md.: Rowman & Littlefield, 2006), 107–21.

2. Owen Lattimore, *The Making of Modern China: A Short History* (New York: Norton, 1944), 186.

3. See Jan Myrdal, *Report from a Chinese Village* (New York: Pantheon, 1965); Ezra Vogel, *Canton under Communism: Programs and Politics in a Provincial Capital, 1949–1968* (Cambridge, Mass.: Harvard University Press, 1969), chap. 3; and Yuan-tsung Chen, *The Dragon's Village* (Middlesex, UK: Penguin Books, 1980). Also see Joseph Fewsmith, "The Elusive Search for Effective Sub-County Governance," in *Mao's Invisible Hand: The Political Foundations of Adaptive Governance*, eds. Sebastian Heilmann and Elizabeth J. Perry (Cambridge, Mass.: Harvard University Asia Center, 2011), 269–96.

4. Ilpyong J. Kim, *The Politics of Chinese Communism: Kiangsi under Soviets* (Berkeley: University of California Press, 1973), 18–19, 114–16, 160–78.

5. Mark Selden, *The Yenan Way in Revolutionary China* (Cambridge, Mass.: Harvard University Press, 1971), chaps. 1–4.

6. For the Yan'an system's flexibility, see Elizabeth Perry, *Rebels and Revolutionaries in North China, 1845–1945* (Stanford: Stanford University Press, 1980), 225–39; and Ralph Thaxton, *China Turned Rightside Up: Revolutionary Legitimacy in the Peasant World* (New Haven: Yale University Press, 1983), 185–90. For a temporal comparison, see Chalmers Johnson, "Chinese Leadership and Mass Response: The Yenan Period and the Socialist Education Campaign

Period," in *China in Crisis*, eds. Ping-ti Ho and Tang Tsou (Chicago: University of Chicago Press, 1968), 1:401–7.

7. See David E. Apter and Tony Saich, *Revolutionary Discourse in Mao's Republic* (Cambridge, Mass.: Harvard University Press, 1994).

8. For a discussion of this environmental contrast, see Sebastian Heilmann, "From Local Experiments to National Policy: The Origins of China's Distinctive Policy Process," *China Journal*, no. 59 (January 2008): 9, 13–15.

9. See Jae Ho Chung, *Central Control and Local Discretion in China* (Oxford: Oxford University Press, 2000), chap. 2.

10. At the dawn of the People's Republic, the number of province-level units amounted to fifty-two as opposed to thirty-three in 2015.

11. See Lowell Dittmer, "Political Development: Leadership, Politics and Ideology," in *The People's Republic after Thirty Years: An Overview*, ed. Joyce E. Kallgren (Berkeley: Center for Chinese Studies, 1979), 27–43; and Wu Li, "Mao Zedong dui xinzhongguo zhongyang yu difang jingji guanxi de tansuo" [An exploration of Mao Zedong on New China's central–local economic relations], *Dang de wenxian* [Literature of the CCP], no. 5 (2006): 49–50.

12. See Frederick C. Teiwes, *Politics and Purges in China: Rectification and the Decline of Party Norms, 1950–1965* (Armonk, N.Y.: M. E. Sharpe, 1979), 349–66; and Peter R. Moody Jr., "Policy and Power: The Career of T'ao Chu, 1956–66," *China Quarterly*, no. 54 (April–June 1973): 267–93. Also see Chung, *Central Control and Local Discretion in China*, 33–35.

13. The quotation is from Alfred L. Chan, "The Campaign for Agricultural Development in the Great Leap Forward: A Study of Policy-Making and Implementation in Liaoning," *China Quarterly*, no. 129 (March 1992): 54–55.

14. See William A. Joseph, "A Tragedy of Good Intentions: Post-Mao Views of the Great Leap Forward," *Modern China* 12, no. 4 (October 1986): 419–57; Jean-Luc Domenach, *The Origins of the Great Leap Forward: The Case of One Chinese Province* (Boulder: Westview, 1995), 157–60; Chu Han, *Sannian ziran zaihai changbian jishi* [Records of natural calamities of the three years of 1959–1961] (Chengdu: Sichuan renmin chubanshe, 1996), 105–42; Li Rui, *Dayuejin qinliji* [Personal recollections of the Great Leap Forward] (Shanghai: Shanghai yuandong chubanshe, 1996), 119–28; and Alfred L. Chan, *Mao's Crusade: Politics and Policy Implementation in China's Great Leap Forward* (Oxford: Oxford University Press, 2001).

15. Victor Falkenheim, "Continuing Central Predominance," *Problems of Communism* 21, no. 4 (1972): 82–83; and David Zweig, "Strategies of Policy Implementation: 'Policy Winds' and Brigade Accounting in Rural China," *World Politics* 37, no. 2 (January 1985): 267–93.

16. For the Maoist norms that were self-policing, see Dorothy J. Solinger, "Politics in Yunnan Province in the Decade of Disorder: Elite Factional Strategies and Central-Local Relations," *China Quarterly*, no. 92 (December 1982): 628–62; Anita Chan, Richard Madsen, and Jonathan Unger, *Chen Village: The Recent History of a Peasant Community in Mao's China* (Berkeley: University of California Press, 1984); Anne F. Thurston, *Enemies of the People: The Ordeals of the Intellectuals in China's Great Cultural Revolution* (Cambridge, Mass.: Harvard

University Press, 1987); and Keith Forster, *Rebellion and Factionalism in a Chinese Province: Zhejiang 1966–1976* (Armonk, N.Y.: M. E. Sharpe, 1990).

17. Sun Qitai and Xiong Zhiyong, *Dazhai hongqi de shengqi yu duoluo* [The rise and fall of Dazhai's red banner] (Huixian: Henan renmin chubanshe, 1990), 258–68; Jae Ho Chung, "The Politics of Agricultural Mechanization in the Post-Mao Era, 1977–1987," *China Quarterly*, no. 134 (June 1993): 264–90; and Marc Blecher and Wang Shaoguang, "The Political Economy of Cropping in Maoist and Dengist China: Hebei Province and Shulu County, 1949–90," *China Quarterly*, no. 137 (March 1994): 73–80.

18. Thomas Lyons, *Economic Integration and Planning in Communist China* (New York: Columbia University Press, 1987), 174.

19. Stuart R. Schram, "Decentralization in a Unitary State: Theory and Practice, 1940–1984," in *The Scope of State Power in China*, ed. S. R. Schram (London: University of London Press, 1985), 98–122; and David S. G. Goodman, "Political Perspectives," in *China's Regional Development*, ed. David S. G. Goodman (London: Routledge, 1989), 22–26.

20. For exemplary assessments of the field, see Jae Ho Chung, "Studies of Central-Provincial Relations in the People's Republic of China: A Mid-Term Appraisal," *China Quarterly*, no. 142 (June 1995): 487–508; Yasheng Huang, "Central-Local Relations during the Reform Era: The Economic and Institutional Dimensions," *World Development* 24, no. 4 (April 1996): 655–72; Dali L. Yang, *Beyond Beijing: Liberalization and the Regions in China* (London: Routledge, 1997); Jae Ho Chung, "Reappraising Central-Local Relations in Deng's China," in *Remaking the Chinese State: Strategies, Society and Security*, eds. Chien-min Chao and Bruce J. Dickson (London: Routledge, 2001), 46–75; Barry Naughton and Dali L. Yang, "Holding China Together: Introduction," in *Holding China Together: Diversity and National Integration in the Post-Deng Era*, eds. Barry Naughton and Dali L. Yang (Cambridge: Cambridge University Press, 2004), 1–28; and Linda C. Li, "Central-Local Relations in the People's Republic of China: Trends, Processes and Impacts for Policy Implementation," *Public Administration and Development* 30, no. 3 (August 2010): 177–90.

21. The "Provincial China" meeting track, which had begun in the mid-1990s with the initiative of David S. G. Goodman to link experts in Australia, Asia, Europe, and the United States, made such valuable contributions as David S. G. Goodman, ed., *China's Provinces in Reform: Class, Community and Political Culture* (London: Routledge, 1997); Feng Chongyi and Hans Hendrischke, eds., *The Political Economy of China's Provinces: Competitive and Comparative Advantages* (London: Routledge, 1999); and John Fitzgerald, ed., *Rethinking China's Provinces* (London: Routledge, 2002). The Asian Network for the Study of Local China (*ANSLoC*), founded in 2006, is another such effort among Asia-based scholars. Its principal outputs include Jae Ho Chung and Tao-Chiu Lam, eds., *China's Local Administration: Traditions and Changes in the Sub-national Hierarchy* (London: Routledge, 2010); and John Donaldson, ed., *Assessing Central-Local Balances of Power in China* (London: Routledge, 2016).

22. See Bo Zhiyue, *Chinese Provincial Leaders: Economic Performance and Political Mobility since 1949* (Armonk, N.Y.: M. E. Sharpe, 2002); Xiaowei Zang, *Elite Dualism and Leadership Selection in China* (London: RoutledgeCurzon,

2003); Susan Whiting, *Power and Wealth in Rural China: The Political Economy of Institutional Change* (Cambridge: Cambridge University Press, 2000); Thomas P. Bernstein and Xiaobo Lu, *Taxation Without Representation in Contemporary Rural China* (Cambridge: Cambridge University Press, 2003); Eric Thun, *Changing Lanes in China: Foreign Direct Investment, Local Governments, and Auto Sector Development* (Cambridge: Cambridge University Press, 2006); Yumin Sheng, *Economic Openness and Territorial Politics in China* (Cambridge: Cambridge University Press, 2010); and Pierre Landry, *Decentralized Authoritarianism in China: The Communist Party's Control of Local Elites in the Post-Mao Era* (Cambridge: Cambridge University Press, 2012).

23. For the former, see Hongbin Cai and Daniel Treisman, "Did Government Decentralization Cause China's Economic Miracle?" *World Politics* 58, no. 4 (July 2006): 505–35; and Minxin Pei, *China's Trapped Transition: The Limits of Developmental Autocracy* (Cambridge, Mass.: Harvard University Press, 2009), 132–35. For the latter, see Gabriella Montinola, Yingyi Qian, and Barry R. Weingast, "Federalism, Chinese Style: The Political Basis for Economic Success in China," *World Politics* 48, no. 1 (October 1995); and Chung, "Reappraising Central-Local Relations in Deng's China," 46–75.

24. See Arthur Waldron, "Warlordism versus Federalism: The Revival of a Debate," *The China Quarterly*, no. 121 (1990): 116–28; David Shambaugh, "Losing Control: The Erosion of State Authority in China," *Current History* 92, no. 575 (1993): 253–59; Edward Friedman, "China's North-South Split and the Forces of Disintegration," *Current History* 92, no. 575 (1993): 270–74; Maria H. Chang, "China's Future: Regionalism, Federation, or Disintegration," *Studies in Comparative Communism* 25, no. 3 (1992): 211–27; Shaoguang Wang, "The Rise of the Regions: Fiscal Reform and the Decline of Central State Capacity in China," *The Waning of the Communist State: Economic Origins of Political Decline in China and Hungary*, ed. Andrew G. Walder (Berkeley: University of California Press, 1995), 87–113; Jack Goldstone, "The Coming Chinese Collapse," *Foreign Policy*, no. 99 (1995): 35–52; Gordon Chang, *The Coming Collapse of China* (New York: Knopf, 2001); Ni Jianzhong, *Daguo zhuhou* [Feudal princes in China] (Beijing: Zhongguo shehui chubanshe 1996); Tong Zhongxin, *Shiheng de diguo* [The empire off balance] (Guiyang: Guizhou renmin chubanshe, 2001); Yang Zaiping and Xiang Dong, *Zhongguo chang bu shuai* [China will not perish but flourish] (Beijing: Jingji kexue chubanshe, 2003); Ma Jianzhong, *Zhengzhi wendinglun* [On political stability] (Beijing: Zhongguo shehuikexue chubanshe, 2003); Zhang Xiaolin, *Wendinglun* [Theory of stability] (Beijing: Zhongyang wenxian chubanshe, 2004); and Li Peilin et al., eds., *Zhongguo shehui hexie wending baogao* [Report on China's social harmony and stability] (Beijing: Shehuikexue wenxian chubanshe, 2008).

25. Chung, "Studies of Central–Provincial Relations in the People's Republic of China," 495–97; and S. Philip Hsu, "Deconstructing Decentralization in China: Fiscal Incentive versus Local Autonomy in Policy Implementation," *Journal of Contemporary China* 13, no. 40 (August 2004): 567–99.

26. Whereas the functional dimension of central–local relations is the focus of this chapter, a structural/institutional dimension is examined in detail in chapter 3.

27. See He Jianzhang and Wang Jiye, *Zhongguo jihua guanli wenti* [Problems of plan control in China] (Beijing: Zhongguo shehuikexue chubanshe, 1984), 48–72; Lyons, *Economic Integration and Planning in Communist China*, 218–22; Huang Yasheng, "Information, Bureaucracy, and Economic Reform in China and the Soviet Union," *World Politics* 47, no. 1 (October 1994): 102–34; and Barry Naughton, *Growing Out of the Plan: Chinese Economic Reform 1978–1993* (Cambridge: Cambridge University Press, 1995), 41–42.

28. See Wu Shaojun, *Guojia fazhan jihua gailun* [Introduction to state development planning] (Beijing: Zhongguo renmin daxue chubanshe, 1999), 84–87; and *Fazhan jihua de zhiding yu guanli* [The making and management of development plans], ed. Cheng Siwei (Beijing: Jingji kexue chubanshe, 2004), 39–41.

29. On China's growing marketization, see Wang Jinbin, "Guanyu woguo shichanghua jincheng de yanjiu" [Study of China's path toward marketization], *Zhongguo jingji shibao* [China economic times], July 20, 2002; and Li Xiaoxi, *Zhongguo shichanghua jincheng* [China's path toward marketization] (Beijing: Renmin chubanshe, 2009), 240.

30. The State Planning Commission, "Woguo zhongyang yu difang jingji guanli quanxian yanjiu" [Boundaries of economic management between China's central and local governments], *Jingji yanjiu cankao* [References for economic research], no. 434/435 (March 1, 1994): 19; and Wu, *Guojia fazhan jihua gailun*, 84–85.

31. Chen Jiagui, ed., *Zhongguo touzi tizhi gaige 30nian yanjiu* [Study of the thirty-year reform of China's investment system] (Beijing: Jingji guanli chubanshe, 2008), 208.

32. See Wang Lixin and Joseph Fewsmith, "Bulwark of the Planned Economy: The Structure and Role of the State Planning Commission," in *Decision-Making in Deng's China: Perspectives from Insiders*, eds. Carol Lee Hamrin and Suisheng Zhao, eds. (Armonk, N.Y.: M. E. Sharpe, 1995), 61; and Wu Renjie, "Zhonggong qidong xinyilun guowuyuan jigou gaige" [Communist China implementing new measures of reforming the state council], *Zhonggong yanjiu* [Studies of communist China] 37, no. 4 (April 2003): 40.

33. On the importance of this change, see Chen Jiagui, ed., *Zhongguo touzi tizhi gaige 30 nian yanjiu*, 211.

34. For details on the earlier reform in this regard, see Zeng Peiyan, *Zhongguo touzi jianshe wushinian* [Fifty years of investment in China] (Beijing: Zhongguo jihua chubanshe, 1999), 233–37; and Chen Jiagui, ed., *Zhongguo touzi tizhi gaige 30nian yanjiu*, 115–16.

35. Zhang Dexin et al., *Zhongguo zhengfu gaige de fangxiang* [Direction of China's government reforms] (Beijing: Renmin chubanshe, 2003), 95–96.

36. In the area of steel production, the threshold was set at the production capacity of 50 million metric tons; and in that of oil exploration, the ceiling was set at the annual production of 1 million tons. See *Guowuyuan guanyu touzi tizhi gaige de jueding* [The state council's decisions regarding the reform of the investment system] (Beijing: Zhongguo shichang chubanshe, 2004), 15–22.

37. Compare Yasheng Huang, *Inflation and Investment Controls in China: The Political Economy of Central-Local Relations during the Reform Era* (Cambridge:

Cambridge University Press, 1996), chap. 8, with Linda C. Li, *Centre and Provinces: China 1978–1993* (Oxford: Oxford University Press, 1998), chap. 7.

38. Gui, *Zhongguo jihua tizhi gaige*, 16; and State Statistical Bureau, ed., *Zhongguo guding zichan touzi tongji nianjian 1950–1995* [Statistical yearbook on China's fixed asset investment 1950–1995] (Beijing: Zhongguo tongji chubanshe, 1997), 91.

39. *Zhongguo tongji ninjian 2003* [Statistical yearbook of China 2003] (Beijing: Zhongguo tongji chubanshe, 2003), 185; and *Zhongguo tongji ninjian 2014* [Statistical yearbook of China 2014] (Beijing: Zhongguo tongji chubanshe, 2014), 153.

40. Huang, *Inflation and Investment Controls in China*, 86; and *Zhongguo tongji nianjian 2014*, 288.

41. For Beijing's efforts during the 1980s, see Shaun Breslin, *China in the 1980s: Centre-Province Relations in a Reforming Socialist State* (London: MacMillan, 1996). For details of the 1994 tax-sharing reform, see Jae Ho Chung, "Beijing Confronting the Provinces: The 1994 Tax-Sharing Reform and Its Implications for Central-Provincial Relations in China," *China Information* 9, no. 2/3 (Winter 1994–95): 1–23; Jiang Weizhuang, *Zhongguo fenshuizhi de juece yu shijian* [The decision and implementation of China's tax-sharing reform] (Beijing: Zhongguo caizheng jingji chubanshe, 1997), chaps. 1–5; and Jing Vivian Zhan, "Explaining Central Intervention in Local Extra-Budgetary Practices in China," *Asian Survey* 51, no. 3 (2011): 500–6.

42. Zhou Tianyong, *Zhongguo zhengzhi tizhi gaige* [China's political system reform] (Beijing: Zhongguo shuili shuidian chubanshe, 2004), 70–71.

43. For positive assessments of the 1994 reform, see Zhao Liming, *Jingji fazhan zhongde zhongguo shuishou yanjiu* [Study of tax collection in China] (Tianjin: Nankai daxue chubanshe, 2001), 119–21; and the Public Finance Task Force of the Chinese Academy of Social Sciences, "Wanshan zhongyang he difang jingji quanli huafen de fenxi ji jianyi" [Analyses of and proposals on better delineating the boundary of economic power between the center and localities], *Lingdao canyue* [References for Leaders], no. 4 (February 5, 2006): 13–15.

44. *Zhongguo tongji nianjian 2014*, 190. For a study that concludes that China's fiscal control is still very much centralized, see Kai-yuen Tsui and Youqing Wang, "Between Separate Stoves and a Single Menu: Fiscal Decentralization in China," *China Quarterly*, no. 177 (March 2004): 71–90; and Becky P. Y. Loo and Sin Yin Chow, "China's 1994 Tax-Sharing Reforms: One System, Different Impact," *Asian Survey* 46, no. 2 (2006): 221–23, 235–37.

45. The share of non-tax revenues for the center, the provinces, and cities/counties is estimated to be less than 10 percent, about 20 percent, and higher than 30 percent, respectively. Zhu Qiuxiang, "Woguo zhongyangdifang shuiquan huafen de zhuanxingqi tezheng ji qi fazhi zouxiang" [Characteristics and directions of China's system of delineating taxation powers between the center and localities during the transitional period], *Tizhi gaige* [System reform], no. 9 (2010): 39.

46. On the rapid rise of nonrevenue incomes of local governments, see Wang Ning, *Difang caizheng gaige yanjiu* [Study of local fiscal reform] (Chengdu:

Xinan caijing daxue chubanshe, 2004), 156–57; Tan Tongxue, *Chuzhen de zhan-suo, Xiangzhen jigou shengzhang de zhengzhi shengtai kaocha* [Stations and offices of Chu Town: A survey of the political environments of township offices and stations] (Beijing: Zhongguo shehuikexue chubanshe, 2006); Graeme Smith, "The Hollow State: Local Governance in China," *China Quarterly*, no. 203 (September 2010): 603–6; and Hiroki Takeuchi, *Tax Reform in Rural China: Revenue, Resistance, and Authoritarian Rule* (Cambridge: Cambridge University Press, 2014), chap. 4.

47. Bernstein and Lu, *Taxation Without Representation*, chaps. 4–5; "Nongcun shuifei gaige" [The tax-for-fee reform in rural China], *Diaocha yanjiu baogao* [Investigative research report], no. 59 (April 16, 2001); Pu Fengcheng, "Dalu shuizhi de gaige yu fazhan" [Reform and development of the tax system in the mainland], *Zhonggong yanjiu* 37, no. 3 (2003): 49; and Tang Huojian and Tan Bowen, "Caizhengzhidu gaige dui zhongyangdifang quanlijiegou de yingxiang" [The impact of the fiscal system reform on central–local power relations], *Tizhi gaige*, no. 1 (2013): 40.

48. Wang Shujie, "Jiaqiang woguo quankoujing yusuan guanli de sikao" [Thoughts on strengthening the unified budgetary management in China], *Caizheng yanjiu* [Fiscal research], no. 1 (2013): 66.

49. Zhu Qiuxiang, "Woguo zhongyangdifang shuiquan huafen de zhuanxingqi tezheng ji qi fazhi zouxiang," 38.

50. Xing Shudong and Chen Lili, "Zengzhishui kuowei gaige hou zhongyang yu difang fenxiang bili wenti yanjiu" [Study of the central–local sharing rate after the reform of expanding the boundary of value-added taxes], *Difang caizheng yanjiu* [Local fiscal research], no. 5 (2013): 13–14.

51. See chapters on Shandong, Fujian, Hainan, and Sichuan in Peter Cheung, Jae Ho Chung, and Zhimin Lin, eds., *Provincial Strategies of Economic Reform in Post-Mao China* (Armonk, N.Y.: M. E. Sharpe, 1998); Jae Ho Chung, ed., *Cities in China: Recipes of Economic Reform in China* (London: Routledge, 1999); and David Zweig, *Internationalizing China: Domestic Interests and Global Linkages* (Ithaca: Cornell University Press, 2003), chap. 2.

52. Chen Yongqin, ed., *Gaibian Zhongguo*, 233–34; and Tang Renwu and Ma Ji, *Zhongguo jingji gaige 30 nian—Duiwai kaifang juan, 1978–2008* [Thirty years of China's economic reforms—Volume on opening, 1978–2008] (Chongqing: Chongqing daxue chubanshe, 2008), chap. 2.

53. See Jae Ho Chung, "A Sub-Provincial Recipe of Coastal Development in China: The Case of Qingdao," *China Quarterly*, no. 160 (December 1999): 944–50.

54. *South China Morning Post*, April 12, 2014.

55. See You-tien Hsing, *Making Capitalism in China: The Taiwan Connection* (New York: Oxford University Press, 1998), chaps. 5–7; and Peter T. Y. Cheung and James T. H. Tang, "The External Relations of China's Provinces," in David M. Lampton, ed., *The Making of Chinese Foreign and Security Policy in the Era of Reform* (Stanford: Stanford University Press, 2001), 91–120.

56. See Ding Lu and William A. W. Neilson, eds., *China's West Regional Development: Domestic Strategies and Global Implications* (London: World Scientific, 2004); Yuan Wenping et al., *Xibu dakaifa zhong difang zhengfu zhineng*

yanjiu [Study of local government functions in the development of the western region] (Chengdu: Xinan caijing daxue chubanshe 2004); Ning Yi and Dong Ning, *Dongbei wenti baogao* [Report on the Northeast problem] (Beijing: Dangdai shijie chubanshe, 2004); David S. G. Goodman, "The Campaign to 'Open Up the West'" and Heike Holbig, "The Emergence of the Campaign to Open Up the West," *China Quarterly,* no. 177 (March 2004): 317–34, 335–57; Hongyi Lai, "Developing Central China," *China: An International Journal* 5, no. 1 (March 2007): 109–28; and Jae Ho Chung, Hongyi Lai, and Jang-Hwan Joo, "Assessing the 'Revive the Northeast' Program: Origins, Policies and Implementation," *China Quarterly,* no. 197 (March 2009): 108–25.

57. See *Zhongguo gaige kaifang shiwunian dashiji* [Chronology of China's fifteen years of reform and opening] (Beijing: Xinhua chubanshe, 1994), 240; Tang Minhao, *WTO yu difang xingzheng guanli zhidu yanjiu* [Study of the local administrative management system and WTO] (Shanghai: Shanghai renmin chubanshe, 2000), chap. 4; Hongyi Harry Lai, "Local Governments and China's WTO Entry," *American Asian Review* 21, no. 3 (Fall 2003): 153–86; and Li Mingjiang, "Local Liberalism; China's Provincial Approaches to Relations with Southeast Asia," *Journal of Contemporary China* 23, no. 86 (2014): 275–93.

58. See John P. Burns, "China's Nomenklatura System," *Problems of Communism* 36, no. 5 (September–October 1987): 38; John P. Burns, "Strengthening Central CCP Control of Leadership Selection: The 1990 *Nomenklatura,*" *China Quarterly,* no. 138 (June 1994): 470–74; Sebastian Heilmann and Sarah Kirchberger, "The Chinese *Nomenklatura* in Transition: A Study Based on Internal Cadre Statistics of the Central Organization Department of the CCP," *China Analysis,* no. 1 (June 2000): 1–13; and Yumin Sheng, "Central–Provincial Relations at the CCP Central Committees: Institutions, Measurements and Empirical Trends, 1978–2002," *China Quarterly,* no. 182 (June 2005): 338–55.

59. According to Zhiyue Bo, provincial leaders with central origins or from such elite provinces as Shanghai, Beijing, Tianjin, Guangdong, Shandong, and Sichuan are likely to be called back to serve on the central stage. See Zhiyue Bo, "The Provinces: Training Ground for National Leaders or a Power in Their Own Right?" in *China's Leadership in the 21st Century: The Rise of the Fourth Generation,* eds. David M. Finkelstein and Maryanne Kivlehan (Armonk, N.Y.: M. E. Sharpe, 2003), 88–89.

60. Zhang Dexin et al., *Zhongguo zhengfu gaige de fangxiang,* 245.

61. See Lance L. P. Gore, *Market Communism: The Institutional Foundation of China's Post-Mao Hyper-Growth* (Hong Kong: Oxford University Press, 1998), chap. 3. For the system of leadership responsibility, see "Liangshi shengzhang fuzezhi" [Governors' responsibility system in grain production], *Jingji yanjiu cankao,* no. 1208 (September 24, 1998): 21–18.

62. See the following for their respective views. Zhou Li'an, Li Hongbin, and Chen Ye, "Xiangdui jixiao kaohe: Zhongguo difang guanyuan jinsheng jizhi de yixiang jiangyan yanjiu" [Relative performance assessments: An empirical study of China's system of local official promotion], *Jingji xuebao* [Studies of economics], no. 1 (2005); Victor Shih et al., "Getting Ahead in the Communist Party: Explaining the Advancement of Central Committee Members in China," *American Political Science Review* 106, no. 1 (February 2012): 167–68, 178; and

Eun Kyong Choi, "Patronage and Performance: Factors in the Political Mobility of Provincial Leaders in Post-Deng China," *China Quarterly*, no. 212 (December 2012): 865–981.

63. State Statistical Bureau, *Zhongguo tongji gongzuo nianjian 1993* [China statistical work yearbook 1993) (Beijing: Zhongguo tongji chubanshe, 1993); I-51–54, III-13–14; and Yasheng Huang, "The Statistical Agency in China's Bureaucratic System: A Comparison with the Former Soviet Union," *Communist and Post-Communist Studies* 29, no. 1 (March 1996): 59–75.

64. Shen Ronghua, "Zhengfu chuizhi guanli handai gaige" [The government's vertical line-control awaits reforms], *Lingdao canyue*, no. 33 (2009): 30–31.

65. See "Zhongguo jingji zhongde mohu shuzi" [Ambiguous figures in China's economy], *Zhongguo minhangbao* [China's aviation news], March 27, 2000; Ge Suhong, "Xuzeng shibei de gongye chanzhi shi ruhe churong de" [On how the false figure of tenfold increase in gross industrial value was derived], *Banyuetan* (Semi-monthly), no. 3 (2001): 30–31; Ernest Kao, "GDP Gap in China the Size of Guangdong Economy," *South China Morning Post*, February 5, 2013; and "Gap in China's Economic Output Data Narrows," *Straits Times*, February 19, 2014.

66. See Yuezhi Zhao, *Market, and Democracy in China: Between the Party Line and the Bottom Line* (Urbana: University of Illinois Press, 1998), 158–60, 168–70, 177; Jae Ho Chung, "Challenging the State: *Falungong* and Regulatory Dilemmas in China," in *Sovereignty Under Challenge: How Governments Respond*, eds. John Montgomery and Nathan Glazer (New Brunswick, N.J.: Transaction, 2002); and Maria Edin, "State Capacity and Local Agent Control in China: CCP Cadre Management from a Township Perspective," *China Quarterly*, no. 173 (March 2003): 35–52.

67. Zhu Guanglei, *Dangdai zhongguo zhengfu guocheng* [Contemporary China's government process], 2nd ed. (Tianjin: Tianjin renmin chubanshe, 2002), 333.

68. See Sen Lin, "A New Pattern of Decentralization in China: The Increase of Provincial Powers in Economic Legislation," *China Information* 7, no. 3 (Winter 1992–93): 27–38; Liu Xingyi, "Zhongyang yu difang de lifaquan huafen" [Delineating the legislative powers between the center and localities] in *Shichang jingji zhong de zhongyang yu difang jingji guanxi* [Central–local economic relations under market economy], ed. Wei Liqun (Beijing: Jingji chubanshe, 1994), 139–40; Zou Keyuan, "Harmonising Local Laws with the Central Legislation," *China Perspectives*, no. 52 (March–April 2004): 44–47; and Jiang Caixun, "Difang lifa shuliang ji xiangmu yanxi" [Study of the volume and category of local legislation], *Renda yanjiu* [Study of the people's congress], no. 11 (2005): 28–32.

69. Randall Peerenboom, *China's Long March Toward Rule of Law* (New York: Cambridge University Press, 2002), 239–59; and Xiao Gongqin, "Jingti defang quanli 'Sudanhua' xianxiang" [The "sultanization" of local power to be forewarned], *Neibu canyue* [Internal references], no. 654 (March 14, 2003): 2–7.

70. In cases of *tiao-kuai* conflicts between local laws and sectoral regulations, the State Council's Legislation Office [*fazhi bangongshi*] is to get involved. If the Office should rule that sectoral regulations are inconsistent with national

laws, it can abolish them immediately. If, on the other hand, local laws should prove problematic, the Office asks the NPC to relinquish them. Personal communications with the late Cai Dingjian in Singapore in August 2005.

71. Ming Xia, "Informational Efficiency, Organizational Development and Institutional Linkages of the Provincial People's Congresses in China," *Journal of Legislative Studies* 3, no. 3 (Autumn 1997): 10–38; and Youngnam Cho, "From 'Rubber Stamps' to 'Iron Stamps': The Emergence of Chinese Local People's Congresses as Supervisory Powerhouses," *China Quarterly*, no. 171 (September 2002): 724–40.

72. Li Yahong, "The Legislative Autonomy of the Localities in China," *China Perspectives*, no. 32 (November–December 2000): 13–21; and Zhang Dexin et al., *Zhongguo zhengfu gaige de fangxiang*, 61.

73. Tan Shigui, *Sifa duli wenti yanjiu* [Study on making the court system independent] (Beijing: Falu chubanshe, 2004), 133–40; and chapter 5 of this volume.

74. See Meng Jianzhu, "Shenhua sifa tizhi gaige" [Deepen the judiciary system reform], *Qiushi Lilunwang* [Website on theory of seeking truth from fact], November 25, 2013, http://www.qstheory.cn; and personal communication with Vice-Minister of Justice Zhao Dacheng in Seoul in January 2015.

75. See chapter 6 for in-depth discussions on this theme.

76. See Grigory Vainshtein, "Totalitarian Public Consciousness in a Post-Totalitarian Society: The Russian Case in the General Context of Post-Communist Developments," *Communist and Post-Communist Studies* 27, no. 3 (1994): 247–59.

77. See, most notably, Bo Yibo's personal recollections about the deleterious symptoms of the "right-aversive disease" [*kongyouzheng*], referring to the popular norm that cadres had to avoid anything that could at any time be perceived as a "rightist" act. See *Ruogan zhongda juece yu shijian de huigu* [Recollections of some crucial decisions and events] (Beijing: Zhonggong zhongyang dangxiao chubanshe, 1993), 2:778.

78. For an excellent overview of this important process, see Ma Licheng and Ling Zhijun, *Jiaofeng: Dangdai zhongguo sanci sixiang jiefang shilu* [Sword-crossing: Records of the three emancipations of ideas in contemporary China] (Beijing: Jinri zhongguo chubanshe, 1998).

79. Chung, *Central Control and Local Discretion in China*, chap. 2; and Sebastian Heilmann, "From Local Experiments to National Policy: The Origins of China's Distinctive Policy Process," *China Journal*, no. 59 (January 2008): 1–30.

80. See Breslin, *China in the 1980s*; Huang, *Inflation and Investment Controls in China*; Jiang Zhen, "Difang zhengfu tudi caizheng hanxu gaige" [Local government's land finance awaits reforms], *Lingdao canyue*, no. 2 (2012): 22–25; and Ciqi Mei and Margaret M. Pearson, "Killing a Chicken to Scare the Monkeys? Deterrence Failure and Local Defiance in China," *China Journal*, no. 72 (July 2014): 75–97.

81. In a nutshell, three factors in particular may constrain or condition the room for local discretion: (1) policy scope (i.e., whether it is targeted at all local units or at only a few), (2) policy nature (i.e., whether it is a resource-related or governance-oriented policy), and (3) whether it requires immediate execution or it is more of a routine. See chapter 6 for more detailed discussions.

82. See Wang Linsheng, *Zhongguo difang zhengfu juece yanjiu* [Study of decision making in China's local governments] (Guangzhou: Huanan ligong daxue chubanshe, 2005), 163–64.

3. THE SUBNATIONAL HIERARCHY IN TIME: INSTITUTIONAL CHANGES (AND CONTINUITIES)

1. Bernard Jouve, "From Government to Urban Governance in Western Europe: A Critical Analysis," *Public Administration and Development* 25, no. 4 (2005): 285–94.

2. See Kent Eaton, *Politics Beyond the Capital: The Design of Subnational Institutions in South America* (Stanford: Stanford University Press, 2004), chap. 6.

3. Jeffrey J. Anderson, *The Territorial Imperative: Pluralism, Corporatism, and Economic Crisis* (Cambridge: Cambridge University Press, 1992), chap. 4.

4. The term "local administrative system" here refers to *difang jianzhi* in Chinese that denotes geographical/spatial [*diyu*], organizational [*jigou*], and political [*zhengzhi*] dimensions of subnational governance. See Tian Suisheng, Luo Hui, and Zeng Wei, *Zhongguo xingzheng quhua gailun* [Overview of China's administrative divisions] (Beijing: Peking University Press, 2005), 7–9.

5. See Jae Ho Chung, "Studies of Central–Provincial Relations in the People's Republic: A Mid-Term Assessment," *China Quarterly*, no. 142 (June 1995): 491–92; Jae Ho Chung, "The Expanding Space of Provincial Politics and Development: Thematic Suggestions for the Future Research Agenda," *Provincial China*, no. 4 (October 1997): 14–16.

6. Frederick Wakeman Jr., *The Fall of Imperial China* (New York: The Free Press, 1975); and Jae Ho Chung, "Assessing the Odds against the Mandate of Heaven: Do the Numbers on Popular Protest Really Matter?" in *Charting China's Future*, ed. Jae Ho Chung (Lanham, Md.: Rowman & Littlefield, 2006), 108–26.

7. See Pu Shanxin, *Zhongguo lidai xingzheng quhua yanjiu* [A study of China's systems of local administration] (Beijing: Zhongguo shehui chubanshe, 1991), 226.

8. See Dorothy J. Solinger, *Regional Government and Political Integration in Southwest China, 1949–1954* (Berkeley: University of California Press, 1977). Other short-lived local units include nine "subprovincial districts" [*xingshuqu*] located in Jiangsu, Anhui, and Sichuan, and "districts" [*qu*] that existed nationwide between the county and the township levels during 1949–1958. See Zhou Zhenhe, *Zhongguo difang xingzheng zhidushi* [History of China's local administrative systems] (Shanghai: Shanghai renmin chubanshe, 2005), 67–68.

9. See Jae Ho Chung and Tao-chiu Lam, "China's 'City System' in Flux: Explaining Post-Mao Administrative Changes," *China Quarterly*, no. 180 (December 2004): 951–52.

10. See the *Constitution of the People's Republic of China*, Article 30. See http://www.gov.cn/gongbao/content/2004/content_62714.htm (accessed February 4, 2015).

11. Since 2009, a new system of provinces directly ruling the counties [*sheng zhiguan xian*] became increasingly popular, diametrically opposed to that of cities leading counties [*shi dai xian* or *shi lingdao xian*]. A detailed discussion of this is provided in a later section.

12. Dai Junliang, *Zhongguo shizhi* [The city system of China] (Beijing: Zhongguo ditu chubanshe, 2000), 104; and Tse-kang Leng, "Centrally Administered Municipalities: Locomotives of National Development," in *China's Local Administration: Traditions and Changes in the Sub-national Hierarchy*, eds. Jae Ho Chung and Tao-Chiu Lam (London: Routledge, 2010), chap. 3.

13. Xinjiang's Tuoputiereke Town is an exceptional case in that it is ruled in order by Jimunai County, Aerdai District [*qu*], Yilihasan Autonomous Zhou [*zizhizhou*], and by the Xinjiang Autonomous Region. In other cases, a special unit called "subcounty district" [*xianxiaqu*] was established between the county and the township, making the structure a five-tier one. See Zhongguo guanlixue yanjiuyuan, ed., *Zhongguo zhengfu cengji yu quhua gaige* [Reforming the levels and boundaries of the Chinese government] (Beijing: Zhongguo guanlixue yanjiuyuan, November 30, 2005), 28, 207.

14. For the need to reform the current three-tier hierarchy, see Pu Shanxin, "Zhongguo shixian fendeng wenti tantao" [Discussion of giving administrative ranks to China's sities and counties], *Zhongguo fangyu* [China's regions], no. 5 (1996): 14–15; Li Wei, "Hebi dou jiao shi" [Why should we call all of them cities?], *Minzheng luntan* [Forum on civil affairs], no. 2 (2001): 36; and Hua Wei, "Xianxing xingzheng quhua de wenti yu gaige" [Problems and reforming of the current local administrative system], *Lingdao wensui* [Selected readings for the leadership], no. 3 (2003): 13.

15. For the concept of mixed unitary system, see Ren Jin, *Zhongou difang zhidu bijiao yanjiu* [A comparative study of local government systems in China and Europe] (Beijing: Guojia xingzheng xueyuan chubanshe, 2007), 29.

16. According to some incomplete—and possibly deflated—statistics, an annual average of forty changes was introduced to China's local administrative system at the county level and above in the post-Mao era. See Zhongguo guanli kexue yanjiuyuan, *Zhongguo zhengfu cengji yu quhua gaige* [China's reform of government ranks and planning] (Internal Report for Discussions, November 30, 2005), 7.

17. Zhou Zhenhe, *Zhongguo difang xingzheng zhidushi*, 73; and Tian Suisheng et al., *Zhongguo xingzheng quhua gailun*, 73.

18. See Feng Chongyi and David S. G. Goodman, "Hainan: Communal Politics and the Struggle for Identity," in *China's Provinces in Reform*, ed. David S. G. Goodman (London: Routledge, 1997), 53–92; Luc Changlei Guo, *Understanding China's Provinces: Chongqing* (Beijing: Intercultural Press, 2013); and Ray Yep, "'One Country, Two Systems' and Special Administrative Regions: The Case of Hong Kong," in *China's Local Administration: Traditions and Changes in the Sub-national Hierarchy*, eds. Jae Ho Chung and Tao-chiu Lam (London: Routledge, 2010), chap. 5.

19. For more detailed discussions of this perceptual dimension, see chapter 4 in this volume.

20. For China's perceptive resistance to a federalist structure, see Tao-chiu Lam, "The Federalist Possibility," in *Charting China's Future*, ed. Jae Ho Chung, 81–106.

21. For the 1953–1954 readjustment, see Tian Suisheng et al., *Zhongguo xingzheng quhua gailun*, 73. And for the case of Sanxia Province, see Zhongguo guanlixue yanjiuyuan, ed., *Zhongguo zhengfu cengji yu quhua gaige*, 56–59.

22. Tian Suisheng et al., *Zhongguo xingzheng quhua gailun*, 94–102; Dai Junliang, *Chengxiang dazhuanxing shiqi de sikao* [Thoughts on the era of great transformation in the city and countryside] (Beijing: Zhongguo shehui chubanshe, 2006), 207–8; Jin Binghao and Zhang Yong, "Chengshi minzuqu de falu diwei handai mingque" [The legal status of the urban ethnic minority districts needs to be clarified], *Neibu canyue* [Internal references], no. 846 (January 26, 2007): 11–18; and *Zhongguo tongji nianjian 2014* [Statistical yearbook of China 2014] (Beijing: Zhongguo tongjichubanshe, 2014), 3.

23. By the end of 2005, 84 percent of the prefecture-level units in China were turned into prefecture-level cities. See *Zhongguo chengshi nianjian 2006* [Yearbook of Chinese cities 2006] (Beijing: Zhongguo chengshi nianjianshe, 2006), 445. For other figures, see *Zhongguo tongji nianjian 2012*, 3; Zheng Dingquan, "Jin20nian woguo difang xingzheng quhua de bianhua" [Changes in China's local administrative structures in the last twenty years], *Zhongguo gaige* [China's reform], no. 9 (2006): 14–15; and Ma Qingyu et al., "Dui Zhejiang sheng zhiguanxian qiangxiankuaquan de diaocha" [A survey of Zhejiang's policies of "putting the provinces in charge of counties" and of "strengthening the power of strong counties"], *Zhengfu guanli cankao* [References for government management], no. 4 (2007): 11.

24. See Pu Shanxin, "Zhongguo shixian fendeng wenti tantao," 14–15; and Hua Wei, "Xianxing xingzheng quhua de wenti yu gaige," 13.

25. For the longevity of the county, see Tian Suisheng et al., *Zhongguo xingzheng quhua gailun*, 29–30; and Han Jingsheng, *Dangdai zhongguo xianzheng gaige yanjiu* [Study of county government reforms in contemporary China] (Tianjin: Tianjin renmin chubanshe, 2007), 53–89.

26. Zhou Zhenhe, *Zhongguo difang xingzheng zhidushi*, 58–84, 207.

27. Diao Tianding, *Zhongguo difang guojia jigou gaiyao* [Summary of China's local government organizations] (Beijing: Falu chubanshe, 1989), 248; Wu Peilun, *Dangdai zhongguo zhengfu gailun* (Beijing: Gaige chubanshe, 1993), 25; and *Zhongguo tongji nianjian 2014*, 3.

28. Zheng Dingquan, "Jin ershinian difang xingzheng quhua de bianhua," 15; and *Zhongguo tongji nianjian 2014*, 3.

29. See Chung and Lam, "China's 'City System' in Flux," 952–55; and Dai Junliang, *Zhongguo shizhi*, 99–112. Detailed discussions of the dynamics involving these processes are provided in a later section of this chapter.

30. Street-level administrative offices—another township-level unit, of which there were 7,566 in 2013—are not an official layer of state administration, but field agencies of the urban districts or city governments without urban districts. See Xu Songtao and Xu Liming, eds., *Zhongguo shizheng— Chengshi xiandaihua de jinyaoshi* [China's city administration—The golden key to urban modernization] (Beijing: Zhongguo renshi chubanshe, 1996), 44.

31. See Zhongguo guanlixue yanjiuyuan, ed., *Zhongguo zhengfu cengji yu quhua gaige*, 6; Li Zhaobo, "Gaige kaifang yilai woguo chengshi fazhan de huigu" [Recollections of urban development in China during the reform era], *Zhongguo chengshi nianjian 2004* [Yearbook of Chinese cities 2004] (Beijing: Zhongguo chengshi nianjianshe, 2004), 244; Dai Junliang, *Chengxiang dazhuanxing shiqi de sikao*, 96, 203; and *Zhongguo tongji nianjian 2014*, 3. Also see Ane Bislev and Stig Thogersen, eds., *Organizing Rural China, Rural China Organizing* (Lanham, Md.: Lexington Books, 2012), chaps. 2 and 6.

32. The category of deputy-provincial cities was for the first time added to the statistical tables published in *Zhongguo chengshi nianjian 1995* [Yearbook of China's cities 1995] (Beijing: Zhongguo chengshi nianjian chubanshe, 1995), 22.

33. There is also an additional category of "quasi-deputy-provincial" [*zhun fushengji*] cities. This label applies to seventeen provincial capitals that are not deputy-provincial cities, as well as ten relatively large cities [*jiaoda de shi*] like Tangshan, Anshan, Fushun, Qiqihar, and Luoyang. See http://wenke.baidu .com/view/fo30c6fb910ef12d2af9e7bd.html.

34. See Liu Junde, "Zhongguo shizhi de huigu yu zhanwang xueshu yantaohui fayan shilu" [Records of the academic discussion meeting on the retrospect and prospect of China's city system], *Zhongguo fangyu*, no. 2 (1999): 2; Hua Wei, "Chengxiang fenzhi yu hezhi" [Divided and unified urban-rural rule], *Zhongguo fangyu*, no. 3 (2000): 15; and "Xianzheng gaige buneng kao xianguan gaopei" [County reforms cannot rely solely on county officials] in *Gaige yaoqing canyue* [Inside information on economic reform], ed. Zhongguo tizhigaige zazhi (Beijing: Xinhua chubanshe, 2010), 80–114.

35. For various special functional zones, see Tian et al., *Zhongguo xingzheng quhua gailun*, 139–43; and David Zweig, *Internationalizing China: Domestic Interests and Global Linkages* (Ithaca: Cornell University Press, 2003), 93–97.

36. See Jae Ho Chung, ed., *Cities in China: Recipes for Development in the Reform Era* (London: Routledge, 1999); and Bian Xuwei, *Zou xiang xiandaihua de xingzheng gaige: Shenzhen zhengfu tizhi chuangxin zhilu* [Toward modernized administrative reform: The road to government system innovations in Shenzhen] (Beijing: Guojia xingzheng xueyuan chubanshe, 2000), 293–302.

37. Mao Shoulong, "Jigou shengji jingsai de zhidu jichu" [The institutional foundation of the competition for administrative upgrading], *Zhongwai qiye wenhua* [Chinese and foreign corporate cultures], no. 16 (2000): 52–55.

38. See Sonny Shiu-Hing Lo, *The Dynamics of Beijing-Hong Kong Relations: A Model for Taiwan?* (Hong Kong: Hong Kong University Press, 2008).

39. Jae Ho Chung, "The Evolving Hierarchy of China's Local Administration: Traditions and Changes," in *China's Local Administration: Traditions and Changes in the Sub-national Hierarchy*, eds. Jae Ho Chung and Tao-chiu Lam (London: Routledge, 2010), 11–13.

40. Ma Shulin, "Lun shengji xingzheng quhua tizhi gaige" [On reforming the provincial-level administrative zoning], *Zhanlue yu guanli* [Strategy and management], no. 2 (1996): 10.

41. The fifteen cities were Beijing, Shanghai, Tianjin, Hangzhou, Dalian, Qingdao, Wuxi, Guangzhou, Wuhan, Chongqing, Shenyang, Changchun, Harbin, Xi'an, and Lanzhou. See Lu Xiyuan, "Dui jingji zhongxin chengshi de chubu

tangao" [A preliminary discussion of the key economic cities], *Hongguan jingji yanjiu* [Macroeconomic research], no. 4 (1982): 26–27.

42. Dalian was the first experimental site, and Chongqing was the first to be approved as such in February 1983. Chongqing was soon followed by Wuhan, Dalian, Guangzhou, Xi'an, and Harbin (1984); Qingdao (1986); Ningbo and Shenyang (1987); Xiamen and Shenzhen (1988); and Chengdu, Nanjing, and Changchun (1989). Eight were provincial capitals [*shenghui*], and the remaining six were either coastal open cities [*yanhai kaifang chengshi*] or special economic zones [*jingji tequ*]. See *Zhongguo chengshi jingji shehui nianjian 1991* [Economic and social yearbook of China's cities] (Beijing: Zhongguo chengshi jingji shehui nianjian chubanshe, 1991), 49; and "Jihua danlie shi zai gaige kaifang zhong xunshu fazhan" [Separately planned cities are developing fast in the midst of reform and opening], *Hongguan jingji guanli* [Macroeconomic management], no. 8 (1992): 32–33.

43. See Zhu Qianwei and Pu Xingzu, eds., *Dangdai zhongguo xingzheng* [Public administration in contemporary China] (Shanghai: Fudan daxue chubanshe, 1993), 327.

44. Unlike the pre-reform era, this time around, the scope of independent planning by these cities was much wider, and the plans for these cities were listed separately in the national plans. See *Zhongguo chengshi jingji shehui nianjian 1991*, 129; and Zhang Menglin, "Wuhanshi jihua danlie huigu" [Retrospect of Wuhan becoming a separately planned city], *Wuhan wenshi ziliao* [Historical materials on Wuhan], no. 2 (2007): 8.

45. For the privileges that came with the separately planned–city designation, see *Zhongguo gaige kaifang shidian* [Compendia of China's reform and opening] (Guangzhou: Guangdong renmin chubanshe, 1993), 133–40; *Zhongguo chengshi jingji shehui nianjian 1991*, 128; and Zhang Menglin, "Wuhanshi jihua danlie huigu," 9.

46. Zhang Menglin, "Wuhanshi jihua danlie huigu," 8; Jae Ho Chung, "Preferential Policies, Local Leadership and Development Strategies: A Comparative Analysis of Qingdao and Dalian," in *Cities in China: Recipes for Economic Development in the Reform Era*, ed. Jae Ho Chung (London: Routledge, 1999), 112; and Zhou Shiya, *Caizheng cengji zhidu yanjiu* [Study of China's local financial institutions] (Beijing: Jingji kexue chubanshe, 2007), 188–90.

47. See Zhou Xuewen and Fang Xun, "Jihua danlie shi yu zhongyang he sheng shiquan huafen wenti zouyi" [Discussion of the issue of delineating the power boundaries between the separately planned cities and the central and provincial governments], *Difang jigou gaige yanjiu* [Study of local government reforms], ed. Ministry of Personnel's Institute for Administrative Management Science (Beijing: Zhonggong zhongyang dangxiao, 1992), 281.

48. Zhongguo guanli kexue yanjiuyuan, *Zhongguo zhengfu cengji yu quhua gaige*, 86–87.

49. Mao Shoulong, "Jigou shengji jingsai de zhidu jichu," 52–55.

50. In 1985 (i.e., prior to the designation), Qingdao's gross value of agricultural and industrial outputs (GVAIO) amounted to 14 percent of Shandong's total. Naturally, Shandong was not willing to let go of Qingdao. See *Fenjin de sishinian—Shandong fence* [Forty years of arduous progress—The Shandong

part] (Beijing: Zhongguo tongji chubanshe, 1989), 109; and *Zhongguo chengshi sishinian* [Forty years of China's cities] (Beijing: Zhongguo tongji xinxi zixun fuwu zhongxin, 1990), 214. For Shandong's opposition to Beijing's designation of Qingdao, see Chung, "Preferential Policies, Local Leadership and Development Strategies," 113.

51. See *Guangzhou nianjian 1991* [Guangzhou yearbook 1991] (Guangzhou: Guangdong renmin chubanshe, 1991), 96; and Christine P. W. Wong, *Financing Local Government in the People's Republic of China* (Hong Kong: Oxford University Press, 1997), 87. For Beijing's measures to minimize losses of Hubei due to the designation of Wuhan as a separately planned city, see Dorothy J. Solinger, *China's Transition to Socialism: Statist Legacies and Market Reforms 1980–1990* (Armonk, N.Y.: M. E. Sharpe, 1993), 177–78.

52. See *Renmin ribao*, April 4, 1985.

53. Paul E. Schroeder, "Territorial Actors as Competitors for Power: The Case of Hubei and Wuhan," in *Bureaucracy, Politics and Decision Making in Post-Mao China*, eds. Kenneth G. Lieberthal and David M. Lampton (Berkeley: University of California Press, 1992), 283–307; and Zhou Xuewen and Fang Xun, "Jihua danlie shi yu zhongyang he sheng shiquan huafen wenti zouyi," 283–85.

54. The actual timing of termination varied as the *jihua danlie* status of Wuhan, for instance, was abolished in 1995. See Zhang Menglin, "Wuhanshi jihua danlie huigu," 11.

55. John P. Burns, "Downsizing the Chinese State: Government Retrenchment in the 1990s," *China Quarterly*, no. 170 (September 2003): 778–79.

56. The Pudong Zone of Shanghai Municipality is also considered to be a deputy-provincial unit. See Xu Songtao and Xu Liming, *Zhongguo shizheng*, 6; and Gu Dong, "Zhongguo chengshihua tixi de goujian" [The construction of China's system of urbanization], *Chengdu xingzheng xueyuan xuebao* [Academic bulletin of Chengdu College of Administration], no. 6 (2002): 44.

57. See Cheng Yitai, "Woguo shiwuge fushengjishi weilai fazhan zhanlue qianxi" [Analysis of the future development strategies of China's fifteen deputy-provincial cities], *Huan Bohai jingji liaowang* [Outlook for the Pan-Bohai region's economy], no. 7 (2003): 1–6.

58. Two compensations were provided for these ten cities. First, they were granted the privileges on a par with the coastal open cities [*yanhai kaifang chengshi*] in conducting foreign trade and soliciting foreign direct investment although only Guangzhou, Hangzhou, Jinan, and Nanjing were coastal by geographical location. Second, personnel decisions pertaining to their top party and government officials were managed directly by the Central Organization Department rather than by the provincial authorities.

59. *Kunming nianjian 1998* [Yearbook of Kunming 1998] (Kunming: Yunnan keji chubanshe, 1998), 65; the 1999 issue, 53; and the 2003 issue, 98.

60. Interview with a knowledgeable scholar in Shanghai in August 2007.

61. Some prefecture-level cities have no districts, but they are more exceptional than typical. See Zhu Qianwei and Pu Xingzu, eds., *Dangdai zhongguo xingzheng*, 322–23.

62. See Liu Junde and Wang Yuming, *Zhidu yu chuangxin—Zhongguo chengshi zhidu de fazhan yu gaige xinlun* [Institution and innovation—New theories

of development and reform in China's urban system] (Nanjing: Dongnan daxue chubanshe, 2000), 11, 47. For a critique of the vaguely defined concept of relatively large cities, see He Bing, "Shilun xianxing xianfa guanyu xingzheng quyu huafen fangshi guiding zhi xiuding" [On revising the current constitution's regulations on administrative zoning], *Zhongguo fangyu*, no. 2 (2002): 4.

63. See Shiuh-Shen Chien, "Prefectures and Prefecture-Level Cities: The Political Economy of Administrative Restructuring," in *China's Local Administration: Traditions and Changes in the Sub-national Hierarchy*, ed. Jae Ho Chung and Tao-chiu Lam (London: Routledge, 2010), 132–34. A different source cites Wuxi and Lanzhou as the first implementers of the scheme. See Hua Wei, "Chengxiang fenzhi yu hezhi," 9.

64. Dai, *Zhongguo shizhi*, 147–48.

65. See Lynn White, "Shanghai-Suburb Relations," in *Shanghai: Revolution and Development in an Asian Metropolis*, ed. Christopher Howe (Cambridge: Cambridge University Press, 1981), 241–68.

66. In Guangdong with twenty-one prefecture-level cities, fifteen had less than a 30 percent ratio of nonagricultural population [*fei nongye renkou*]. Chen Mingxun and Li Yun, "Woguo jianzhishi shezhi cunzai de yixie wenti" [Some problems of city systems in China], *Zhongguo fangyu*, no. 2 (1998): 8.

67. Pu and Zhu, eds., *Dangdai zhongguo xingzheng*, 322; Dai, *Zhongguo shizhi*, 163; Hua Wei, "Shizhi congtan" [Overview of the city system], *Zhongguo fangyu*, no. 3 (2000): 9; The Ministry of Civil Affairs, ed., *Zhonghua renmin gongheguo xingzheng quhua jiance 2001* [Quick guide to administrative zoning in the People's Republic of China 2001] (Beijing: Zhongguo ditu chubanshe, 2001), 1; Chien, "Prefectures and Prefecture-Level Cities" in *China Local Administration*, eds. Chung and Lam, 128; and *Zhongguo tongji nianjian 2014*, 3.

68. Diao Tianding, *Zhongguo difang guojia jigou gaiyao* [Survey of local government organizations in China] (Beijing: Falu chubanshe, 1989), 169; and Dai, *Zhongguo shizhi*, 148.

69. Diao, *Zhongguo difang guojia jigou gaiyao*, 205.

70. Contrary to the original objective of reducing bureaucratic redundancy, some county-level cities and even counties first acquired the status of prefecture-level cities and then sought to merge with rural prefectures.

71. See Liu and Wang, *Zhidu yu changxin*, 10–11, 40, 47, 138; Dai, *Zhongguo shizhi*, 82; and Cong Senquan, "Chezhen sheshi" [On establishing cities out of townships], *Zhongguo fangyu*, no. 1 (2002): 2–5.

72. Interviews with MCA officials in Beijing in 2002. Also see "Zhongguo shizhi huigu yu zhanwang xueshu yantaohui fayan shilu," 7.

73. In the case of Guangdong in the late 1990s, for instance, of its thirty-three county-level cities, only one (Sanshui) had a 50 percent ratio of nonagricultural population, whereas those of the eleven county-level cities were less than 20 percent. See Chen and Li, "Woguo jianzhishi shezhi cunzai de yixie wenti," 8.

74. Tao-chiu Lam, "The County System and County Governance," in *China's Local Administration: Traditions and Changes in the Sub-national Hierarchy*, eds. Jae Ho Chung and Tao-chiu Lam (London: Routledge, 2010), 158.

75. Wang Yuxi, Ji Lijia, and Lin Yang, "Liaoningsheng chexian sheshi gongzuo youguan wenti de diaocha yu sikao" [Investigation on Liaoning's work in the

establishment of cities by abolishing counties], *Zhongguo fangyu*, no. 1 (1998): 10; and Shen Liren, *Difang zhengfu de jingji zhineng he jingji xingwei*, 243.

76. Liu and Wang, *Zhidu yu changxin*, 40.

77. "Woguo xianji chengshi de fazhan" [The development of county-level cities in China], *Diaocha yanjiu baogao* [Report on survey and research], no. 4362 (June 28, 2013): 4.

78. See Yu Xueming, "Qiantan woguo xingzheng quyu zhongde feidi wenti" [On the "flying territory" in China's administrative zoning], *Zhongguo fangyu*, no. 4 (1999): 22.

79. See Liu and Wang, *Zhidu yu chuangxin*, 179; Dai, *Zhongguo shizhi*, 97; *Jingji yanjiu cankao*, no. 86 (2000): 41; and Cong Senquan, "Zouyi dijishi shixiaqu de xingzheng qubie tiaozheng" [On administrative readjustment of urban districts in prefecture-level cities], *Zhongguo fangyu*, no. 3 (2002): 8–9.

80. See, for instance, Li Xingdi, "Maixiang guoji chengshi de Qingdao jichu sheshi jianshe" [Infrastructure construction in Qingdao aspiring to become an international city], *Dongbeiya luntan* [Northeast Asia forum], no. 4 (1994): 70.

81. See Zhang Zhichang, "Shixiaqu: Jidai guifan he tiaozheng" [Urban districts: Needing standards and adjustments], *Zhongguo fangyu*, no. 1 (1999): 10.

82. Although Shanghai at one point sought to turn a few of its counties into prefecture-level cities, the bid proved futile since the Constitution stipulates that no centrally administered municipalities are authorized to have cities under them. See Dai, *Zhongguo shizhi*, 109–12; Lam, "The County System and County Governance," 159; and "Woguo xianji chengshi de fazhan," 5.

83. Dai, *Zhongguo shizhi*, 110, 112; and Liu Junde, *Zhongguo xingzheng quhua de lilun yu shijian* [Theory and practice in administrative zoning in China] (Shanghai: Huadong shifan daxue chubanshe, 1996), 141.

84. Chan Kam Wing and Li Zhang, "The Hukou System and Rural–Urban Migration in China: Processes and Changes," *China Quarterly*, no. 160 (December 1999): 836–37; and Lisa Hoffman and Liu Zhongquan, "Rural Urbanization on the Liaodong Peninsula: A Village, a Town, and a Nongmin Cheng," in *Farewell to Peasant China: Rural Urbanization and Social Change in the Late Twentieth Century*, ed. Gregory Eliyu Guldin (Armonk, N.Y.: M. E. Sharpe, 1997), 175.

85. Zhou Yixing and Meng Yanchun, "Zhongguo dachengshi jiaoquhua qushi" [The trend of suburbanization of big cities in China], *Chengshi guihua huikan* [Journal of urban planning), no. 3 (1998): 22–27.

86. Ren Jie and Liang Ling, *Gongheguo jigou gaige yu bianqian* [Organizational reforms in the People's Republic] (Beijing: Huawen chubanshe, 1999), 112–13; Wang Wen, "Guangdong xingzheng quhua de xinqingkuang he xinwenti," 8; "Zhongguo shizhi huigu yu zhanwang xueshu yantaohui fayanshilu," 3, 5, 12; Song Junling and Huang Xu, eds., *Zhongguo chengzhenhua zhishi shiwu jiang*, 234–35; and Xia Hai, *Zhongguo zhengfu jiagou* [The structure of Chinese government] (Beijing: Qinghua daxue chubanshe, 2001), 46.

87. Dai, *Zhongguo shizhi*, 68. Political motives were also at work since the party secretaries and mayors of newly created county-level cities were often upgraded to a deputy-prefecture level status. Interviews with MCA officials in Beijing in 2002.

88. See Dai, *Zhongguo shizhi*, 112; and Hua Wei, "Xinxingshi yu xingouxiang" [New situations and new ideas], *Zhongguo fangyu*, no. 4 (2000): 14.

89. For the budgetary and fiscal authority of prefecture-level cities, see Cong Senquan, "Lueshu chexiao diqu sheli dijishi de fazhi yiyi" [On the legal meanings of establishing prefecture-turned-cities], *Zhongguo fangyu*, no. 2 (2002): 8–9.

90. The situation was sarcastically dubbed as "small horses (poor counties) pulling a large cart (prefecture-level city)" [*xiaoma la dache*]. See Liu and Wang, *Zhidu yu chuangxin*, 134; Shen Liren, *Difang zhengfu de jingji zhineng he jingji xingwei* [Economic functions and behavior of local government] (Shanghai: Shanghai yuandong chubanshe, 1998), 242; and Hua Wei, "Xinxingshi yu xingouxiang," 18.

91. Dai, *Zhongguo shizhi*, 66, 99–101, 112; and Luo Hao, "Diyuxing zhengqu ji juluoxing zhengqu zouyi" [Discussions of two types of administrative units], *Zhongguo fangyu*, no. 5 (1999): 16. According to an interviewee, county-level cities had better terms for receiving loans than counties. Interview in Beijing in June 2002. Of course, cities enjoy more opportunities for foreign investment than rural counties.

92. Once county-level cities or counties were redesignated as urban districts, they immediately lost independent decision-making powers in urban planning, construction projects approval, foreign exchange management, and land-related issues as stipulated in Article 17 of the Constitution. See Pu Shanxin, "Dui shi lingdao xian tizhi de fansi" [Reflections on the system of putting cities in charge of counties], *Zhongguo fangyu*, no. 5 (1999): 2–7; and Wu Yongming, "Guangzhou shiyu jianshe mubiao moshi he xingzheng quhua" [The goal, model, and administrative zoning in Guangzhou's municipal development], *Zhongguo fangyu*, no. 4 (1999): 14–16.

93. See Jin Ergang, ed., *Zhongguo chengshihua zouxiang yanjiu*, 40; Wang Hongjin, "Guanyu woguo chengshi buju tiaozheng yu chengshihua wenti de sikao" [Thoughts on the problems of city designation and urbanization in China], *Chengshi kaifa* [Urban development], no. 11 (2000): 20; and Zweig, *Internationalizing China*, 51–52.

94. See Dai, "Lun sheshi moshi yu shizhi gaige," 194.

95. Wang Yuanzheng, "Zhongguo chengshihua daolu de xuanze he zhang'ai," 36–37. According to Pu Shanxin (MCA), radiation effects were most optimal when a large well-developed city led small poor counties as opposed to a small city leading poor counties or a large city leading—and competing with—a large county. See "Dui shi lingdao xian tizhi de tantao" [Discussions on the system of "cities leading counties"], *Zhongguo fangyu*, no. 5 (1995): 7.

96. For the former, see Chen Xiushan and Song Jiechen, "Chongxin jieding dijishi de diwei yu gongneng" [On newly delineating the status and functions of the prefecture-level cities], *Juece zixun* [Consultation for decision making], no. 7 (2004): 12–14; and Lu Hongchang, "Jiben weichi wuji xianzhuang zui wei yi" [It is the best to maintain the current five-tier system], in *Zhongguo zhengfu cengji yu quhua gaige*, 194–96.

97. Dai Junliang, "Xingzheng quhua ying shixing shengxian erjizhi" [The administrative structure must be a two-tier system of provinces and counties],

Zhongguo gaige [China's reform], no. 9 (2001): 38–39; and Hua Wei, "Xianxing xingzheng tizhi de wenti yu gaige," 13–18.

98. Wang Xiaoguang, "Zhongguo chengshi de xingzheng quhua tiaozheng yu gaige," 231; Cao He, "Chexiao dijishi neng jiejue duoda wenti" [Abolishing the prefecture level can solve a lot of problems], in *Zhongguo zhengfu cengji yu quhua gaige*, 191–93; and Li Youwei, "Guanyu xingzheng tizhi gaige de sikao yu jianyi" [Thoughts and suggestions on reforming China's administrative system], *Zhongguo chengshi nianjian 2004* [Yearbook of China's cities 2004] (Beijing: Zhongguo chengshi nianjianshe, 2004), 28–30.

99. Item 24 of Part 6 in "Zhonggong zhongyang guowuyuan guanyu tuijin shehuizhuyi xinnongcun jianshe de ruogan yijian" [Central Document (2006) no. 1]; and Jiang Xiumin and Dai Shengliang, "Woguo sheng zhiguan xian tizhi gaige de zhuli ji shixian lujing jiexi" [Analysis of impediments to and solutions for China's reform of provinces directly ruling counties], *Tizhi gaige*, no. 11 (2010): 20.

100. See item 26 of "Zhonggong zhongyang guowuyuan guanyu 2009nian cujin nongye wending fazhan nongmin chixu zengshou de ruogan yijian" [Some opinions of the party center and the state council on promoting stable development of agriculture and increasing peasant incomes], Central Document [2009] no. 1.

101. Different sources offer somewhat different estimates because the scheme entailed a couple of variants (up to seven). The two most important modes were that of "fiscal control only" and that of relinquishing full administrative control to the provinces. Zhou Xiangzhi, "Woguo sheng zhiguan xian yanjiu zhong de jige wenti" [Some questions regarding the research on China's provinces-directly-ruling-counties policy], *Tizhi gaige*, no. 3 (2010): 22–24; and Wang Liya, "Zhongguo shengguanxian tizhi gaige de xianshi shenshi" [Looking into the realities of China's provinces-directly-ruling-counties reform], *Tizhi gaige*, no. 5 (2011): 9–11.

102. Yang Zhiyong, "Caizheng de sheng zhiguan xian gaige buyi yidaoqie" ["One cut of a knife" should not be allowed in implementing the provinces-directly-ruling-counties scheme in fiscal terms], *Lingdao canyue*, no. 11 (2012): 13–17. Also see chapter 6 in this volume.

103. Xiao Qingwen, "Shengguanxian tizhi gaige de zhengfu xingwei chayi yu tuijin celue xuanze" [Variations in government behavior of implementing the provinces-directly-ruling-counties reform and means to promote the reform], *Tizhi gaige*, no. 11 (2011): 21; and Pan Xiaojuan, "Guanyu tuixing sheng zhiguan xian gaige de diaocha he sikao" [Research and thoughts on promoting the reform of provinces directly ruling counties], *Tizhi gaige*, no. 7 (2012): 65.

104. Sun Xueyu, *Chuizhi quanli fenhe—Sheng zhiguanzhi tizhi yanjiu* [Vertical power division—Study of the provinces-directly-ruling-counties policy] (Beijing: Renmin chubanshe, 2013), 141–54.

105. Meng Bai, "Sheng zhiguan xian shidian zhong de wenti yu duice—Yi henan sheng wei li" [Problems of and solutions for the experimental sites for the provinces-directly-ruling-counties policy—The case of Henan], *Lilun dongtai*, no. 1942 (November 30, 2012): 20–22.

106. See Chien, "Prefectures and Prefecture-Level Cities," 128; Jiang Xiumin and Dai Shengliang, "Woguo sheng zhiguan xian tizhi gaige de zhuli ji shixian lujing jiexi," 22; Xiao Qingwen, "Shengguanxian tizhi gaige de zhengfu xingwei chayi yu tuijin celue xuanze," 23; Wang Zhanyang, "Dabuding jiaju shengxian shikong" [A supplementary measure may actually cause the loss of control over counties] and Xiong Wenzhao, "Sheng zhiguan xian xuyao tongpan guihua" [The provinces-leading-counties policy needs an across-the-board planning], *Gaige neican*, no. 18 (2010): 1–4, 5.

107. On the other hand, Indonesia and India have thirty-four and thirty-five provinces or states, respectively, whereas Australia has only eight.

108. See Ma Shulin, "Lun shengji xingzheng quhua tizhi gaige," 10–11; and Zhou Zhenhe, *Zhongguo difang xingzheng zhidushi*, 418.

109. See Dai Junliang, *Chengxiang dazhuanxing shiqi de sikao* [Thoughts on the era of great transformations in China's cities and countryside] (Beijing: Zhongguo shehui chubanshe, 2006), 127; and Zhang Zhanbin, "Zhengfu cengji gaige yu sheng zhiguan xian shixian lujing yanjiu" [Study of the road to reforming the local administrative ranks and materializing the policy of "putting the provinces in charge of counties"], *Jingji yu guanli yanjiu* [Economic and management research], no. 4 (2007): 24–26. For a proposal to set up a total of ten centrally administered municipalities (based on the precedent that there were thirteen during the Republican era), see Luo Tianhao, *Daguo zhucheng—21 shiji zhongguo chengshi yu quyu jingzheng* [Cities of a great power—China's cities and regional competition] (Hangzhou: Zhejiang daxue chubanshe, 2012), 68–72.

110. Wang Chuanlan, *Jingzheng yu yichun zhong de quyu hezuo xingzheng—Jiyu changjiang sanjiaozhou dushi quan de shizheng yanjiu* [Regional cooperative administration in the midst of competition and interdependency: Empirical research on the metropolitan region of the Yangtze River Delta] (Shanghai: Fudan daxue chubanshe, 2008).

111. Shi Weimin, "Xiangzhen gaige de lujing xuanzhe" [The choices of paths for township reform] in Shi Weimin, Pan Xiaojuan, Guo Weiqing, and Guo Zhenglin, *Xiangzhen gaige: Xiangzhen xuanju, tizhi chuangxin yu xiangzhen zhili yanjiu* [Township reform: Research on township election, institutional innovation and township governance] (Beijing: Zhongguo shehui kexueyuan chubanshe, 2008), 510–16.

112. Zhou Zhenhe, *Zhongguo difang xingzheng zhidu shi*, 416–18; and Pu Shanxin, *Zhongguo xingzheng quhua gaige yanjiu* [A study of reforming China's administrative division] (Beijing: Shangwu yinshuguan, 2006), 56–60.

113. In Central Document [1999] no. 2, the policy of creating prefecture-level cities received a very positive assessment, whereas the practice of turning counties into cities was suspended in 1997. See Dai Junliang, Liu Junde, and Wang Yuming, "Shi xia shi" [Cities ruling cities], *Zhongguo fangyu*, no. 3 (2000): 2, 4.

114. See Douglass North, *Institutions, Institutional Change and Economic Performance* (New York: Cambridge University Press, 1990).

115. Pu Shanxin, *Zhongguo xingzheng quhua gaige yanjiu*, 153–56; Dai Junliang, *Zhongguo shizhi*, 101–5; Liu Junde and Wang Yuming, *Zhidu yu chuangxin*, 182–84; and Dai Junliang, *Chengxiang dazhuanxing shiqi de sikao*, 317–28.

116. Joel Samoff, "Decentralization: The Politics of Interventionism," *Development and Change* 21, no. 3 (1990): 514–24.

117. See Tan Tongxue, *Chuzhen de zhansuo: Xiangzhen jigou shengzhang de zhengzhi shengtai kaocha* [Stations and offices of Chu town: A survey of the political environment of township offices and stations] (Beijing: Zhongguo shehuikexueyuan chubanshe, 2006); Zeng Ming, "Wending yadao yiqie xia de xiangzhen zhengfu" [Township/town governments under the condition of "stability precedes everything else"], *Tizhi gaige*, no. 5 (2011): 28–35; and Hiroki Takeuchi, "Survival Strategies of Township Governments in Rural China: From Predatory Taxation to Land Trade," *Journal of Contemporary China*, 22, no. 83 (2013): 755–72.

4. THE CENTER'S PERCEPTIONS OF LOCAL BUREAUCRACY IN CHINA: A TYPOLOGICAL FIRST-CUT

1. The central state refers to the Communist Party and government apparatus at the central (national) level, and the local state denotes the subnational party and government organizations below the central level and above the "self-governing" villages and the equivalent units. For a comprehensive discussion of the Chinese local state, see Jae Ho Chung and Tao-chiu Lam, eds., *China's Local Administration: Traditions and Changes in the Sub-national Hierarchy* (London: Routledge, 2010).

2. The provinces here refer to all province-level units, inclusive of centrally administered cities and ethnic minority regions.

3. Central government officials rarely think or speak in these abstract scholarly terms, but this triple typology appears to contain more analytical components without losing the evaluative sentiments embedded in those more popular and often vulgar vocabularies.

4. Definitions of the three terms (agent, representative, and principal) are adapted, with some modifications, from http://dictionary.reference.com; and Vernon Bogdanor, ed., *The Blackwell Encyclopedia of Political Science* (Oxford: Blackwell, 1991), 531–32.

5. A large number of studies take this view when characterizing the local bureaucracy of the Maoist era. For a comprehensive literature review, see Jae Ho Chung, "Studies of Central–Provincial Relations in the People's Republic of China: A Mid-Term Appraisal," *China Quarterly*, no. 142 (June 1995): 491–94. For Chinese writings that identify local government leaders as agents of the center, see Ren Jin, "Lun difang xingzheng shouzhang de falu diwei yu fangshi" [On the legal status and the mode of producing local administrative leaders], *Zhengfu guanli cankao* [References for government management], no. 79 (2008): 1–6; and Li Ruichang, *Zhengfujian wangluo zhili* [Intergovernmental networked governance] (Shanghai: Fudan daxue chubanshe, 2012), 95.

6. Amos Perlmutter, *Modern Authoritarianism: A Comparative Institutional Analysis* (New Haven: Yale University Press, 1981).

7. The totalitarian ideological system in which everyone watches everyone else was an effective supplement for the central state's insufficient capacity for

administrative monitoring. See Anne F. Thurston, *Enemies of the People: The Ordeal of the Intellectuals in China's Great Cultural Revolution* (Cambridge, Mass.: Harvard University Press, 1983); and Bo Yibo, *Ruogan zhongda juece yu shijian de huigu* [Recollections of some crucial decisions and events] (Beijing: Zhonggong zhongyang dangxiao chubanshe, 1993), 2:777–78.

8. For such a strategic calculus of the local bureaucracy, see Frederick C. Teiwes, "Provincial Politics: Themes and Variations," in *China: Management of a Revolutionary Society*, ed. John M. H. Lindbeck (Seattle: University of Washington Press, 1971), 172. The dynamics of in-advance implementation is discussed in Jae Ho Chung, *Central Control and Local Discretion in China: Leadership and Implementation During the Post-Mao Decollectivization* (Oxford: Oxford University Press, 2000), 33–42.

9. How vulnerable localities were to the whims of Beijing's fiscal and material control during the Maoist era is well illustrated in *Zhongguo caizheng wushinian* [China's finance in the last fifty years], ed. Xiang Huaicheng (Beijing: Zhongguo caizheng jingji chubanshe, 1999).

10. See Melanie Manion, *Retirement of Revolutionaries in China: Public Policies, Social Norms, Private Interests* (Princeton: Princeton University Press, 1993); and Hon S. Chan, "Cadre Personnel Management in China: The Nomenklatura System, 1990–1998," *China Quarterly*, no. 179 (2004): 703–34.

11. For a view that focuses on economic growth as a key factor in career advancement, see Zhou Li'an, Li Hongbin, and Chen Ye, "Xiangdui jixiao kaohe: Zhongguo difang guanyuan jinsheng jizhi de yixiang jiangyan yanjiu" [Relative performance assessments: An empirical study of China's system of local official promotion], *Jingji xuebao* [Studies of economics], no. 1 (2005). For an interesting view that economic performance is more important to the promotion of governors than that of provincial party secretaries, see Eun Kyong Choi, "Patronage and Performance: Factors in the Political Mobility of Provincial Leaders in Post-Deng China," *China Quarterly*, no. 212 (December 2012): 865–981. For a weak linkage between provincial economic performance and the selection of Central Committee members, see Victor Shih et al., "Getting Ahead in the Communist Party: Explaining the Advancement of Central Committee Members in China," *American Political Science Review* 106, no. 1 (February 2012): 167–68, 178. For a study focusing on the "homophily" factors of joint origin, joint education, and joint work experience, see Sonja Opper, Victor Nee, and Stefan Brehn, "Homophily in the Career Mobility of China's Political Elite," *Social Science Research*, no. 50 (2015): 332–52.

12. See Yasheng Huang, "Administrative Monitoring in China," *China Quarterly*, no. 143 (September 1995): 828–43; and Chung, *Central Control and Local Discretion in China*, 39–40, 45–46.

13. Local governments are often dubbed as bridges or corridors that allow the flow of popular views to the center, thus signifying a somewhat passive nature of this representative role. See Yi Chonghua, *Zhongguo difangzhengfu zhuanxing* [Transformation of China's local government] (Beijing: Zhongguo shehuikexue chubanshe, 2008), 29–30.

14. Many examples of going against the tenet of "viewing the whole nation as a single chessboard" [*quanguo yipanqi*] are available. The cases of Li Jingquan

of Sichuan, Tao Zhu of Guangdong, Zeng Xisheng of Anhui, and Yang Yichen of Heilongjiang during the 1950s, 1960s, and early 1980s, respectively, are most notable in this regard.

15. These are called "local collective interests" [*difang qunti liyi*] as opposed to the center's interests or local government interests [*difang zuzhi liyi*]. See Yi Chonghua, *Zhongguo difangzhengfu zhuanxing*, 230–31; and Shen Liren, *Difang zhengfu de jingji zhineng he jingji xingwei* [Economic functions and behavior of local government] (Shanghai: Shanghai yuandong chubanshe, 1998), 133–35.

16. Heilongjiang's provincial party secretary, Yang Yichen, put up fierce resistance to the household responsibility reform during 1981–1982 due to his firm belief that the scheme of large machinery-based farming was more suitable for the province. See Chung, *Central Control and Local Discretion in China*, chap. 6.

17. This may easily lead to collective corruption within the local state. See Ben Hillman, "Factions and Spoils: Examining Political Behavior within the Local State in China," *China Journal*, no. 64 (July 2010): 1–18.

18. See Shaun Breslin, *China in the 1980s: Centre-Province Relations in a Reforming Socialist State* (New York: MacMillan, 1996), chap. 4.

19. See Zhu Guanglei, *Dangdai zhongguo zhengfu guocheng* [Contemporary China's political process] (Tianjin: Tianjin renmin chubanshe, 1997), 372; Liu Haiying, *Difang zhengfu jian caizheng guanxi yanjiu* [Study of fiscal relations between local governments] (Beijing: Zhongguo caizheng jingji chubanshe, 2006), 121; Zhang Jianping, *Zhongguo quyu kaifa wenti yanjiu* [Study of regional development in China] (Beijing: Zhongguo jingji chubanshe, 2009), 11–12; and Yu dongshan, *Zhuanxingqi zhongguo difang zhengfu: Jingzheng yanjiu* [Study of competition among local governments in China] (Shenyang: Dongbei daxue chubanshe, 2012), 82–86.

20. See Andrew G. Walder, "Local Governments as Industrial Firms: An Organizational Analysis of China's Transitional Economy," *American Journal of Sociology* 101, no. 2 (1995): 263–301; Wang Hua, *Zhongguo difang zhengfu jixiao chaju yanjiu* [Study of performance differentials among China's local governments] (Shanghai: Shanghai shehuikexueyuan chubanshe, 2011), 63–66; and He Hualing and Zhang Chen, "Xiandaiguojia goujian yuxia de zhongguo difangzhengfu zhili zhuanxing" [The transformation of China's local governance from a perspective of modern state-building], *Tizhi gaige*, no. 8 (2013): 32–36.

21. Jae Ho Chung, "Reappraising Central–Local Relations in Deng's China," in *Remaking the Chinese State: Strategies, Society and Security*, eds. Chien-min Chao and Bruce J. Dickson (London: Routledge, 2001), 50–52.

22. Most notable measures in this direction included the downward delegation of economic planning, the "localization" [*difanghua*] of local development strategies, and the "diversification" [*duoyanghua*] of local development models. See Shen Liren, *Difang zhengfu de jingji zhineng he jingji xingwei*, chaps. 12–13.

23. See Kai-yuen Tsui and Youqiang Wang, "Between Separate Stoves and Single Menu: Fiscal Decentralization in China," *China Quarterly*, no. 177 (March 2004): 71–90; and Barry Naughton and Dali L. Yang, eds., *Holding China*

Together: Diversity and National Integration in the Post-Deng Era (Cambridge: Cambridge University Press, 2004), chaps. 4, 7, and 8.

24. See the appendix in Peter Cheung, Jae Ho Chung, and Zhimin Lin, eds., *Provincial Strategies of Economic Reform in Post-Mao China: Leadership, Politics and Implementation* (Armonk, N.Y.: M. E. Sharpe, 1998); Peter Cheung and James Tang, "The External Relations of China's Provinces," in *The Making of Chinese Foreign and Security Policy in the Era of Reform*, ed. David M. Lampton (Stanford: Stanford University Press, 2001), 91–120; and Mingjiang Li, "Local Liberalism: China's Provincial Approaches to Relations with Southeast Asia," *Journal of Contemporary China* 23, no. 86 (March 2014).

25. During the Maoist era, there was little discrepancy in the agent imagery in terms of what Beijing thought the local bureaucracy was and ought to be. During the reform era, however, with the principalization of the local state, the discrepancy has widened rather considerably.

26. See Luo Yiping, *Difang zhengfu juece yanjiu* [A study of local government decision making] (Xiangtan: Xiangtan daxue chubanshe, 2011), 36–88.

27. Many scholars discuss a lot about regulation, supervision, and service provision but hardly regard the "representation of popular interests" [*minyi biaoda*] as a key function of local governments. See, for instance, Xu Bijiu, "Guanyu difang zhengfu jingji zhineng de jige wenti" [Some questions on the economic function of local governments], *Lilun dongtai* [Dynamics of theory], no. 1752 (August 20, 2007): 24–28.

28. This drastic reform, called the tax-sharing reform [*fenshuizhi*], was implemented in 1994, one year ahead of the announced schedule due to Beijing's growing sense of urgency and concern with rampant localism. For more details, see chap. 6 in this volume.

29. Zheng Lin, *Difang zhengfu diwei—Caili peizhi wenti yanjiu* [The place of local governments—A study of allocating fiscal powers] (Beijing: Renmin fayuan chubanshe, 2008), 68.

30. Zhang Fei and Qu Futian, "Cong difang zhengfu zhi jian boyi de jiaodu kan tudi shichang zhixu" [The land market order as seen from an interlocal game-theoretic perspective], *Jingji wenti tansuo* [Exploring economic problems], no. 6 (2005): 19–22; and You-tien Hsing, *The Great Urban Transformation: Politics and Land and Property in China* (Oxford: Oxford University Press, 2010).

31. Recurring cycles of central–local feuds over macroeconomic stabilization since the late 1980s is a vivid case in point. See Yashng Huang, *Inflation and Investment Controls in China: The Political Economy of Central–Local Relations in China* (Cambridge: Cambridge University Press, 1996); Breslin, *China in the 1980s*; Sarah Tong and Yao Jielu, "China's Rising Local Government Debts Spark Concerns," *East Asian Policy* 2, no. 4 (October–December 2010): 38–49; and "Overheating Fears Grow as China's Local Governments Set GDP Targets High," *Xinhua*, January 25, 2011.

32. Yi Chonghua, *Zhongguo defang zhengfu zhuanxing*, 59, 61–62, 236–39; and Cai Yongshun, "Irresponsible State: Local Cadres and Image-Building in China," *Journal of Communist Studies and Transition Policies* 20, no. 4 (December 2004): 20–41.

33. Joseph Fewsmith, "The Elusive Search for Effective Sub-County Governance," in *Mao's Invisible Hand: The Political Foundations of Adaptive Governance in China*, eds. Sebastian Heilmann and Elizabeth J. Perry (Cambridge, Mass.: Harvard University Asia Center, 2011), 278.

34. Xin Xiangyang, *Zhongguo fazhanlun* [On China's development] (Jinan: Shandong renmin chubanshe, 2006), 134; and Zhou Zhenchao, *Dangdai zhongguo zhengfu tiaokuai guanxi yanjiu* [Study of vertical–horizontal government relations in contemporary China] (Tianjin: Tianjin renmin chubanshe, 2009), 81–97.

35. See Victor Shih, "Dealing with Non-Performing Loans: Political Constraints and Financial Policies in China," *China Quarterly*, no. 180 (December 2004): 933–35; and Li Xiaoxi, *Zhongguo jingji gaige 30nian—Shichanghua jincheng juan 1978–2008* [Thirty years of China's economic reform—Volume on the process of marketization 1978–2008] (Chongqing: Chongqing daxue chubanshe, 2008), 204.

36. See Richard Louis Edmonds, "The Sanxia Project: The Environmental Argument Surrounding China's Super Dam," *Global Ecology and Biography Letters*, no. 1 (1991): 105–24. Also see Guo Rongxing, "Interprovincial Border Disputes: The Case of Lake Weishan," *Journal of Contemporary China* 21, no. 75 (2012): 531–50; and Scott Moore, "Hydropolitics and Inter-Jurisdictional Relationships in China: The Pursuit of Localized Preferences in a Centralized System," *China Quarterly*, no. 219 (September 2014): 760–75.

37. See "Guowuyuan bangongting guanyu yinfa shuilibu zhineng peizhi neishe jigou he renyuan bianzhi guiding de tongzhi" [The state council's circular on the regulations governing the internal organs and personnel arrangements within the ministry of water management: 1998], cited in Maria Saleth and Ariel Dinar, "Water Challenge and Institutional Response," *World Bank Policy Research Working Paper 2045* (Washington, D.C.: World Bank, January 1999), 25–27.

38. Zhongguo xingzheng guanli xuehui, ed., *Zhengfu cengji guanli* [Intergovernmental management] (Beijing: Renmin chubanshe, 2009), 69, 97–98; and Shen Ronghua, "Zhengfu chuizhi guanli handai gaishan" [Vertical control needs some improvement], *Lingdao canyue* [References for leadership], no. 33 (2009): 30–31.

39. Xiao Gongqin, "Jingti difang quanli sudanhua xianxiang" [Be wary of the sultanization of local power], *Neibu canyue* [Internal references], no. 10 (March 14, 2003): 6–7.

40. Yang Xuedong, "Zhongguo difang zhengfu gaige 30nian," in *Difang de fuxing* [The re-rise of localities], eds. Yang Xuedong and Lai Hairong (Beijing: Shehuikexue wenxian chubanshe, 2009), 8.

41. Admittedly, the central state is hardly a single or uniform entity either. Yet, to focus more effectively on how the local government is viewed by Beijing, it is assumed here that the central state is more cohesive in dealing with localities than it really is.

42. Beijing's view of each of the thirty-three province-level units may presumably differ as, for instance, the Chinese generally regard Shandong as a docile province while viewing Guangdong as a rebellious one. Beijing's perception of a province may also change over time as the Chinese seem to regard Shanghai

as less compliant now than before. Yet, such political-anthropological endeavors fall outside the purview of this study.

43. Among the four tiers of subnational administration, the provinces appear to be the least compliant with the center. In a survey conducted in 2010 on 2,523 provincial and city officials, the number of respondents who chose "provinces unconditionally carrying out central policy" was the lowest, with only 14.8 percent, whereas the comparable figures for the prefectures/cities, counties /cities, and townships/towns were 20.4 percent, 23.8 percent, and 23.9 percent, respectively. See Zhongguo zhengfa daxue ketizu, "Congxiang zhengfu guanxi diaocha" [A survey on vertical inter-governmental relations], *Gaige neican* [Internal references for reform], no. 20 (2010): 5–7.

44. For Beijing's dualistic perception of the provinces, see John Donaldson, "Provinces: Paradoxical Politics, Problematic Partners," in *China's Local Administration: Traditions and Changes in the Sub-national Hierarchy*, eds. Jae Ho Chung and Tao-chiu Lam (London: Routledge, 2010), 14, 38.

45. For the former trend, see Andrew Mertha, "China's 'Soft' Centralization: Shifting *Tiao/Kuai* Authority Relations," *China Quarterly*, no. 184 (December 2005): 791–810; and for the latter, see Jae Ho Chung, "Vertical Support, Horizontal Linkages, and Regional Disparities in China: Typology, Incentive Structure, and Operational Logic," *Issues and Studies* 37, no. 4 (July–August 2001): 121–46.

46. See Zhongguo xingzheng guanli xuehui, ed., *Zhengfu cengji guanli*, 242.

47. See Wei Hsiu-mei, *Qingdai zhi huibi zhidu* [The system of avoidance in the Qing dynasty] (Taipei: Academia Sinica, 1992). Also see Jae Ho Chung, "Central-Local Dynamics: Historical Continuities and Institutional Resilience," in *Mao's Invisible Hand: The Political Foundation of Adaptive Governance in China*, eds. Sebastian Heilmann and Elizabeth J. Perry (Cambridge, Mass.: Harvard University Asia Center, 2011), 308–9.

48. Zhiyue Bo, *Chinese Provincial Leaders: Economic Performance and Political Mobility Since 1949* (Armonk, N.Y.: M. E. Sharpe, 2002), 44.

49. Bo, *Chinese Provincial Leaders*, 45.

50. See Cheng Li and David Bachman, "Localism, Elitism, and Immobilism: Elite Formation and Social Change in Post-Mao China," *World Politics* 42, no. 1 (October 1989): 71; and Xiaowei Zang, "Provincial Elite in Post-Mao China," *Asian Survey* 31, no. 6 (June 1991): 516.

51. In terms of five-year average, the respective ratio was 45 percent for 1984–1989, 38 percent for 1990–1994, 45 percent for 1995–1999, 40 percent for 2000–2004, and 41 percent for 2005–2009. These figures were calculated using the data in *Zhonggong yanjiu* [Studies of communist China] (Taipei: Zhonggong yanjiu zazhishe, various years). I thank Myung-jong Chun for research assistance.

52. The decline of natives during the 1990s is noted in Bo, *Chinese Provincial Leaders*, 45. For the figures for the native provincial party secretaries in 1999 and 2002, see Dali L. Yang, *Remaking the Chinese Leviathan: Market Transition and the Politics of Governance in China* (Stanford: Stanford University Press, 2004), 5.

53. This is stipulated in the amended Law of Regional Autonomy (2001). See Hongyi Lai, "Ethnic Autonomous Regions: A Formula for a Unitary Multiethnic

State," in *China's Local Administration: Traditions and Changes in the Sub-national Hierarchy*, eds. Jae Ho Chung and Tao-chiu Lam (London: Routledge, 2010), 74, 82. Perhaps this is why the promotion of governors relied more on their economic performance than that of party secretaries. See Choi, "Patronage and Performance."

54. See Jae Ho Chung and Tao-chiu Lam, "China's 'City System' in Flux: Explaining Post-Mao Administrative Changes," *China Quarterly*, no. 180 (December 2004): 951–52; and Sun Xueyu, *Chuizhi guanli fenhe—Sheng zhiguanzhi tizhi yanjiu* [Vertical management—A study of the provinces-directly-ruling-counties system] (Beijing: Renmin chubanshe, 2013), 141–54.

55. See Shiuh-Shen Chien, "Prefectures and Prefecture-Level Cities: The Political Economy of Administrative Restructuring" and Tao-Chiu Lam, "The County System and County Governance," in *China's Local Administration: Traditions and Changes in the Sub-national Hierarchy*, eds. Jae Ho Chung and Tao-chiu Lam (London: Routledge, 2010), 128, 179, respectively.

56. See "Zhonggong zhongyang guowuyuan guanyu 2009nian cujin nongye wending fazhan nongmin chixu zengshou de ruogan yijian" [Some opinions regarding the CCP Central Committee and State Council on promoting the steady development of agriculture and increasing peasant incomes in 2009], February 1, 2009, http://news.xinhuanet.com/newscenter/2009-02-01/content _10746024_3.htm.

57. By the end of 2013, the rate of province-wide implementation in Sichuan, Shandong, and Henan was 43.7, 22.0, and 9.2 percent, respectively. The comparable figures for Zhejiang, Fujian, and Hainan were all 100 percent. See chapter 6 for details.

58. See He Xianming, *Sheng guan xian gaige* [The reform of provinces directly ruling counties] (Shanghai: Xuelin chubanshe, 2009), chaps. 3–4.

59. Although the status and names (*sheng, dao, zhou,* and *lu*) of the provincial level changed frequently, the county (*xian*) remained virtually unchanged from the Qin to the People's Republic. See Zhou Zhenhe, *Tiguo jingye zhidao—Zhongguo xingzheng quhua yange* [The way of zoning and ruling the nation—Changes and continuities in China's administrative zoning] (Shanghai: Shanghai shudian chubanshe, 2009), 27–28.

60. See Hua Wei, "Xianzhi: Xiangtu zhongguo de xingzheng jichu" [The county system: The administrative foundation of rural China], *Zhanlue yu guanli* [Strategy and management], no. 6 (2001): 54, 57. A Chinese scholar characterizes the province as the "most crucial" [*zui zhuyao*] level of local administration while calling the county as the "most fundamental" [*zui jichu*]. Xiong Wenzhao, "Sheng zhiguan xian xuyao tongpan guihua" [The provinces-directly-ruling-counties policy requires overall planning], *Gaige neican*, no. 18 (2010); 5.

61. *Zhongguo tongji nianjian 2014* [China statistical yearbook of 2014] (Beijing: Zhongguo tongji chubanshe, 2014), 3.

62. Chu Tung-tsu, *Local Government in China under Ch'ing* (Cambridge, Mass.: Harvard University Press, 1962), xi.

63. See Lam, "The County System and County Governance," 149, 154. Some refer to the county as a "semi-grassroots level" [*zhun jiceng*]. See Bao Jingsheng,

Dangdai zhongguo xianzheng gaige yanjiu (Tianjin: Tianjin renmin chubanshe, 2007), 50.

64. According to *China Survey,* conducted in 2008 by Texas A & M University, the share of the respondents who replied "don't trust" was 13.9 percent for the central level, 24.3 percent for the provincial level, and 34.8 percent for the county level. I thank Bruce J. Dickson for sharing these data. Also see Ji Jianlin, "Shehui guanli yu chengzhi fubai ying xietong tuijin" [Social management and the persecution of corruption must proceed in mutual coordination], *Lilun dongtai,* no. 1920 (April 20, 2012): 25; and Yongshun Cai, *State and Agents in China: Disciplining Government Officials* (Stanford: Stanford University Press, 2015), 73.

65. Wang Shengyong, *Xianji zhengfu guanli moshi chuanxin tantao* [An exploration of renovating the management of county-level governments] (Beijing: Renmin chubanshe, 2006), 127; and Wang Zhanyang, "Dabuding jiaju shengxian shikong" [Supplementary measures may actually contribute to the loss of control over provinces and counties], *Gaige neican,* no. 18 (2010): 2–3.

66. Wang Jiamin, "Zhongyang litui sheng zhiguan xian—Xianwei shuji jiang you shengwei zhijie renmin" [The center pushes hard the provinces-directly-ruling-counties reform—County party secretaries are to be appointed directly by the provinces], *Zhongguo xinwen zhoukan* (July 23, 2009), http://news.sina.com .cn/c/sd/2009-07-23/095718281105.shtml (accessed on March 14, 2011).

67. See Ian Seckington, "County Leadership in China: A Baseline Survey," *China: An International Journal* 5, no. 2 (September 2007): 205, 223; and *South China Morning Post,* May 15, 2009.

68. According to a rare government survey conducted in 231 counties of four provinces in 1987, 53 percent of the county-level leading officials were assigned to their native localities. The leading officials here refer to party secretaries, magistrates, mayors, and heads of the organization department, courts, procuratorate, and public security units. For the survey result, see Liu Junsheng, *Zhongguo renshizhidu gaiyao* [Overview of China's personnel management system] (Beijing: Qinghua daxue chubanshe, 2009), 126.

69. "Guojia gongwuyuan zhanxing tiaoli" [Tentative measures for the government officials: August 14, 1993]; and Liu Junsheng, *Zhongguo renshizhidu gaiyao,* 128–29.

70. Hillman reports that the rule of avoidance was more or less suspended in his two case townships since 2004. It remains uncertain, however, how generalizable the finding is for China as a whole. See Ben Hillman, *Patronage and Power: Local State Networks and Party-State Resilience in Rural China* (Stanford: Stanford University Press, 2014), 47–48.

71. Wang Peng and Zhang Yongtao, "Yidi weiguan ehuo gailiu guitu?" [Is elite circulation being reversed?] in *Ningxia dangxiao xuebao* [Academic bulletin of Ningxia University], no. 5 (2010): 1.

72. The popular old saying that "the sky is high and the emperor is far away" [*tian gao huangdi yuan*] is generally geared to the counties, and therefore the townships are deemed farther away from the center. Qin Hui, "Zhongguo difang zhili jieguo de lishi yu zhuanxing" [The history and transformation of China's local governance structure], *Gaige neican,* no. 7 (2003): 31–33.

73. Yang Zhong, "Chinese Township Government: Between a Rock and a Hard Place," in *China's Local Administration: Traditions and Changes in the Subnational Hierarchy*, eds. Jae Ho Chung and Tao-chiu Lam (London: Routledge, 2010), 175.

74. See Graeme Smith, "Political Machination in a Rural County," *China Journal*, no. 62 (July 2009): 29–59; Hilman, "Factions and Spoils"; and Zhou Xueguang, "The Institutional Logic of Collusion among Local Governments in China," *Modern China* 5, no. 1 (January 2010): 47–78.

75. People's trust in the party committees at the township level was the lowest, with only 16 percent, whereas the comparable figures for those at the county and provincial levels were 26 percent and 42 percent, respectively. Lianjiang Li, "Political Trust in Rural China," *Modern China* 30, no. 2 (2004): 234.

76. See Hillman, *Patronage and Power*, 90–91; and Gunter Schubert and Anna L. Ahlers, "County and Township Cadres as Strategic Groups: 'Building a New Countryside' in Three Provinces," *China Journal*, no. 67 (January 2012): 67–86.

77. Zhou Tianyong, *Zhongguo zhengzhi tizhi gaige* [The reform of China's political system] (Beijing: Zhongguo shuili shuidian chubanshe, 2004), 101–2, 117; Graeme Smith, "The Hollow State: Local Governance in China," *China Quarterly*, no. 203 (September 2010): 603–6; and An Chen, "How Has the Abolition of Agricultural Taxes Transformed Village Governance in China? Evidence from Agricultural Regions," *China Quarterly*, no. 219 (September 2014): 721–31.

78. See Tan Tongxue, *Chuzhen de zhansuo, Xiangzhen jiguo shengzhang de zhengzhi shengtai kaocha* [Stations and offices of Chu town: A survey of the political environment of township offices and stations] (Beijing: Zhongguo shehuikexue chubanshe, 2006); Zhongguo xingzheng guanli xuehui, ed., *Zhengfu cengji guanli*, 236–37; and Wu Licai, "Xingzhen gaige" [Reforms of townships] in *Difang de fuxing*, eds. Yang Xuedong and Lai Hairong, 229–47. Also see Zheng Lin, *Difang zhengfu diwei*, 189–92; and Zhou Tianyong, *Zhongguo zhengzhi tizhi gaige*, 109.

79. Liu Chengli, "Zhongyang yu difang caizheng guanxi de tiaozheng yu difang zhengfu xingwei de bianhua" [Readjustment of central–local fiscal relations and the changes in local government behavior] in *Difang de fuxing*, eds. Yang Xuedong and Lai Hairong, 207–9.

5. THE CENTER'S INSTRUMENTS OF LOCAL CONTROL

1. See Robert Rotberg, ed., *When States Fail: Causes and Consequences* (Princeton: Princeton University Press, 2003); and Robert Bates, *When Things Fell Apart: State Failure in Late-Twentieth Century Africa* (Cambridge: Cambridge University Press, 2008).

2. Sixty-six years may not be a very long time for a state's lifespan in general terms, but it certainly is for the regimes in many newly established developing nations in the contemporary era.

3. For the quote, see John Fitzgerald, "Reports of My Death Have Been Greatly Exaggerated," in *China Deconstructs: Politics, Trade and Regionalism*,

eds. David S. G. Goodman and Gerald Segal (London: Routledge, 1994), 21–58. For assessments that are supportive of Beijing's sustained capacity for local governance, see Yasheng Huang, *Inflation and Investment Controls in China: The Political Economy of Central–Local Relations during the Reform Era* (Cambridge: Cambridge University Press, 1996); Jae Ho Chung, *Central Control and Local Discretion: Leadership and Implementation During Post-Mao Decollectivization* (Oxford: Oxford University Press, 2000); Barry Naughton and Dali L. Yang, eds., *Holding China Together: Diversity and National Integration in the Post-Deng Era* (Cambridge: Cambridge University Press, 2004); Sheng Yumin, *Economic Openness and Territorial Politics in China* (Cambridge: Cambridge University Press, 2010); and Pierre Landry, *Decentralized Authoritarianism in China: The Communist Party's Control of Local Elites in the Post-Mao Era* (Cambridge: Cambridge University Press, 2012).

4. Refer to chapter 2 of this volume.

5. The quotation is from Amos Perlmutter, *Modern Authoritarianism: A Comparative Institutional Analysis* (New Haven: Yale University Press, 1981), 71.

6. See *Guanyu jianguo yilai dang de ruogan lishi wenti de jueyi* [Resolutions on some historical problems of the party since 1949] (Beijing: Renmin chubanshe, 1985); and Bo Yibo, *Ruogan zhongda juece yu shijian de huigu* [Recollections of some crucial decisions and events] (Beijing: Zhonggong zhongyang dangxiao chubanshe, 1993), 2:777–79.

7. See Dai Yuanchen, "Sixiang jiefang tuidongle gaige kaifang he jingji fazhan" [The "emancipation of mind" pushed forward the reform, opening, and economic development], *Shehuikexue yanjiu cankao ziliao* [Reference materials for social science research], no. 588 (February 20, 1999): 1–6; and Jae Ho Chung, "Reappraising Central–Local Relations in Deng's China: Decentralization, Dilemmas of Control and Diluted Effects of Reform," in *Remaking the Chinese State: Strategies, Society ad Security*, eds. Bruce J. Dickson and Chien-min Chao (London: Routledge, 2001), 47–52.

8. See Sebastian Heilmann, "Policy-Making Through Experimentation: The Foundation of a Distinctive Policy Process," in *Mao's Invisible Hand: The Political Foundations of Adaptive Authoritarianism in China*, eds. Sebastian Heilmann and Elizabeth J. Perry (Cambridge, Mass.: Harvard University Asia Center, 2011), 62–101.

9. Sun Qitai and Xiong Zhiyong, *Dazhai hongqi de shengqi yu duoluo* [The rise and fall of the Dazhai model] (Huixian: Henan renmin chubanshe, 1990), 285–363.

10. See Hong Yung Lee, *From Revolutionary Cadres to Bureaucratic Technocrats* (Berkeley: University of California Press, 1991), chaps. 7 and 8.

11. "Guanyu zhongguo shichanghua jincheng de yanjiu" [Study of China's marketization processes], *Diaocha yanjiu baogao* [Investigative research report], no. 1747 (July 26, 2002): 5. Also see chapter 2 for details.

12. Liu Guoguang, ed., *Zhongguo Shige wunian jihua yanjiu baogao* [Research report on China's 10 Five-Year Plans] (Beijing: Renmin chubanshe, 2006), chaps. 11 and 12.

13. See Zhao Suisheng, "From Coercion to Negotiation: The Changing Central-Local Economic Relationship in Mainland China," *Issues and Studies* 28,

no. 10 (October 1992): 1–22; Shaun Breslin, *China in the 1980s: Centre-Province Relations in a Reforming Socialist State* (London: MacMillan, 1996), chaps. 4, 6, and 7; Ciqi Mei and Margaret M. Pearson, "Killing a Chicken to Scare the Monkeys? Deterrence Failure and Local Defiance in China," *China Journal*, no. 72 (July 2014): 75–97; and Tucker Van Aken and Orion A. Lewis, "The Political Economy of Noncompliance in China: The Case of Industrial Energy Policy," *Journal of Contemporary China* 24, no. 95 (2015): 798–822.

14. For issue-based variations in the extent of local discretion, see Jae Ho Chung, "Studies of Central–Provincial Relations in the People's Republic of China: A Mid-Term Appraisal," *China Quarterly*, no. 142 (June 1995): 497–501. Also see chapter 6 for detailed discussions.

15. See Wang Linsheng, *Zhongguo difang zhengfu juece yanjiu* [Study of decision making in China's local governments] (Guangzhou: Huanan ligong daxue chubanshe, 2005), 163–64.

16. See Chung, *Central Control and Local Discretion in China*, chaps. 4–6; and Chen Guanren, *17 gesheng zizhiqu he zhixiashi gaige qidong jishi* [Records on the start of reform in seventeen provinces, autonomous regions, and centrally administered cities] (Beijing: Zhonggong dangshi chubanshe, 2009), chap. 2.

17. In traditional China, too, the number of provinces was highly stable as it was 16, 15, and 18, respectively, during the Yuan, Ming, and Qing dynasties. See Zhou Zhenhe, *Zhongguo difang xingzheng zhidushi* [History of China's local administrative institutions] (Shanghai: Shanghai renmin chubanshe, 2005), chap. 3.

18. Zhang Jicai, *Zhongguo jindai lianbangzhuyi yanjiu* [Study of federalism in modern China] (Beijing: Zhongguo shehuikexue chubanshe, 2012), 223.

19. See Stuart R. Schram, "Decentralization in a Unitary State: Theory and Practice, 1940–1984," in *The Scope of State Power in China*, ed. S. R. Schram (London: University of London Press, 1985), 82–95, 98. Also see Jin Ji, *Banglianzhi—Zhongguo de zuijia chulu* [The confederation—The best option for China] (Hong Kong: Baixing chuban gongsi, 1992); Wang Liping, *Lianbangzhi yu shijie zhixu* [Federalism and the world order] (Beijing: Beijing daxue chubanshe, 2000), chaps. 8 and 10; Song Xiaozhuang, *Lun yiguo liangzhi xia zhongyang he xianggang tequ de guanxi* [On the center–Hong Kong relations under the one country, two systems framework] (Beijing: Zhongguo renmin daxue chubanshe, 2003), chap. 3; and Zhang Jicai, *Zhongguo jindai de lianbangzhuyi yanjiu*, 250–51.

20. For the two principles of regional boundary demarcation, see Zhou Zhenhe, *Zhongguo difang xingzheng zhidushi*, 236–49. And for the case of Shandong, see Dorothy J. Solinger, *Regional Governments and Political Integration in Southwest China, 1949–1954* (Berkeley: University of California Press, 1977), 29. Also see Zhou Zhenhe, *Tiguo jingye zhi dao—Zhongguo xingzheng quhua yange* (Shanghai: Shanghai shudian chubanshe, 2009), 27.

21. Tian Suisheng, Luo Hui, and Zeng Wei, *Zhongguo xingzheng quhua gailun* [Overview of China's administrative divisions] (Beijing: Peking University Press, 2005), 94–102; Dai Junliang, *Chengxiang dazhuanxing shiqi de sikao* [Thoughts on the era of great transformation in the city and countryside] (Beijing: Zhongguo shehui chubanshe, 2006), 207–8; Jin Binghao and Zhang Yong, "Chengshi minzuqu de falu diwei handai mingque" [The legal status of the urban ethnic

minority districts need to be clarified], *Neibu canyue* [Internal references], no. 846 (January 26, 2007): 11–18; and *Zhongguo tongji nianjian 2013* [Statistical year of China 2013] (Beijing: zhongguo tongjichubanshe, 2013), 3.

22. The *loci classicus* on this subject include John P. Burns, *The Chinese Communist Party's Nomenklatura System* (Armonk, N.Y.: M. E. Sharpe, 1989); Melanie Manion, *Retirement of Revolutionaries in China: Public Policies, Social Norms, Private Interests* (Princeton: Princeton University Press, 1993); and Xu Songtao and Sun Jianli, eds., *Zhongguo renshi zhidu gaige 1978–2008* [Reforms of China's personnel system, 1978–2008] (Beijing: Zhongguo renshi chubanshe, 2008).

23. For the traditional system of avoidance, see Wei Hsiu-mei, *Qingdai zhi huibi zhidu* [The system of avoidance in the Qing dynasty] (Taipei: Academia Sinica, 1992).

24. For Beijing's distrust of local cadres in Southern China during the 1950s, see Yang Kuisong, "CCP Cadre Policy in the Early Years of the PRC," paper presented at the conference on "Adaptive Authoritarianism" held at Harvard University during July 14–16, 2008.

25. See table 4.1.

26. Also related is the extent of cross-provincial mobility of provincial leaders. According to some 2012 data, a higher level of cross-provincial mobility was discernible for the provincial party secretaries than for the governors. See Xufeng Zhu, "Geographical Political Mobility, Local Bureaucratic Entrepreneurship and Laboratories of Governance Paradigms," paper presented at the 9th Annual Workshop of the Asian Network for the Study of Local China (*ANSLoC*), Seoul National University, May 2, 2014, Tables 1 and 2.

27. See Jae Ho Chung, "Vertical Support, Horizontal Linkages, and Regional Disparities in China," *Issues and Studies* 37, no. 4 (July–August 2001): 121–46. Also see chapter 7 of this volume.

28. For details, see Michel Oksenberg, "Methods of Communication within the Chinese Bureaucracy," *China Quarterly*, no. 57 (January–March 1974): 1–39; and Yasheng Huang, "The Statistical Agency in China's Bureaucratic System: A Comparison with the Former Soviet Union," *Communist and Post-Communist Studies* 29, no. 1 (March 1996): 59–75.

29. See Kenneth Lieberthal, *Central Documents and Politburo Politics in China* (Ann Arbor: Center for Chinese Studies, University of Michigan, 1978), 26, 32, 51, 63, 71; and Michael Schoenhals, *Doing Things with Words in Chinese Politics* (Berkeley: Institute for East Asian Studies, 1992), chap. 1.

30. Michael Schoenhals, "Elite Information in China," *Problems of Communism* 25, no. 5 (September–October 1985): 65–71; Michael Schoenhals. *Doing Things with Words in Chinese Politics*, 37–44; and Wu Guoguang, "Command Communication: The Politics of Editorial Formulation in the People's Daily," *China Quarterly*, no. 137 (March 1994): 194–211.

31. See State Statistical Bureau, *Zhongguo tongji gongzuo nianjian 1993* [China statistical work yearbook 1993] (Beijing: Zhongguo tongji chubanshe, 1993); I-51–54, III-13–14; Yasheng Huang, "The Statistical Agency in China's Bureaucratic System," 59–75; and Shen Ronghua, "Zhengfu chuizhi guanli handai gaige" [The government's vertical line-control awaits reforms], *Lingdao canyue*, no. 33 (2009): 30–31.

32. Ge Suhong, "Xuzeng shibei de gongye chanzhi shi ruhe churong de" [On how the false figure of tenfold increase in gross industrial output value was derived], *Banyuetan* (Semi-Monthly), no. 3 (2001): 30–31; Ernest Kao, "GDP Gap in China the Size of Guangdong Economy," *South China Morning Post*, February 5, 2013; and "Gap in China's Economic Output Data Narrows," *Straits Times*, February 19, 2014.

33. Given that Mao carried out more inspection trips during the catastrophic Great Leap Forward than any other times, those trips were certainly used more for the purpose of imposing his ideals and preferences than for getting better tuned to local situations.

34. For the increase in the frequency of inspection trips by these leaders, see http://www.xinhuanet.com/newscenter/ldrbdzj.

35. Ilpyong J. Kim, *The Politics of Chinese Communism: Kiangsi Under Soviets* (Berkeley: University of California Press, 1973), 226.

36. Different names were given to this post under different dynasties—i.e., *cishi* in the Han, *anchashi* in the Tang, *zhenglian fangsi* in the Song, and *jiancha yushi* in the Ming and Qing. See Long Guangfu, *Zhongguo xianzhengfu xingzheng jiandu* [Administrative supervision over the county administration in China] (Beijing: Zhongguo shehuikexue chubanshe, 2012), 31–32.

37. Available studies include Lawrence R. Sullivan, "The Role of the Control Organs in the Chinese Communist Party, 1977–1983," *Asian Survey* 24, no. 6 (1984): 597–667; Ting Gong, "The Party Discipline Inspection in China: Its Evolving Trajectory and Embedded Dilemmas," *Crime, Law and Social Change* 49 (2008): 139–52; and Guo Yong, "The Evolvement of the Chinese Communist Party Discipline Inspection Commission in the Reform Era," *China Review* 12, no. 1 (2012): 1–24.

38. "Shengji jiwei lingdao you zhongjiwei timing" [Provincial-level discipline inspection commissioners are to be appointed by the central discipline commission] (March 28, 2014), http://news.sohu.com/20140328/n397379517.shtml; and Xuezhi Guo, "Controlling Corruption in the Party: China's Central Discipline Inspection Commission," *China Quarterly*, no. 219 (August 2014): 608–12.

39. Yukyung Yeo, "Complementing the Local Discipline Inspection Commissions of the Party: Empowerment of the Central Inspection Groups," paper presented at the 9th Annual Workshop of the Asian Network for the Study of Local China (*ANSLoC*), Seoul, May 2, 2014. Also see Zhu Yongjia, "Guanyu zhongyang xunshiyuan zhidu de lishi huigu" [A historical review of the central inspector system], *Guanchazhe* [Observer], June 3, 2013, http://www.guancha .cn/Zhuyongjia/2013_06_03_14; and "Zuiqiang zhongjiwei liangnian xunbian quanguo zhujin zhongyang yanguan difang" [The omnipotent central discipline inspection commission inspects the whole nation just in two years, moves into the center and oversees localities], *Ming Pao*, January 12, 2015.

40. Long Guangfu, *Zhongguo xianzhengfu xingzheng jiandu*, 152–76, 207–25.

41. For more detailed discussions of this case, see chapter 6 of this volume.

42. See the issue of March 21, 1994.

43. Xin Xiangyang, *Zhongguo fazhanlun* [On China's development] (Jinan: Shandong renmin chubanshe, 2006), 134; and Zhou Zhenchao, *Dangdai*

zhongguo zhengfu tiaokuai guanxi yanjiu [Study of vertical–horizontal government relations in contemporary China] (Tianjin: Tianjin renmin chubanshe,
2009), 81–97.

44. See Victor Shih, "Dealing with Non-Performing Loans: Political Constraints and Financial Policies in China," *China Quarterly*, no. 180 (December
2004): 933–35; and Zhongguo jingji tizhi gaige zazhishe, ed., *Gaige yaoqing
canyue* [Inside information on economic reform] (Beijing: Xinhua chubanshe,
2010), 29–34.

45. Zhongguo xingzheng guanli xuehui, ed., *Zhengfu cengji guanli* [Inter-
governmental management] (Beijing: Renmin chubanshe, 2009), 69, 97–98;
and Shen Ronghua, "Zhengfu chuizhi guanli handai gaige," 30–31.

46. For such an assessment, see Li Ruichang, *Zhengfujian wangluo zhili*
[Intergovernmental networked governance] (Shanghai: Fudan daxue chunbanshe, 2012), chap. 4.

47. Yu Jianrong, "Dangqian bufen diqu nongcun quntixing shijian de zhuyao
tedian" [Major characteristics of collective protests in some rural areas],
Lingdao canyue, no. 21 (July 25, 2002): 14–15; Dennis J. Blasko, *The Chinese
Army Today: Tradition and Transformation for the 21st Century* (London: Routledge, 2006), 17, 66; Xu Shihong, "Shenhua wujing jiazhi renshi" [Deepen our
understanding of the value of PAP], *Guofang* [National defense], no. 2 (2008):
66–67; Jae Ho Chung, "Managing Political Crises in China: The Case of Collective Protests," in *China's Crisis Management*, ed. Jae Ho Chung (London: Routledge, 2011), 147–51; and Francois Godement et al., "Control at the Grassroots:
China's New Toolbox," *China Analysis* (London: Asia Center, June 2012), 3–4.

48. David Shambaugh, *Modernizing China's Military: Progress, Problems
and Prospects* (Berkeley: University of California Press, 2002), 22; and Blasko,
The Chinese Army Today, 67.

49. Academy of Military Sciences, *Zhongguo renmin jiefangjun gaige fazhan
30nian* [Reform and development of PLA in the last 30 years] (Beijing: Jiefangjun chubanshe, 2008), 371–73. Also see Yang Yi, ed., *Zhongguo guojia anquan zhanlue gouxiang* [Ideas and plans for China's national security strategy]
(Beijing: Shishi chubanshe, 2009), 397–407; and *Guofang*, no. 9 (2009): 13–14.

50. In late 2015, the total number of the PLA's regional commands was reduced from seven to five. For the rumored return of the great administrative
regions, see Dorothy J. Solinger, "Some Speculations on the Return of the Regions: Parallels with the Past," *China Quarterly*, no. 75 (September 1979):
623–38.

51. Kim, *The Politics of Chinese Communism*, 160.

52. Michael D. Swaine, "Chinese Regional Forces as Political Actors," in *Chinese Military Regionalism: The Security Dimension*, eds. Richard H. Yang et al.
(Boulder: Westview Press, 1994), 63–67.

53. Wei-chin Mu, *Provincial-Central Government Relations and the Problem
of National Unity in Modern China* (PhD diss., Princeton University, 1948), reprinted by the University Microfilm (Ann Arbor: University of Michigan, 1965),
56; and S. A. M. Adshead, *Province and Politics in Late Imperial China: Viceregal
Government in Szechwan, 1898–1911* (London: Curzon Press, 1984), 10–11. Also
see David Shambaugh, "China's Military in Transition: Politics, Professionalism,

Procurement and Power Projection," *China Quarterly*, no. 146 (June 1996): 283; and Shambaugh, *Modernizing China's Military*, 22, 29.

54. Mu, *Provincial-Central Government Relations and the Problem of National Unity in Modern China*, 59; and Zhou Zhenhe, *Tiguo jianye zhi dao*, 27.

55. Shambaugh, "China's Military in Transition," 283.

56. See Bruce J. Dickson, "The Future of the Chinese Communist Party: Strategies of Survival and Prospects for Change," in *Charting China's Future*, ed. Jae Ho Chung, chap. 2; and Jae Ho Chung, "China's Local Governance in Perspective: Instruments of Central Government Control," *China Journal*, no. 75 (January 2016), 38–60.

57. See Elizabeth Perry and Mark Selden, eds., *Chinese Society: Change, Conflict and Resistance* (London: Routledge, 2000); Peter H. Gries and Stanley Rosen, eds., *State and Society in 21st Century China: Crisis, Contention and Legitimation* (London: RoutledgeCurzon, 2004); and Jae Ho Chung, Hongyi Lai, and Ming Xia, "Mounting Challenges to Governance in China: Surveying Collective Protestors, Religious Sects and Criminal Organizations," *China Journal*, no. 56 (July 2006): 1–31.

58. See Jae Ho Chung, "Challenging the State: Regulatory Dilemmas and *Falungong* in China," in *Sovereignty Under Challenge: How Governments Respond*, eds. John Montgomery and Nathan Glazer (New Brunswick, N.J.: Transaction, 2002), 83–106; and Eric Harwit, "Spreading Telecommunications to Developing Areas in China: Telephones, the Internet and the Digital Divide," *China Quarterly*, no. 180 (December 2004): 1010–30.

6. DETERMINANTS OF LOCAL DISCRETION
IN IMPLEMENTATION: EXPLORING
POLICY-CONTINGENT VARIATION

1. See Parris Chang, *Power and Policy in China* (University Park: Penn State University Press, 1978); Keith Forster, *Rebellion and Factionalism in a Chinese Province: Zhejiang, 1966–76* (Armonk, N.Y.: M. E. Sharpe, 1990); Dorothy J. Solinger, "Politics in Yunnan Province in the Decade of Disorder: Elite Factional Strategies and Central-Local Relations, 1967–1980," *China Quarterly*, no. 92 (December 1982): 628–62; Frederick C. Tewis, *Leadership, Legitimacy and Conflict in China* (London: Palgrave MacMillan, 1984); and David S. G. Goodman, *Centre and Province in the People's Republic of China: Sichuan and Guizhou, 1955–1965* (Cambridge: Cambridge University Press, 1986). For a summary of their views, see Jae Ho Chung, "Studies of Central–Provincial Relations in the People's Republic of China: A Mid-Term Appraisal," *China Quarterly*, no. 142 (June 1995): 487–490.

2. Yasheng Huang, *Inflation and Investment Controls in China: The Political Economy of Central–Local Relations During the Reform Era* (Cambridge: Cambridge University Press, 1996); Susan Whiting, *Power and Wealth in Rural China; The Political Economy of Institutional Change* (Cambridge: Cambridge University Press, 2000); Sheng Yumin, *Economic Openness and Territorial Politics in China* (Cambridge: Cambridge University Press, 2010); and Pierre

Landry, *Decentralized Authoritarianism in China: The Communist Party's Control of Local Elites in the Post-Mao Era* (Cambridge: Cambridge University Press, 2012).

3. Daniel Kelliher, *Peasant Power in China: The Era of Rural Reform, 1979–1989* (New Haven: Yale University Press, 1992); and Kate Zhou, *How the Farmers Changed China: Power of the People* (Boulder: Westview, 1996).

4. See Yi Chonghua, *Zhongguo difangzhengfu zhuanxing* [Transformation of China's local government] (Beijing: Zhongguo shehuikexue chubanshe, 2008), 29–30.

5. The case of Yang Yichen, the first provincial party secretary of Heilongjiang during the early 1980s, is most notable in this regard. Yang put up fierce resistance to the household responsibility reform during 1980–1982 due to his firm belief that decollectivization was not suitable for the province's schemes of large machinery-based farming. See Jae Ho Chung, *Central Control and Local Discretion in China: Leadership and Implementation During Post-Mao Decollectivization* (Oxford: Oxford University Press), chap. 6.

6. These are called "local collective interests" [*difang qunti liyi*] as opposed to the center's interests or local government interests [*difang zuzhi liyi*]. See Yi Chonghua, *Zhongguo difangzhengfu zhuanxing*, 230–31; and Shen Liren, *Difang zhengfu de jingji zhineng he jingji xingwei* [Economic functions and behavior of local government] (Shanghai: Shanghai yuandong chubanshe, 1998), 133–35.

7. See Andrew G. Walder, "Local Governments as Industrial Firms: An Organizational Analysis of China's Transitional Economy," *American Journal of Sociology* 101, no. 2 (1995): 263–301; Peter Cheung, Jae Ho Chung, and Lin Zhimin, eds., *Provincial Strategies of Economic Reform in Post-Mao China: Leadership, Politics and Implementation* (Armonk, N.Y.: M. E. Sharpe, 1998); and Wang Hua, *Zhongguo difang zhengfu jixiao chaju yanjiu* [Study of performance differentials among China's local governments] (Shanghai: Shanghai shehuikexueyuan chubanshe, 2011), 63–66.

8. See Zhu Guanglei, *Dangdai zhongguo zhengfu guocheng* [Contemporary China's political process] (Tianjin: Tianjin renmin chubanshe, 1997), 372; Liu Haiying, *Difang zhengfu jian caizheng guanxi yanjiu* [Study of fiscal relations between local governments] (Beijing: Zhongguo caizheng jingji chubanshe, 2006), 121; and Zhang Jianping, *Zhongguo quyu kaifa wenti yanjiu* [Study of regional development in China] (Beijing: Zhongguo jingji chubanshe, 2009), 11–12.

9. Kai-yuen Tsui and Youqiang Wang, "Between Separate Stoves and Single Menu: Fiscal Decentralization in China," *China Quarterly*, no. 177 (March 2004): 71–90; and Barry Naughton and Dali L. Yang, eds., *Holding China Together: Diversity and National Integration in the Post-Deng Era* (Cambridge: Cambridge University Press, 2004), chaps. 4, 7, and 8; and Jae Ho Chung, "China's Local Governance in Perspective: Instruments of Central Government Control," *China Journal*, no. 75 (January 2016): 38–62.

10. Case studies of one or a few provinces, of course, must attain key information on such networks in order to explain cross-provincial variations in implementation. See Chung, *Central Control and Local Discretion in China*, chaps. 4–6.

11. Chung, "Studies of Central–Provincial Relations in the People's Republic of China," 487–508; and John Donaldson, *Small Works: Poverty and Economic Development in Southwestern China* (Ithaca: Cornell University Press, 2010), chaps. 3–6.

12. In continent-sized nations like China, the center's capacity for administrative monitoring is limited due to the problem of information asymmetry even in an era of modern technology. At the same time, the central government is generally obliged to treat all local units more or less equally so as to avoid criticisms of regional biases. Therefore, a selective policy with a few targets is generally less standardized and allows more room for local discretion. Max O. Stephenson Jr. and Gerald M. Pops, "Conflict Resolution Method and the Policy Process," *Public Administration Review* 49, no. 5 (1989): 466–67; and Ruth Hoogland DeHoog, "Competition, Negotiation, or Cooperation? Three Alternative Models for Contracting for Services," in *Conflict Resolution and Public Policy*, ed. Miriam K. Mills (New York: Greenwood Press, 1990), 155–76.

13. Susan Barrett and Michael Hill, "Policy, Bargaining and Structure in Implementation," in *New Research in Central-Local Relations*, ed. Michael Goldsmith (Aldershot: Gower, 1986), 50–52.

14. Merilee S. Grindle, "Policy Content and Context in Implementation," in Merilee S. Grindle, *Politics and Policy Implementation in the Third World* (Princeton: Princeton University Press, 1980), 9; and Brian W. Hogwood and Lewis A. Gunn, *Policy Analysis for the Real World* (New York: Oxford University Press, 1984), 206, 213–14.

15. See Kenneth Lieberthal and Michel Oksenberg, *Policy Making in China: Leaders, Structures and Processes* (Princeton: Princeton University Press, 1988), chap. 6; Cheung, Chung, and Lin, eds., *Provincial Strategies of Economic Reform in Post-Mao China*; Jae Ho Chung, "Challenging the State: Regulatory Dilemmas and *Falungong* in China," in *Sovereignty under Challenge: How Governments Respond*, eds. John Montgomery and Nathan Glazer (New Brunswick, N.J.: Transaction, 2002), 83–106; Arthur Kleinman and James L. Watson, eds., *SARS in China* (Stanford: Stanford University Press, 2006), chaps. 3–4; and James W. Tong, *Revenge of the Forbidden City: The Suppression of the Falungong in China* (Oxford: Oxford University Press, 2009).

16. Unlike the totalitarian Maoist period when strict standardization and nationwide single-model imposition were pervasive, the authoritarian post-Mao era has consistently emphasized—if not always acted upon—the principle of implementing according to local conditions [*yindi zhiyi*]. Therefore, to a certain extent, this change produced an effect of reducing the overall number of "encompassing" policies in reality. See Chung, *Central Control and Local Discretion in China*, 40–45; and Sebastian Heilmann, "Policy Experimentation in China's Economic Rise," *Studies in Comparative International Development* 43, no.1 (March 2008): 1–26.

17. This is based on a simple application of value 1 and 0 in accordance with the respective feature of each policy. According to this calculation, the local discretion score for the stability maintenance policy is zero and that for the "Revive the Northeast" scheme is 3, and that for the provinces-directly-ruling-counties

policy is 2, while that for the remaining three—the "Guangdong/Hainan policy," the household responsibility scheme, and the tax-sharing reform—is 1 in each case.

18. See, for instance, David S. G. Goodman, "The Campaign to 'Open Up the West'" and Heike Holbig, "The Emergence of the Campaign to Open Up the West," *China Quarterly*, no. 177 (March 2004): 317–34, 335–57; and Hongyi Lai, "Developing Central China," *China: An International Journal* 5, no. 1 (March 2007): 109–28.

19. Cheng Yang, "Woguo hongguan quyu jingji fazhan zhanlue de lishi yanbian" [Historical evolution of China's macroregional development strategies], *Qiusuo* [Exploration], no. 9 (2004): 15–18.

20. See Li Jingyu, "Dongbei diqu chengzhang wei zhongguo disida jingji zengzhangji de zhanlue sikao" [Strategic thinking toward making Northeast China's fourth economic engine], *Jingji yanjiu cankao* [Reference materials for economic research], no. 6 (2004): 31–32; and Liu Jian and Cheng Rui, "Tongchou quyu fazhan zhanlue de siwei shihuo" [Thoughts on the centrally coordinated regional development strategies], *Dangdai caijing* [Contemporary finance and economy], no. 2 (2005): 98–99.

21. See Danny Schechter, *Falun Gong's Challenge to China* (New York: Akashic Books, 2000), chap. 5; and interviews at the State Council Office for Reviving the Northeast, November 23, 2004.

22. See "Sanzhong quanhui de buxieyin" [Discords at the Third Plenum of the 15th Central Committee], *Zhengming* [Contend], November 1998, 14–16; and Ning Yi and Dong Ning, *Dongbei zhazheng—Dongbei wenti baogao* [How to fix the Northeast: Report on the Northeast problem] (Beijing: Dangdai shijie chubanshe, 2004), 42–43.

23. Tan Ailing, "Dongbei zhenxing guoce chutai qianhou" [The stories behind the launch of the "Revive the Northeast" scheme], *Ershiyi shiji jingji daobao* [Twenty-first-century economic herald] August 13, 2003; and Xia Wensi, "Hu Jintao zhuazhu dongbei daji Shanghaibang" [Hu Jintao grasps the Northeast and strikes the Shanghai gang], *Kaifang* [Open], November 2003, 18–19.

24. See "Guanyu shishi dongbei diqu deng laogongye jidi zhenxing zhanlue de ruogan yijian" [Certain opinions regarding implementing the strategies of reviving the old industrial bases including the Northeast; hereafter certain opinions], *Zhongfa* (2003), no. 11, part XII; and interviews in Beijing in February 2006.

25. "Zhang Guobao zai guoxinban jizhehui shang de jianghua" [Zhang Guobao's speech at the press conference held by the state council's information office], *Xinhuawang*, March 2, 2005, http://news.xinhuanet.com/2005-03/02/content_2638389.htm (last accessed on October 17, 2005).

26. They included (1) accelerating ownership reforms and separating welfare provision from enterprise management, (2) rationalizing state-owned industrial sectors (e.g., downsizing the primary sectors like mining), and (3) expanding the share of non-state economy in the region. See "Certain Opinions," especially parts III, IV, VI, VII, and XI; and "Dui Zhonggong zhenxing dongbei laogongye jidi zhanlue zhi fenxi" [An analysis of the CCP's strategy of reviving

Northeastern old industrial bases], *Zhonggong yanjiu* [Studies of Chinese communism], October 2003, 51.

27. See Zhang Guohong, "Waishang zhijie touzi yu jingji zengzhang—jianlun dongbei laogongye jidi zhenxing zhong liyong waizi wenti" [Foreign direct investment and economic growth—In the context of reviving the Northeast old industrial base"], *Xueshu jiaoliu* [Scholarly exchange], July 2005: 83–84.

28. See Sun Shiqiang, "Wajue guojia zhengce xiaoying zhenxing dongbei jingji de zhanlue fenxi" [An analysis of strategies for utilizing the national policy of "reviving the Northeast"], *Qianyan* [Front], no. 6 (2004): 43; and "Luoshi zhenxing dongbei laogongye jidi qiye suodeshui youhui zhengce chutai" [Favorable enterprise income tax policies for materializing the revival of Northeastern old industrial bases are revealed], October 9, 2004, http://www .XINHUANET.com (accessed on February 4, 2006).

29. The winner was Liaoning, which got fifty-two of the one hundred projects approved by Beijing. It should be noted that the shipbuilding sector could not be claimed by landlocked Heilongjiang and Jilin.

30. Jae Ho Chung, Hongyi Lai, and Jang-Hwan Joo, "Assessing the 'Revive the Northeast' Program: Origins, Policies and Implementation," *China Quarterly*, no. 197 (March 2009): 108–25; and Guowuyuan zhenxing dongbei diqu deng laogongye jidi lingdao xiaozu bangongshi, ed., *Zhenxing dongbei diqu deng laogongye jidi 2004niandu baogao* [The 2004 report on the scheme of "reviving the Northeast and old industrial bases"] (Beijing: Zhongguo caizheng jingji chubanshe, 2005), 95, 116–17, 129.

31. Guowuyuan zhenxing dongbei diqu deng laogongye jidi lingdao xiaozu bangongshi, ed., *Zhenxing dongbei diqu deng laogongye jidi 2004niandu baogao*, 103–4, 120, 131.

32. For the Hainanese desire to set up an independent province, see Feng Chongyi and David S. G. Goodman, "Hainan Province in Reform: Political Dependence and Economic Interdependence," in *Provincial Strategies of Economic Reform in Post-Mao China*, eds. Peter Cheung, Jae Ho Chung, and Lin Zhimin (Armonk, N.Y.: M.E. Sharpe, 1998), 344.

33. One thing remains unclear, though, as to whether, at that early point, Beijing was already thinking of Hainan in terms of the South China Sea and related maritime strategic issues.

34. See Feng Chongyi and David S. G. Goodman, "Hainan: Communal Politics and the Struggle for Identity," in *China's Provinces in Reform: Class, Community and Political Culture*, ed. David S. G. Goodman (London: Routledge, 1997), 60.

35. On this notorious scandal, see Richard Baum, *Burying Mao: Chinese Politics in the Age of Deng Xiaoping* (Princeton: Princeton University Press, 1994), 168, 175.

36. Feng and Goodman, "Hainan," 61; and "Guowuyuan pizhuan <Guanyu Hainandao jinyibu duiwai kaifang jiakuai jingji kaifa jianshe de zuotanhui jiyao> de tongzhi" [State council approves the circular on the summary of the discussion meeting on further opening Hainan and accelerating economic construction there], April 14, 1988: *Guofa* (1988), no. 24 in Guowuyuan tequ

bangongshi, ed., *Zhongguo duiwai kaifang zhinan—Dang he zhengfu duiwai kaifang wenjian xuanbian* [Guide to China's opening—Collection of party and government documents on opening] (Kunming: Yunnan renmin chubanshe, 1992), 65.

37. For the institutional evolution in this sector, see Jae Ho Chung, "Beijing Confronting the Provinces: The 1994 'Tax-Sharing Reform' and Implications for Central-Provincial Relations," *China Information* 9, no. 2/3 (1994): 1–23; and Tsui and Wang, "Between Separate Stoves and a Single Menu," 71–90.

38. Shaun Breslin, *China in the 1980s: Centre-Province Relations in a Reforming Socialist State* (London: MacMillan, 1996), chap. 4.

39. Sixteen budget-deficit provinces (including eight ethnic minority and border provinces) were given fixed central subsidies, and fixed-sum transfer arrangements were granted to three fiscal-surplus provinces of Shandong, Heilongjiang, and Shanghai. Hebei, Liaoning, Beijing, Jiangsu, Zhejiang, and Henan were to increase their contracted baseline figures at a rate ranging from 3.6 to 6.5 percent per annum while enjoying a 100 percent marginal retention rate. Anhui, Tianjin, and Shanxi would continue with a system of overall revenue sharing. Guangdong and Hunan were to progressively increase their remittances according to the stipulated rate of 9 and 7 percent per annum, respectively.

40. EBFs are the revenues that fall outside the purview of the state budget and collected by local governments according to some set rules. Although three-fourths (76.4 percent) of EBFs resided with enterprises in 1991, local governments easily tapped enterprise funds by imposing levies or by shifting administrative costs to enterprises under their control. See Yu Tianxin, "Guipin he shudao yusanwai zijin de gaigeshi zai bixing" [The reform of merging and channeling the extra-budgetary funds is inevitable], *Jingji yanjiu cankao* [Reference for economic research], no. 417 (May 7, 1994): 30–31.

41. Song Xinzhong, *Zhongguo caizheng tizhi gaige yanjiu* [A study of China's fiscal reform] (Beijing: Zhongguo caizheng jingji chubanshe, 1992), 63, 65, 68–70; and Yang Zhiyong, "Fenshuizhi gaige shi zhenyang kaishide" [How did the tax-sharing reform come about?], *Difang caizheng yanjiu* [Studies of local finance], no. 10 (2013): 5–7.

42. For the 1993 budget report, see "China's Finance Minister Hints at Dangers Ahead," *Far Eastern Economic Review*, March 24, 1994, 48.

43. The reform stipulated that the value-added tax was to be imposed on the entire process of commodity production as well as its circulation, and that it was to be shared between the central and provincial governments in the ratio of 7.5 and 2.5 rather than half and half. See "Guowuyuan guanyu shixing fenshuizhi caizheng guanli tizhi de jueding" [State council's decision on implementing the "tax-sharing" system], State Council Document no. 85, issued on December 15, 1993, in *Caizheng* [Finance], no. 2 (1994): 19.

44. Foreign-funded and foreign wholly owned enterprises were already enjoying this favorable rate, although certain enterprises in the Special Economic Zones and Economic and Technological Development Zones enjoyed a rate as low as 15 percent.

45. See *Renmin ribao*, November 23, 1993; *Ming Pao*, March 14, 1994; and Cao Bolong, "Mingnian shixing de xinshuizhi yu xianxing shuizhi de bijiao fenxi" [A comparative analysis of the current tax system and the tax-sharing system] in *Hebei caihui*, reprinted in *Baokan soyin ziliao: caizheng yu shuiwu* [Newspaper index materials: Fiscal and tax matters], no. 2 (1994): 50–51.

46. "Caizhengtingzhang tan fenshuizhi gaige" [Fiscal bureau chiefs discuss the tax-sharing reform] in *Caizheng*, no. 2 (1994): 11–13; "Shengqu dangzheng lingdao tan caishui gaige" [Provincial leaders discuss the fiscal and tax reform] in *Caizheng*, no. 4 (1994): 2–3; *Ming Pao*, March 15, 1994; and *Wenwei Po*, February 3 and March 21, 1994; and "Shixing fenshuizhi difang caizheng zenmoban" [What about local finance after the tax-sharing reform?], *Caizheng yanjiu*, no. 7 (1994): 47.

47. In the case of Guizhou and Yunnan, 92 and 60 percent, respectively, of the marginal increase in the provincial tax revenues were to be remitted to the center. See *Ming Pao*, March 14, 1994; and *Wenwei Po*, March 22, 1994.

48. *Jinrong shibao* [Financial times], December 6, 1993.

49. See the issue of March 21, 1994.

50. Provinces sarcastically branded Beijing's stance as "iron-fist policy" [*tie-wan zhengce*], "when persuasion fails, imposition predominates" [*shuobufu jiu-yafu*], and "a big stone crushing small crabs to death" [*dashi yasi xie*].

51. Xiang Huaicheng, *Jiushiniandai caizheng fazhan zhanlue* [Strategies of developing China's finance] (Beijing: Zhongguo caizheng jingji chubanshe, 1991), 16; and *South China Morning Post*, December 20, 1993.

52. See State Council Documents no. 85, 19; *Wenwei Po*, February 3, 1994; and Ning Xueping, "Ping caishui tizhi gaige fang'an" [Commentary on the fiscal and tax reform measures] in *Gaige* [Reform], no. 2 (1994) reprinted in *Baokan soyin ziliao: Caizheng yu shuiwu*, no. 4 (1994): 60.

53. For the swift process of nationwide implementation, see *Renmin ribao*, December 13, 1993; and *Guangming ribao*, March 21, 1994.

54. See chapter 2 of this volume.

55. The repeated failures during the 1980s might have prompted Beijing to be much more assertive and demanding than it would have otherwise. For fears that the whole reform might repeat the failures of the 1980s, see "Fenshuizhi yu difang zhuli" [The tax-sharing reform encounters local opposition], *Guangji-aojing* [Wide angle], January 1994, 11.

56. The full name of the policy was initially *caizheng sheng zhiguan xian*, often abbreviated as *sheng zhiguan xian*.

57. For the problems with the cities-ruling-counties scheme as a source of the new policy, see Pan Xiaojuan, "Guanyu tuixing sheng zhiguan xian gaige de diaocha he sikao" [Research and thoughts on promoting the reform of provinces directly ruling counties], *Tizhi gaige*, no. 7 (2012): 66–67.

58. The Ministry of Civil Affairs, ed., *Zhonghua renmin gongheguo xingzheng quhua jiance 2001* [Quick guide to administrative zoning in the People's Republic of China 2001] (Beijing: Zhongguo ditu chubanshe, 2001), 1; and Chris Chien, "Prefectures," in *China's Local Administration: Traditions and Changes in the Sub-national Hierarchy*, eds. Jae Ho Chung and Tao-chiu Lam (London: Routledge, 2010), 128.

59. Item 24 of Part 6 in "Zhonggong zhongyang guowuyuan guanyu tuijin shehuizhuyi xinnongcun jianshe de ruogan yijian" [Opinions of the party center and the state council on the construction of a socialist new countryside], Central Document [2006] no. 1; and item 26 of "Zhonggong zhongyang guowuyuan guanyu 2009nian cuin nongye wending fazhan nongmin chixu zengshou de ruogan yijian" [Opinions of the party center and the state council on promoting stable rural development and increasing agricultural production], Central Document [2009] no. 1.

60. See Zhongguo guanlixue yanjiuyuan, ed., *Zhongguo zhengfu cengji yu quhua gaige* [Reforming the levels and boundaries of the Chinese government] (Beijing: November 30, 2005); and Zhou Xiangzhi, "Woguo sheng zhiguan xian yanjiu zhong de jige wenti" [Some questions regarding the research on China's provinces-directly-ruling-counties policy], *Tizhi gaige*, no. 3 (2010): 22–24.

61. Due to the multiple (some mixed) modes of the scheme, different figures are available for the same periods/provinces, but no sources refer to the completion of nationwide implementation. Yang Zhiying, "Caizheng de sheng zhiguan xian gaige buyi yidaoqie" [The policy of provinces directly ruling counties in finance should not be standardized for every locality], *Lingdao canyue*, no. 11 (2012): 13–17.

62. Hong Xiaojing, "Sheng zhiguan xian: kaoyan zhengfu zhihui" [The provinces-directly-ruling-counties policy: Testing the government's wisdom], *Gaige neican*, no. 18 (2010): 8.

63. Sun Xueyu, *Chuizhi quanli fenhe—Shengzhiguanzhi tizhi yanjiu* [Vertical power division—A study of the province-leading-county policy] (Beijing: Renmin chubanshe, 2013): 141–54.

64. Meng Bai, "Sheng zhiguan xian shidian zhong de wenti yu duice—Yi henan sheng wei li" [Problems of and solutions for the experimental sites for the provinces-leading-counties policy—The case of Henan], *Lilun dongtai*, no. 1942 (November 30, 2012): 20–22.

65. See Wang Zhanyang, "Dabuding jiaju shengxian shikong" [A supplementary measure may actually cause the loss of control over counties]; Xiong Wenzhao, "Sheng zhiguan xian xuyao tongpan guihua" [The provinces-leading-counties policy needs an across-the-board planning], *Gaige neican*, no. 18 (2010): 1–4, 5; and Xiao Qingwen, "Shengguanxian tizhi gaige de zhengfu xingwei chayi yu tuijin celue xuanze" [Variations in government behavior of implementing the provinces-directly-ruling-counties reform and means to promote the reform], *Tizhi gaige*, no. 11 (2011): 23–24.

66. Pan Xiaojuan, "Guanyu tuixing sheng zhiguan xian gaige de diaocha he sikao," 65.

67. The compliance rate (the number of production teams under the new household-based systems divided by the total number of teams in China) was 1.0 percent in January 1980 and 98.3 percent in December 1983. See Guo Shutian, *Zhongguo nongcun gaige yu fazhan shinian* [Ten years of rural reform and development in China] (Beijing: Nongye chubanshe, 1990), 7, 10.

68. Exceptions were allowed for three situations: (1) those engaged in special sideline occupations; (2) areas that were peripheral, distant, and mountainous;

and (3) single households living in isolation due to transportation difficulties. See *Zhongguo nongye nianjian 1980* [China agricultural yearbook 1980] (Beijing: Nongye chubanshe, 1981), 56–62.

69. See Lu Xueyi, *Lianchan chengbao zerenzhi yanjiu* [Study of production-linked responsibility systems] (Shanghai: Shanghai renmin chubanshe, 1986), 80; and Jae Ho Chung, *Central Control and Local Discretion in China: Leadership and Implementation During Post-Mao Decollectivization* (Oxford: Oxford University Press, 2000), chaps. 3–4.

70. Xiang Xiyang and Shen Chong, eds., *Shinianlai lilun zhengce shijian—Ziliao xuanbian* [Theory, policy, and implementation in last ten years—Select materials] (Beijing: Qiushi chubanshe, 1988), 2:36.

71. *Renmin ribao*, August 4, 1981.

72. For the early experiments of the 1960s, see Wang Gengjin et al., *Xiangcun sanshinian: Fengyang nongcun shehui jingji fazhan shilu* [Thirty years in the countryside: Records of social economic development in Fengyang county] (Beijing: Nongcun duwu chubanshe, 1989), 272–365.

73. Chung, *Central Control and Local Discretion in China*, 64–65. Also see Chen Guanren, *17gesheng zizhiqu he zhixiashi gaige qidong jishi* [Chronicles of initiating reforms in seventeen provinces, autonomous regions and centrally administered cities] (Beijing: Zhonggong dangshi chubanshe, 2009), chap. 2.

74. Jae Ho Chung, "The Politics of Agricultural Mechanization in the Post-Mao Era, 1977–1987," *China Quarterly*, no. 134 (June 1993): 284–88; and Chung, *Central Control and Local Discretion in China*, 71–76, 128.

75. *Heilongjiang ribao* [Heilongjiang daily], August 16, 1981.

76. *Heilongjiang ribao*, January 29, 1982; and "Zhengque renshi nongye jitijingji de youyuexing' [Correctly recognize the advantages of the collective economy in agriculture], *Fendou* [Struggle], March 1982, 18–19.

77. *Nongmin bao* [Peasant daily], March 22, 1983; *Liaoning jingji tongji nianjian 1984* [Liaoning economic statistical yearbook 1984] (Shenyang: Liaoning renmin chubanshe, 1984), III-63; and *Dangdai zhongguo de Jilin* [Contemporary China's Jilin] (Beijing: Dangdai zhongguo chubanshe, 1991), 182–84.

78. Information from the author's interviews in Beijing and Harbin in July 1994.

79. *Renmin ribao*, October 20, 1982.

80. The speech was delivered in November but published in *Renmin ribao*, December 23, 1982.

81. *Heilongjiang ribao*, December 25, 1982.

82. Chung, *Central Control and Local Discretion in China*, 161–62.

83. See Li Liangdong and Hou Shaowen, *Wending: Yadao yiqie de daju* [Stability: The foremost goal that overrides everything else] (Beijing: Zhongyang dangxiao chubanshe, 1999); and Chen Peixiao and Xia Liping, eds., *Xinshiji jiyuqi yu zhongguo guoji zhanlue* [Opportunities of the new century and China's international strategies] (Beijing: Shishi chubanshe, 2004).

84. Although the term "accidental incidents" [*tufa shijian*] is often used interchangeably with collective protests, the former is a broader concept that

encompasses natural disasters, industrial accidents, endemics/pandemics, environmental catastrophes, and terrorist attacks, as well as collective protests. See the Writing Team, ed., *Yingdui tufa shijian* [Coping with accidental incidents] (Beijing: Xinhua chubanshe, 2008), i, 1. For Chinese glossary that refers to collective protests, see The Task Force Team, ed., *Zhongguo quntixing tufa shijian—Chengyin ji duice* [Collective and accidental incidents in China—Reasons and responses] (Beijing: Guojia xingzheng xueyuan chubanshe, 2009), 2.

85. See Hu Lianhe et al., *Dangdai zhongguo shehui wending wenti* [Problems of social stability in contemporary China] (Beijing: Hongqi chubanshe, 2009), 57, 139.

86. This is the data reportedly released by the Central Commission on the Comprehensive Management of Public Security (*Zhongyang shehui zhian zonghe zhili weiyuanhui*). See http://www.renminbao.com/rmb/articles/2004/6/21/3157.html (last accessed on July 7, 2004).

87. See the Task Force Team, "Jingji jiegou tiaozhengqi quntixing shijian fazhan qushi tezheng ye yufang" [The development, characteristics and prevention of collective protests during the period of economic structural adjustment], *Lilun dongtai*, no. 1853 (June 10, 2010): 2.

88. Although the average annual occurrence of large-scale protests was 15.8 for 2003–2006, that for 2007–2009 rose to 61.7. Tong Yanqi and Lei Shaohua, "Large-Scale Mass Incidents in China," *East Asian Policy* (April–June 2010): 24.

89. Zhang Wancheng, *Nongcun zhian yu goujian hexie shehui* [Public security and the construction of harmonious society in the countryside] (Beijing: Zhongguo renmin gongan daxue chubanshe, 2008), 259–60.

90. The Task Force Team, ed., *Zhongguo quntixing tufa shijian*, 272–76, 299–313; "China Issues Statute on 'Large-Scale Mass Activities,'" *Xinhua*, September 21, 2007, http://news.xinhuanet.com/english/2007-09/21/content_766524.htm; Jiang Xun, "Zhonggong miandui guanzhi weiji" [China faces a governance crisis], *Yazhou zhoukan*, December 23, 2007, 32; and The Writing Team, *Yingdui tufa shijian*, Appendix 1, 184–85.

91. Guojia jihua weiyuanhui hongguan jingji yanjiuyuan, *Woguo shehui xingshi genzong fenxi yu duice yanjiu* [In-depth analysis of China's social conditions and measures] (Beijing: Macroeconomic Research Institute, December 2000), 97.

92. Jae Ho Chung, Hongyi Lai, and Ming Xia, "Mounting Challenges to Governance in China: Surveying Collective Protestors, Religious Sects and Criminal Organizations," *China Journal*, no. 56 (July 2006): 21; and Tong and Lei, "Large-Scale Mass Incidents in China," 24.

93. "Erlingyaoer nian quntixing shijian yanjiu baogao" [The 2012 study report on collective protests], 2, posted on December 27, 2012, on *Fazhiwang*, http://legaldaily.com.cn.

94. Not only have the reasons for collective protests diversified—social conflicts (24.4 percent), land misappropriation (22.2 percent), clashes between the police and people (22.2 percent), clashes between officials and people (13.3 percent), environmental issues (8.9 percent)—but also both city dwellers

(51.1 percent) and peasants (46.7 percent) actively took part in them. See "Erlingyaoer nian quntixing shijian yanjiu baogao," 3, 5.

95. Generally, the government regulations stress two seemingly contradictory principles: quick reaction [*kuaishu fanying*] versus careful use of force [*chenyong jingli*], as well as efficiency [*xiaolu*] versus legality [*hefaxing*]. See Kong Lingdong and Ma Ben, eds., *Tufa gonggong shijian yingji guanli* [Emergency management of public incidents] (Jinan: Shandong daxue chubanshe, 2009), 237–38; and Zhang Lianbo and Ren Xiaodong, eds., *Difang zhengfu yingji guanli* [Emergency management by local governments] (Dalian: Dalian ligong daxue chubanshe, 2009), 112–13.

96. See The Task Force Team of Qinghua University, "Weiwen zhiduhua zhuangui zhong de fengxian yingdui" [Coping with the risk of carrying out the task of institutionalizing the maintenance of stability], *Gaige neican*, no. 15 (2010): 13.

97. See Liu Zhenhua, *Nongcun diqu shehui zhian fangkong tixi yanjiu* [Study of the public security and control system in the rural society] (Beijing: Zhongguo renmin gongan daxue, 2008), 44.

98. See Zhan Wancheng, *Nongcun zhian yu goujian hexie shehui*, 254; and Guan Wujun, "Tianjia weiwen bushi changjiu zhi ji" [Maintaining stability at whatever cost is not a reasonable option), *Gaige neican*, no. 15 (2010): 7.

99. Zhan Wancheng, *Nongcun zhian yu goujian hexie shehui*, 23–25; and Liu Zhenhua, *Nongcun diqu shehui zhian fangkong tixi yanjiu*, 46, 49.

100. See Andrew Jacobs and Jonathan Ansfield, "Well-Oiled Security Apparatus in China Stifles Calls for Change," *New York Times*, March 1, 2011; "China's Internal Security Spending Jumps Past Army Budget," *Reuters*, March 5, 2011; and "China Riot Informers Promised Cash and Residency for Tipoffs," *Guardian*, June 20, 2011.

101. The Task Force Team, ed., *Zhongguo quntixing tufa shijian*, 55, 77, 81, 96, 107; "Zhiyao yinfa quntixing shijian jiu mianzhi" [Causing a collective protest is a cause of dismissal], *Lingdao juece xinxi*, no. 2 (November 2006): 14; and *South China Morning Post*, July 14, 2009.

102. See Chung, "Challenging the State: Falungong and Regulatory Dilemmas in China," 83–106; Maria Hsia Chang, *Falungong: The End of Days* (New Haven: Yale University Press, 2004); and Tong, *Revenge of the Forbidden City*, chaps. 6 and 8.

103. See Koan Kaufman, "SARS and China's Health-Care Response: Better to be Both Red and Expert" and Tony Saich, "Is SARS China's Chernobyl or Much Ado about Nothing?" in *SARS in China*, eds. Arthur Kleinman and James L. Watson (Stanford: Stanford University Press, 2006), 62–68, 73–84. Also see Hongyi Lai, "Managing Pandemic/Epidemic Crises: Institutional Setup and Overhaul," in *China's Crisis Management*, ed. Jae Ho Chung (London: Routledge, 2011), chap. 5.

104. For a full-page report on the provinces' swift compliance with Beijing's efforts to track down and repatriate corruption- and bribery-related criminals, see Jiang Jie, "Zhuitao zhuizong: Sheng yiji zhengfali" [Pursuing criminals: Provinces are in full gear], *Renmin ribao*, May 5, 2015.

7. THE POLITICAL ECONOMY OF VERTICAL SUPPORT AND HORIZONTAL NETWORKS

1. John Williamson, ed., *Economic Consequences of Soviet Disintegration* (Washington, D.C.: Institute for International Economics, 1993), chaps. 4 and 5; and Gernot Grabher and David Stark, eds., *Restructuring Networks in Post-Socialism: Legacies, Linkages, and Localities* (Oxford: Oxford University Press, 1997).

2. For local protectionism and market fragmentation in China, see Chen Dongqi et al., *Dapuo difang sichang fenge* [Breaking the fragmented local markets] (Beijing: Zhongguo jihua chubanshe, 2002), chaps. 2, 5; Andrew Wedeman, *From Mao to Market: Rent-Seeking, Local Protectionism, and Marketization in China* (New York: Cambridge University Press, 2009), chaps. 3–5; Yu Dongshan, *Zhuanxingqi Zhongguo difang zhengfu jingzheng yanjiu* [Study of competition between local governments in China] (Shenyang: Dongbei daxue chubanshe, 2012), 51–59; and Wang Junmin, *State–Market Interactions in China's Reform Era: Local State Competition and Global Market Building in the Tobacco Industry* (London: Routledge, 2013), chap. 3.

3. Benjamin Higgins and Donald J. Savoie, *Regional Development Theories and Their Application* (New Brunswick, N.J.: Transaction, 1997), chaps. 2, 5, 8; and Liu Peilin, "Difang baohuzhuyi he shichang fenge de shunshi" [Local protectionism and the loss inflicted by market fragmentation], *Zhongguo gongye jingji* [China's industrial economy], no. 4 (2005).

4. See Richard J. Samuels, *The Politics of Regional Policy in Japan: Localities Incorporated?* (Princeton: Princeton University Press, 1983), 9–17; Gernot Grabher, ed., *The Embedded Firm: On the Socioeconomics of Industrial Networks* (London: Routledge, 1993); and Anna Lee Saxenian, *Regional Advantage: Culture and Competition in Silicon Valley and Route 128* (Cambridge, Mass.: Harvard University Press, 1994).

5. Beijing's concern for regional disparities was largely a political gesture during the 1980s. No explicit concern as such was expressed in Zhao Ziyang's speech at the National People's Congress in May 1984. The 7th Five-Year Plan for 1986–1990 had the development of the eastern region as its key priority, although Beijing did consider some support for "old, minorities, border, and poor" regions. See *Zhengfu gongzuo baogao* [Government work report] (Hong Kong: Sanlian, 1984), 15–16; and *Zhonghua renmin gongheguo guomin jingji he shehui fazhan diqige wunian jihua 1986–90* [The 7th Five-Year Plan for the national economic and social development in the PRC] (Beijing: Renmin chubanshe, 1986), 91–108.

6. See *Guanyu guomin jingji he shehui fazhan jiuwu jihua he 2010nian yuanjing mubiao gangyao de baogao* [Report on the 9th Five-Year Plan for the national economic and social development and the long-term goals for 2010] (Beijing: Renmin chubanshe, 1996), 21–22, 99–103; and Xu Guodi, "Shiwu he zhi 2020nian woguo diqu jingji xietiao fazhan jiben silu yanjiu" [Study of the principal path toward a regionally coordinated economic development for the 10th Five-Year Plan and 2020], *Jingji yanjiu cankao* [References for economic research], no. 1282 (May 4, 1999): 2–13.

7. David S. G. Goodman, "The Campaign to 'Open Up the West'" and Heike Holbig, "The Emergence of the Campaign to Open Up the West," *The China Quarterly,* no. 177 (March 2004): 317–34, 335–57; Hongyi Lai, "Developing Central China," *China: An International Journal* 5, no. 1 (March 2007): 109–28; and Jae Ho Chung, Hongyi Lai, and Jang-Hwan Joo, "Assessing the 'Revive the Northeast' Program: Origins, Policies and Implementation," *China Quarterly,* no. 197 (March 2009): 108–25.

8. In the case of the fourth option, it is imperative for the center to "allow" these voluntarily formed networks to exist (i.e., survive).

9. For these measures of vertical resource support, see Jae Ho Chung, "Regional Disparities, Policy Choices, and State Capacity in China," *China Perspectives,* no. 31 (September–October 2000): 37–41.

10. See Jeffrey J. Anderson, *The Territorial Imperative: Pluralism, Corporatism, and Economic Crisis* (Cambridge: Cambridge University Press, 1992), 61–97.

11. Such Chinese terms as "economic stimuli" [*jingji ciji*], "direct control" [*zhijie kongzhi*], and "public location" [*gonggong quwei*] belong to the domain of vertical policy support. See Chen Yao, *Guojia zhongxibu fazhan zhengce yanjiu* [Study of China's policy of developing the central and western regions] (Beijing: Jingji guanli chubanshe, 2000), 74–77.

12. For such variations, see Peter T. Y. Cheung, Jae Ho Chung, and Zhimin Lin, eds., *Provincial Strategies of Economic Reform in Post-Mao China* (Armonk, N.Y.: M. E. Sharpe, 1998); and Jae Ho Chung, ed., *Cities in China: Recipes for Economic Development in the Reform Era* (London: Routledge, 1999).

13. See Gary Miller, *Managerial Dilemma: The Political Economy of Hierarchy* (Cambridge: Cambridge University Press, 1992), chaps. 4–6.

14. This type is popularly found in many federal systems. See, for instance, Robert Agranoff and Michael McGuire, *Collaborative Public Management: New Strategies for Local Government* (Washington, D.C.: Georgetown University Press, 2003); and Ann O'M. Bowman, "Horizontal Federalism: Exploring Interstate Interactions," *Journal of Public Administration Research and Theory,* 14, no. 4 (2004): 535–46.

15. See Chris Pickvance, "Mediating Institutions in the Transition from State Socialism: The Case of Local Government," in *Restructuring Networks in Post-Socialism: Legacies, Linkages, and Localities,* eds. Gernot Grabher and David Stark (Oxford: Oxford University Press, 1997), 305–23.

16. In reality, any regime at one point relies on multiple alternatives, but the relative weight to each may vary as the center's capacity changes over time. See Anderson, *The Territorial Imperative,* 62–65, 81–83.

17. Wei Wei, *Zhongguo jingji fazhanzhong de quyu chadao yu quyu xietiao* [Regional disparities and coordination in China's economic development] (Hefei: Anhui renmin chubanshe, 1995), 75.

18. Development Research Center of the State Council, *Zhongguo quyu xietiao fazhan zhanlue* [Strategies for China's coordinated regional development] (Beijing: Zhongguo jingji chubanshe, 1994), 16–17.

19. Despite the "self-reliance" rhetoric, quite a large portion of funds was actually provided by the central government to support local economic

development. See Christine P. W. Wong, "The Maoist Model Reconsidered: Local Self-Reliance and the Financing of Rural Industrialization," in *New Perspectives on the Cultural Revolution*, eds. William Joseph, Christine P. W. Wong, and David Zweig (Cambridge, Mass.: Harvard University Press, 1991), 183–96.

20. Chinese sources note that Beijing sought to establish interregional networks on three occasions in 1954, 1961, and 1970. See Zhang Wanqing, *Quyu hezuo yu jingji wangluo* [Interregional cooperation and economic networks] (Beijing: Jingji kexue chubanshe, 1987), 26. For the geographical limitations of "lateral exchanges" even in the early years of the reform era, see Dorothy J. Solinger, "Urban Reform and Relational Contracting in Post-Mao China," in *China's Transition from Socialism: Statist Legacies and Market Reforms 1980–1990* (Armonk, N.Y.: M. E. Sharpe, 1993), 119.

21. Thomas Lyons, *Economic Integration and Planning in Communist China* (New York: Columbia University Press, 1987), 51, 174.

22. For Beijing's near-total control over fiscal and material resources allocation during the pre-reform era, see Michel Oksenberg and James Tong, "The Evolution of Central–Provincial Fiscal Relations in China, 1971–1984: The Formal System," *China Quarterly*, no. 125 (March 1991): 1–12; and Penelope B. Prime, "Central-Provincial Investment and Finance: The Cultural Revolution and Its Legacy in Jiangsu Province," in *New Perspectives on the Cultural Revolution*, eds. Joseph, Wong, and Zweig, 197–215.

23. Wu Zhe, *Qingxie de guotu: Zhongguo quyu jingji bupingheng fazhan de xianshi yu qushi* [Uneven regional economic development in China: Realities and trends] (Beijing: Zhongguo jingji chubanshe, 1995), 101.

24. See Sang Baichuan, *Quyu kaifang zhanlue lun: Qingxie zhengce yu quanfangwei kaifang* [On the strategy of regional opening—Discriminate policies and omnidirectional opening] (Beijing: Zhongguo qingnian chubanshe, 1996), 40–50; and Chen Dongsheng, *Kuashiji de zhongguo quyu fazhan* [Regional development for the next century] (Beijing: Jingji guanli chubanshe, 1999), 203–4.

25. See Woo Tun-oy, "Regional Economic Development and Disparities," *China Review 1996* (Hong Kong: Chinese University Press, 1996), 283–84; and Wang Shaoguang and Hu Angang, *The Political Economy of Uneven Development: The Case of China* (Armonk, N.Y.: M. E. Sharpe, 1999), 42–50.

26. See Barry Naughton, "The Decline of Central Control over Investment in Post-Mao China," in *Policy Implementation in Post-Mao China*, ed. David M. Lampton (Berkeley: University of California Press, 1987), 76–77.

27. *Zhongguo tongji nianjian 1996* [Statistical yearbook of China 1996] (Beijing: Zhongguo tongji chubanshe, 1996), 22–23, 223.

28. Ding Xianjiao, "Jiben jianshe touzi lingyu de fazhan yu biange" [Development and changes in the realm of basic construction investment], *Zhongguo caizheng* [China's finance], October 1999, 11–12; and *Zhongguo tongji nianjian 2000*, 167.

29. *Dangdai zhongguo caizheng* [Contemporary China's finance] (Beijing: Zhongguo shehui kexue chubanshe, 1988), 1:309–11; author's interviews in Beijing in July 2004; and Barry Naughton, *The Chinese Economy: Transitions and Growth* (Cambridge, Mass.: MIT Press, 2006), chap. 4.

30. Gui Shiyong, ed., *Zhongguo jihua tizhi gaige* [Reform of China's plan system] (Beijing: Zhongguo caizheng jingji chubanshe, 1994), 9, 10, 60; *Dangdai zhongguo de wuzi liutong* [Contemporary China's materials allocation] (Beijing: Zhongguo shehuikexue chubanshe, 1993), 103–4; Lu Jiang, *Neimao daili chutan* [A preliminary discussion of the internal trade agency system] (Beijing: Zhongguo wuzi chubanshe, 1995), 17–23, 45–49; and Wu Shaojun, *Guojia fazhan jihua gailun* [Introduction to state development planning] (Beijing: Zhongguo renmin daxue chubanshe, 1999), 84–87.

31. See "Learning the Rules of Foreign Trade," *China News Analysis*, no. 1464 (July 15, 1992): 1–9.

32. *Zhongguo duiwai kaifang diqu touzi huanjing he zhengce* [Investment environments and policies for China's open areas] (Beijing: Yunnan renmin chubanshe, 1993), 184, 217; Liu Baorong and Liao Jiasheng, eds., *Zhongguo yanbian kaifang yu zhoubian guojia shichang* [The opening of China's border areas and the neighboring markets] (Beijing: Falu chubanshe, 1993); and Tang Renwu and Ma Ji, eds., *Zhongguo jingji gaige 30nian—Duiwaikaifang juan* [Thirty years of China's economic reforms—Volume on opening, 1978–2008] (Chongqing: Chongqing daxue chubanshe, 2008), 65–67.

33. The comeback of Beijing's vertical resource support in the 2000s is discussed in a later section.

34. See *Jingji ribao* [Economic daily], March 12, 1986; and *Renmin ribao* [People's daily], August 6, 1989.

35. *World Tibet Network News*, September 21, 1994; and *Liaowang* [Outlook], no. 558 (September 26, 1994): 14–23.

36. Interviews in Jinan, Qingdao, and Dalian in July 1997 and June 1999; and Shandong Provincial Leadership Small Group on Aiding the Three Gorges Dam Region, "Guanyu duikou zhiyuan sanxia kuqu yimin gongzuo qingkuang de baogao" [Report on supporting the refugees in the Three Gorges Dam region], (Jinan: January 6, 1997), 1–3.

37. The networks were arranged as follows: Shandong-Beichuan County, Guangdong-Wenchuan County, Zhejiang-Qingchuan County, Jiangsu-Mianzhu City, Beijing-Shenfang City, Shanghai-Dujiangyan City, Hebei-Pingwu County, Liaoning-An County, Henan-Jiangyou City, Fujian-Pengzhou City, Shanxi-Mao County, Hunan-Li County, Jilin-Heishui County, Anhui-Songpan County, Jiangxi-Xiaojin County, Hubei-Hanyuan County, Chongqing-Congzhou City, Heilongjiang-Jiange County, Shenzhen with affected areas in Gansu, and Tianjin with affected areas in Shaanxi. Interviews in Chengdu in September 2012.

38. "Guowuyuan bangongting guanyu yinfa wenchuan dizhen zhaihou huifu chongjian duikou zhiyuan fangan de tongzhi" [State council circular on providing collective support for recovering and reconstructing in Wenchuan seriously affected by the earthquake] (State Council Office [2008] no. 53, June 18, 2008), http://www.gov.cn/zwgk/2008-06/18/content_1019966.htm.

39. By 2010, the accumulated total since 1995 of the cadres transferred to Tibet amounted to 4,741. See Yasheng Huang, "China's Cadre Transfer Policy toward Tibet in the 1980s," *Modern China*, 21, no. 2 (April 1995): 184–204; Zheng Shaozhong, "Zhongyang shiyinian xianhou pai 2894ming yuanzang ganbu"

[The center has dispatched 2,894 cadres to Tibet in the last 11 years], *Renmin ribao*, December 3, 2006; Yu Hongchang et al., "Yuanzang shisinian" [Supporting Tibet for the last fourteen years], http://www.chinatibetnews.com/yuanzang/2009-10/25/content_319064.htm; and "Zhongyang he guojiajiguan yangqi diliupi yuanzang ganbu cong Beijing qicheng" [The party center and government units cheer for the sixth dispatch of cadres in support of Tibet], August 1, 2010, http://fianance.ifeng.com/roll/20100801/2466562.shtml.

40. By 2010, the accumulated total of the cadres transferred to Xinjiang since 1997 was 6,980. See "Yuanjiang ganbu chengwei dongxibu hezuo niudai" [The work of cadre transfer in support of Xinjiang has become the nexus of east–west cooperation], *Urumuqi wanbao* [Urumqi evening news], September 22, 2005; and "Diqipi yuanjiang ganbu dijiang" [The seventh batch of cadres in support of Xinjiang arriving], *Xinjiang ribao* [Xinjiang daily], August 26, 2011.

41. See http://renshi.people.com.cn/n/2012/0801/c139617-18645213.htm; http://renshi.people.com.cn/n/2012/1012/c140761-19247143.htm; http://renshi.people.com.cn/n/2012/1111/c140761-19541066.htm.

42. For these dyadic pairs, see He Jianzhang and Wang Jiye, eds., *Zhongguo jihua guanli wenti* [Problems of plan management in China] (Beijing: Zhongguo shehuikexue chubanshe, 1984), 166–67; Xu Bingwen et al., *Zhongguo xibei diqu fazhan zhanlue gailun* [Introduction to the development strategies of China's Northwest] (Beijing: Jingji guanli chubanshe, 1992), 247; and Wang Yiming, *Zhongguo quyu jingji zhengce yanjiu* [Study of China's regional economic policy] (Beijing: Zhongguo jihua chubanshe, 1998), 46.

43. Zhang Junkuo and Hou Yongzhi, *Xietiao quyu fazhan* [Coordinated regional development] (Beijing: Zhongguo fazhan chubanshe, 2008), 88–89.

44. See http://renshi.people.com.cn/n/2012/0726/c139617-18605584.htm; and http://renshi.people.com.cn/n/2012/1105/c140761-19503689.htm.

45. See the relevant document by the Yunnan Provincial Government listed in http://sh.eastday.com/eastday/node6336/node 6337/ula208758.html.

46. http://www.56-china.com.cn/china2012/201-12/12-6q/12-06mz8/html.

47. *Dangdai zhongguo de wuzi liutong*, 132–35.

48. Zhang, *Quyu hezuo yu jingji wangluo*, 34–50, 100–17; Wang, *Zhongguo quyu jingji zhengce yanjiu*, 153; Lynn T. White III, *Unstately Power: Local Causes of China's Economic Reforms* (Armonk, N.Y.: M. E. Sharpe, 1998), 373–88; and Wang Weiquan, *Difang zhengfu hezuo* [Cooperation among local governments] (Beijing: Zhongyang bianyi chubanshe, 2013), chap. 2.

49. Tang Yalin, *Changjiang sanjiaozhou quyu zhili de lilun yu shijian* [Theory and practice in the governance of Yangzi River Delta region] (Shanghai: Fudan daxue chubanshe, 2014), 2–4, 81, 83–94.

50. See http://www.sdpc.gov.cn/zcfb/zcfbtz/2009tz/t20090703_289358.htm; http://bgt.ndrc.gov.cn/zcfb/t20110602_498624.htm; and http://news.daihe.cn/2012/12-03/101800581.html.

51. "Xinchangtai xia woguo quyu zhengce de tiaozheng fangxiang yu jucuo" [The future direction and policy toward readjusting China's regional strategy under the new normal], *Diaocha yanjiu baogao* [Investigative research report], no. 4700 (January 30, 2015): 7–11.

52. See Dorothy J. Solinger, "Uncertain Paternalism: Tensions in Recent Regional Restructuring in China," *International Regional Science Review*, 11, no. 1 (1987): 35.

53. See Xu Bingwen et al., *Zhongguo xibei diqu fazhan zhanlue gailun* [Survey of economic development strategies in China's Northwest region] (Beijing: Jingji guanli chubanshe, 1992), 254; *Zhongguo zhengfu jigou minglu* [Directory of government organizations in China] (Beijing: Xinhua chubanshe, 1996), 1:8–9; and *Zhongyang zhengfu zuzhi jigou* [Organizations of the central government] (Beijing: Gaige chubanshe, 1998), 113–14.

54. See Chen Yongjun, *Zhongguo diqu zhi jian shichang fengsuo wenti yanjiu* [Study of market enclosure among China's regions] (Fuzhou: Fujian renmin chubanshe, 1994), 94.

55. In January 1997, Dalian was assigned to support five cities and counties in Guizhou (Zunyi and Liupaishui), Hubei (Xingshan), Tibet (Naqu), and Liaoning (Chaoyang). Without specific incentives and close monitoring by Beijing, Dalian either evaded this heavy burden or simply offered token donations to these cities. This information comes from interviews in Dalian in 1997. For Shenzhen's similar response to Beijing's imposed donations, see *South China Morning Post International Weekly*, July 13, 1996, and February 8, 1997.

56. The pairing of Shandong with Qinghai, for instance, was allegedly decided on the grounds that Liang Buting, the party chief of Qinghai, was from Shandong and sought to get linked up with his native province. Although Liang later became Shandong's party chief, the fifteen-year cooperation between the two provinces was deemed less than ideal. The information on the Shandong–Qinghai pairing is from interviews in Jinan in July 1999. For the problems associated with the lack of interdependence and information asymmetry in horizontal cooperation, see Miller, *Managerial Dilemma*, 57.

57. In this overhaul, nine coastal provinces (Shandong, Fujian, Liaoning, Zhejiang, Jiangsu, Guangdong, Shanghai, Tianjin, and Beijing) were newly paired with nine inland provinces (in corresponding order, Xinjiang, Ningxia, Qinghai, Sichuan, Shaanxi, Guangxi, Yunnan, Gansu, and Neimenggu); and four coastal open cities of Dalian, Qingdao, Shenzhen, and Ningbo were paired with Guizhou. See *Ming Pao*, October 14, 1996; and "Quanguo fupin kaifa gongzuo qingkuang" [The current situation of the national poverty alleviation work], *Jingji yanjiu cankao*, no. 1001 (January 1, 1997): 8.

58. See Yong-Nian Zheng, "Perforated Sovereignty: Provincial Dynamism and China's Foreign Trade," *Pacific Review* 7, no. 3 (1994): 313–14; Pak K. Lee, "Local Economic Protectionism in China's Economic Reform," *Development Policy Review* 16, no. 3 (September 1998): 281–303; Li Shantong, "Zhonggu guonei difang baohu wenti de diaocha yu fenxi" [Investigation and analysis of local protectionism in China], *Jingji yanjiu* [Economic studies]: no. 11 (2004): 78–84; and Yu Dongshan, *Zhuanxingqi zhongguo difang zhengfu jingzheng yanjiu*, 34–45.

59. In 1987, the number of such linkages was estimated to be less than one hundred, which rose to several hundred by 1991. See Zhang, *Quyu hezuo yu jingji wangluo*, 27, 271–80. Also see Zhang Jingen, *Dangdai zhongguo zhengfujian guanxi daolun* [Introduction to intergovernmental relations in contemporary China] (Beijing: Shehuikexue wenxian chubanshe, 2009), 141.

60. A 1996 report by the State Planning Commission indicated that horizontal cooperative linkages were formed predominantly "among western localities" [*xixi hezuo*]. See *Woguo diqu jingji xietiao fazhan yanjiu*, 24.

61. For an earlier list of these networks, see *Zhongguo hengxiang jingji nianjian 1992* [1992 yearbook on China's horizontal economic linkages] (Beijing: Zhongguo shehui kexue chubanshe, 1993); and Yu Dongshan, *Zhuanxingqi zhongguo difang zhengfu jingzheng yanjiu*, 109–10.

62. For discussions of the Regional Economic Coordination Association of Southwest China, see Zheng, *Institutional Change, Local Developmentalism, and Economic Growth*, 222–51; and Chen Dongsheng, *Xibu jingji juequi zhi lu* [The road to boosting the economy of the western region] (Shanghai: Shanghai yuandong chubanshe, 1996), 193–96.

63. See *South China Morning Post*, May 20 and August 23, 1994; Xu, *Zhongguo xibei diqu fazhan zhanlue gailun*, 9–10; *Zhongguo daxinan zai jueqi* [The rise of China's Southwest] (Nanning: Guangxi jiaoyu chubanshe, 1994), 14, 55; and Zheng Yongnian, *De Facto Federalism in China: Reforms and Dynamics of Central-Local Relations* (London: World Scientific, 2007), 295–312.

64. See Chen, *Xibu kaifa dazhanlue yu xinsilu*, 264–74; and Lin Jiabin, "Gaige kaifang yilai diqu fazhan de huigu yu zhanwang" [Retrospect and prospect for regional development in the era of reform and opening], *Jingji yanjiu cankao*, no. 1249 (January 25, 1999): 30.

65. "Yu Shaan Lu sansheng shengzhang tan chongzhen huanghe jingji" [Governors of Henan, Shaanxi, and Shandong discuss how to revive the economies along the Yellow River], *Liaowang zhoukan* [Outlook weekly: overseas edition], June 24, 1991, 14–15; The "westward" strategy task force group, "Guanyu Huanghe jingji xiezuoqu lianhe fazhan wenti" [On jointly developing the Yellow River economic cooperative association], *Jingji yanjiu cankao*, no. 835 (March 2, 1996): 22–28; and interviews in Jinan in 1999.

66. See http://finance.sina.com.cn/roll/20101018/09358794661.shtml; http://www.ah.xinhuanet.com/ahzw2006/2011-09/21/content_23746962.htm; and http://www.chinaeast.gov.cn/2011-07/26/c_131010081.htm; and Zhang Junkuo and Hou Yongzhi, *Xietiao quyu fazhan*, 227–30.

67. Because the jump in the number of provincial organizers during 1999–2000 coincided with the start of the "Develop the West" scheme, the shadow of Beijing was lingering in the backgrounds. Yet the increases in investment—particularly during 2009–2014—also tell us that there certainly was more to it than just Beijing's push.

68. *Woguo diqu jingji xietiao fazhan yanjiu*, 45; Fei Hongping, *Zhongguo quyu jingji fazhan* [Regional economic development in China] (Beijing: Kexue chubanshe, 1998), 132; and Zhang Yaohui, *Quyu jingji lilun yu diqu jingji fazhan* [Regional economic theories and local economic development] (Beijing: Zhongguo jihua chubanshe, 1999), 204.

69. The dyadic cooperation between Yunnan and Guangdong was later expanded to a multimember network encompassing Guangxi, Guizhou, the Ministry of Electrical Power, and the China Development Bank. See Chen, *Xibu jingji jueqi zhi lu*, 194. For other dyadic networks, see *South China Morning Post*, July 7, 1995; Chen, *Xibu jingji jueqi zhi lu*, 195–96; and Gao Yufang, *Quyu jingji fazhan*

yu woguo shehuizhuyi shichang jingji [Regional economic development and the socialist market economy in China] (Wuhan: Hubei jiaoyu chubanshe, 1995), 177.

70. *Sichuan ribao*, April 22, 2010.

71. http://www.gx.chinanews.com/2013/1607_0307/70467.html.

72. Interviews in Jinan in 1997; for the Huaihai Zone, see Zhang, *Quyu hezuo yu jingji wangluo*, 71–83; and for the Pan-Bohai Zone, see Sang, *Quyu kaifang zhanluelun*, 225–35.

73. For county-level networks, see *Zhongguo hengxiang jingji nianjian 1992*, 178–82; for interfirm networks, see Xu, *Zhongguo xibei diqu fazhan zhanlue gailun*, 256–60; and for intertownship and intervillage networks, see Zhu Fengchi et al., *Zhongguo fan pinkun yanjiu* [Study of China's antipoverty campaign] (Beijing: Zhongguo jihua chubanshe, 1996), 138–47. For the active involvement of firms from the coastal region (especially, Zhejiang) in the western region, see Lu Lijun and Zheng Yanwei, *Dongbu qiye xijin de moshi yu xingwei* [The mode and behavior in eastern firms' march into the western region] (Beijing: Zhongguo jingji chubanshe, 2004), 107–25, 198–99.

74. Chen Wenshan, *Zhongguo jingji tequ yanjiu* [Study of China's special economic zones] (Shanghai: Fudan daxue chubanshe, 1996), 142–43.

75. See *Qingdao nianjian 1992* [Qingdao yearbook 1992] (Qingdao: Zhongguo baike quanshu chubanshe, 1993), 70–71; interviews in Jinan, Qingdao, and Dalian in 1997 and 1999; for Henan's case, see Liu Menglin, ed., *Henan zhuwai gongzuo huigu yu zhanwang* [Retrospect and prospects for Henan's external liaison work] (Zhengzhou: Henan renmin chubanshe, 1994), 8; and *South China Morning Post*, January 19, 1996.

76. According to a survey conducted in 1995 with eighty-four leading cadres and experts and academics, only 5 percent of those representing the coastal region supported more preferential policies for the inland, whereas the comparable figure representing the inland region amounted to 83 percent. See State Planning Commission, *Woguo diqu jingji xietiao fazhan yanjiu* [Study of regionally coordinated economic development in China] (Beijing: Gaige chubanshe, 1996), 128. Selective target policies would produce maximum impact only if their target areas were small. That is, as the geographical area of "open zones" increased, the very "specialness" of preferential policies would be diluted. Unless the privileges granted to the inland region were far more special and exclusive than those for the coastal region so as to offset the former's inferior endowments, their positive impact would most likely be minimal at best. Then, again, the coastal region would strongly oppose such measures, and Beijing would find it difficult to ignore their voices. For Beijing's will to limit free-trade zones (FTZs) to a very small number of localities, for instance, see "Cities Wrong to Bank on FTZ Status," *China Daily*, April 21, 2014; and "China Halts FTZ Applications," *Global Times*, June 4, 2014.

77. "Guowuyuan guanyu guifan caizheng zhuanyi zhifu qingkuang de baogao" [State council report on the situation regarding the changes to fiscal transfer] (June 27, 2007), http://www.gov.cn/zxft/ft98/content_903353.htm; Wang Yiming, *Zhongguo quyu jingji zhengce yanjiu*, 28–41; and Jia Kang and Liang Ji, "Zhongyang difang caili fenpei guanxi de tizhi luoji yu biaoxiang"

[Analysis of systemic logic and image in central–local fiscal distribution], *Tizhi gaige* [System reform], no. 5 (2011): 38.

78. *Zhongguo tongji nianjian 2012* (Beijing: Zhongguo tongji chubanshe, 2012), 291.

79. Xie Xuren, "Dangqian caizheng fazhan gaige youguan de wenti" [Some problems pertaining to fiscal reforms at present], *Zhonggong zhongyang dangxiao baogaoxuan* [Selected reports of the central party school], no. 2 (2012): 9; Su Ming, "Baorongxing fazhan yu caizheng zhengce xuanze" [Fiscal policy options for more accommodating development], *Lilun dongtai*, no. 1944 (December 20, 2012): 8–9; and Hu Zuquan, "Woguo zhongyang dui difang zhuanyi zhifu yanjiu" [Study of China's system of central–local fiscal transfer], *Difang caizheng yanjiu* [Studies of local finance], no. 10 (2013): 36–37.

80. The interprovincial sales tax revenues in total national sales tax revenues rose from 41.9 percent in 2003 to 43.2 percent in 2005. The interprovincial trade dependence ratio also increased from 65.4 percent in 2003 to 75.9 percent in 2004. See Zhang Junkuo and Hou Yongzhi, *Xietiao quyu fazhan*, 227, 228, 232. Also see Lu Zheng and Deng Xiang, *Zhongguo diqu fengong yu zhuanyehua yanjiu*, 76–77.

81. Gernot Grabher, "Rediscovering the Social in the Economics of Interfirm Relations," in *The Embedded Firm: On the Socioeconomics of Industrial Networks*, ed. Gernot Grabher (London: Routledge, 1993), 8–11.

8. CONCLUSION

1. For a similar line of foreign-policy related analysis of domestic problems in China, see Zhao Kejin, "Zhongguo waijiao mianlin tiaozhan xuyao biange" [Chinese foreign policy is facing challenges and needs changes], *Lilun dongtai* [Observing theories], no. 1941 (November 20, 2012): 20–21.

2. Also see Martin K. Whyte, *Myths of the Social Volcano: Perceptions of Inequality and Distributive Injustice in Contemporary China* (Stanford: Stanford University Press, 2010). According to the Fragile States Index, China's ranking has been moving in a "less fragile" direction over the years. See http://ffp .statesindex.org/rankings-2014.

3. This perhaps constitutes an explanation for the adoption of such new practices as "putting the provinces back in charge of counties" and "placing township finance under county control."

4. See Jude Howell, *China Opens Its Doors: The Politics of Economic Transition* (Hertfordshire: Lynne Rienner, 1993), 5–6; and Jae Ho Chung, "Reappraising Central–Local Relations in Deng's China: Decentralization, Dilemmas of Control and Diluted Effects of Reform," in *Remaking the Chinese State: Strategies, Society and Security*, eds. Chien-min Chao and Bruce J. Dickson (London: Routledge, 2001), 66. Also see Ciqi Mei and Margaret M. Pearson, "Killing a Chicken to Scare the Monkeys? Deterrence Failure and Local Defiance in China," *China Journal*, no. 72 (July 2014): 75–97.

5. See Wanning Sun, "Discourses of Poverty: Weakness, Poverty and Provincial Identity in Anhui," in *Rethinking China's Provinces*, ed. John Fitzgerald (London: Routledge, 2002), 153–77; and Ding Kaijie, "The Crucial Role of Local Governments in Setting Up a Social Safety Net," *China Perspectives*, no. 48 (July–August 2003): 37–49.

6. I was sensitized to this by Vivienne Shue, "Grasping Reform: Economic Logic, Political Logic, and the State–Society Spiral," *China Quarterly* 144 (December 1995): 1174–85.

7. "Woguo cailixing zhuanyi zhifu zhidu de fenxi yu wanshan jianyi" [Analyses and proposals on improving China's system of fiscal transfer payments], *Diaocha yanjiu baogao* [Investigative research report], no. 188 (November 10, 2005): 9–11; and Xie Xuren, "Dangqian caizheng fazhan gaige youguan wenti" [Some problems on the current fiscal development reform], in *Zhonggong zhongyang dangxiao baogao wenxuan* [Selected works at the CCP's central party school], no. 2 (2012): 8–9.

8. The Grassroots Finance Task Force of the Chinese Academy of Social Sciences, "Xiangcai xianguan gaige pingshu" [On the reform of counties managing townships' finance], *Lingdao canyue* [References for leadership], no. 7 (March 5, 2006): 22–24; and "Zhongyang-difang zhengfu ziyuan youhua de yuanze silu ji guanjian huanjie" [Some thoughts and key tasks regarding better delineating the power and responsibilities between central and local governments], *Diaocha yanjiu baogao*, no. 4374 (July 18, 2013): 1–11.

9. See Borge Bakkan, "State Control and Social Control in China," in *State Capacity in East Asia*, eds. Kjeld Erik Brodsgaard and Susan Young (Oxford: Oxford University Press, 2000), chap. 9; and Jae Ho Chung, Hongyi Lai and Ming Xia, "Mounting Challenges to Governance in China: Surveying Collective Protestors, Religious Sects and Criminal Organizations," *China Journal*, no. 56 (July 2006): 1–31.

10. See Joseph Fewsmith and Gao Xiang, "Local Governance in China: Incentives and Tensions," *Daedalus* 143, no. 2 (Spring 2014): 170–83.

11. For this line of argument, see Uradyn E. Bulag, "Ethnic Resistance with Socialist Characteristics," in *Chinese Society: Changes, Conflict and Resistance*, eds. Elizabeth J. Perry and Mark Selden (London: Routledge, 2000), 195; and Remi Castets, "The Uyghurs in Xinjiang: The Malaise Grows," *China Perspectives*, no. 49 (September–October 2003): 34–48.

12. Many of these problems are identified as key sources of China's "crack-up" in the coming future. See David Shambaugh, "The Coming Chinese Crack-up," *Wall Street Journal*, March 6, 2015. For a Chinese counterargument, see "Shen Dawei tuhan: Zhongguo bengkui weinaban" [David Shambaugh's sudden call-out for China's collape doesn't mean much], *Huanqiu shibao* [Global times], May 9, 2015.

13. Gabriella Montinola, Yingyi Qian, and Barry R. Weingast, "Federalism, Chinese Style: The Political Basis for Economic Success in China," *World Politics* 48, no. 1 (October 1995): 50–81; and Evan A. Feigenbaum and Damien Ma, "Federalism, Chinese Style," *Foreign Affairs* 93, no. 3 (May 6, 2014).

14. For the pros and cons of federalism from Chinese perspectives, compare Liu Junning, "Liansheng zizhi" [Joint provincial self-rule], *Zhanlue yu guanli*,

no. 5 (2002): 17–28 with Lin Zhiyuan, "Zhongyang jiquan he difang fenquan: lianbangzhuyi de jingyan yu jiaoxun" [Centralization and decentralization: The experiences and lessons of federalism], *Zhanlue yu guanli*, no. 1 (2003): 82–85. For China's overall "allergy" to the federalist possibility, see Zhang Jicai, *Zhongguo jindai lianbangzhuyi yanjiu* [Study of federalism in modern China] (Beijing: Zhongguo shehuikexue chubanshe, 2012), 58–64, 250–51.

15. Kathryn Stoner-Weiss, *Local Heroes: The Political Economy of Russian Regional Governance* (Princeton: Princeton University Press, 1997), chap. 3; Liu Yawei, "Local Electoral Reforms and the Rule of Law," in *Charting China's Future: Political, Social and International Dimensions*, ed. Jae Ho Chung (Lanham, Md.: Rowman & Littlefield, 2006), chap. 3; and Lam Tao-chiu, "Competition in a Glasshouse: Local Governments and *gongxuan* in China," paper presented at the inaugural workshop of the Asian Network for the Study of Local China (ANSLoC), Seoul, May 5–6, 2006.

16. As long as the respective responsibilities of Beijing and localities are divided by the lump sum [*zonge*], rather than by the specific functional domain, central–local tension is bound to remain. See Yan Tingrui, *Zhongguo xingzheng tizhi gaige wenti baogao* [Report on the problems of administrative system reforms in China] (Beijing: Zhongguofazhanchubanshe, 2004), 252.

17. Jae Ho Chung, "Forecasting China's Future: Scenarios, Uncertainties and Determinants," in *Charting China's Future: Political, Social and International Dimensions*, ed. Jae Ho Chung (Lanham, Md.: Rowman & Littlefield, 2006), 1–19.

18. Although some suggest that these forecasts have already proved incorrect, they are mostly misleading or distort the essence of the key arguments posited. See, for instance, David Shambaugh, "China's Immediate Future: Stable or Unstable?" in *Charting China's Future: Domestic and International Challenges*, ed. David Shambaugh (London: Routledge, 2013), 173–74.

19. China is keenly aware of the importance of stable central–local relations in its drive toward a great-power status. See Yang Yi, ed., *Zhongguo guojia anquan zhanlue gouxiang* [Ideas and plans for China's national security strategy] (Beijing: Shishi chubanshe, 2009), 397–407.

20. See Jae Ho Chung, ed., *Assessing China's Power* (London: PalgraveMacMillan, 2015). Also see Andrew J. Nathan, "Authoritarian Resilience," in *Will China Democratize?*, eds. Andrew J. Nathan, Larry Diamond, and Moore F. Plattner (Baltimore: Johns Hopkins University Press, 2013), chap. 7.

21. See, respectively, Christopher Layne, "The Unipolar Illusion: Why New Great Powers Will Rise," *International Security* 17, no. 4 (Spring 1993): 5; and Kenneth Waltz, "Structural Realism after the Cold War," *International Security* 25, no. 1 (Summer 2000): 32. For a similar line of reasoning in the Chinese context, see Ge Jianxiong, *Tongyi yu fenlie: Zhongguo lishi de qishi* [Unification and disintegration—Insights from China's history] (Beijing: Xinhua Shudian, 1994), 31–35.

22. Fareed Zakaria, *The Post-American World* (New York: Norton, 2009).

23. In the West and the United States, federalism has been going through a process of evolution where the so-called "coercive federalism" (where the federal government is the dominant policy maker and able to assert its will unilaterally, thereby blurring the line with unitary systems) is coming into exis-

tence. See Jack W. Meek and Kurt Thurmeier, eds., *Networked Governance: The Future of Intergovernmental Management* (Thousand Oaks, Calif.: CQ Press, 2012), 13–25.

24. Many signs of centralization are discernible under Xi Jinping's rule, although it is not totally clear if they represent Beijing's firm control over localities or, alternatively, Beijing's persistent responses to successful local resistance.

25. See Grigore Pop-Eleches, "Historical Legacies and Post-Communist Regime Change," *Journal of Politics* 69, no. 4 (November 2007): 908–26; Victoria Tin-bor Hui, "How China Was Governed," *The American Interest*, Spring 2008, 53–65; and R. Kent Guy, *Qing Governors and Their Provinces: The Evolution of Territorial Administration in China, 1644–1796* (Seattle: University of Washington Press, 2010).

Index

Central Organization Department (COD), 27, 56, 68, 78, 167n58
Central Party School, 68
centrifugal forces, 6, 11, 15, 18, 36, 64, 72–73, 77–78, 141–42, 145–48
Changchun, 38
Chengdu, 38, 40, 41
China East–West Trade Fair (*Xiqiahui*), 133–34
Chinese Communist Party (CCP), 17, 72, 73, 77, 86, 145
Chongqing, 4, 35, 40, 41, 46, 64, 109, 166n42
cities-ruling-counties policy, 7, 43, 46, 66, 100, 163n11, 193n57
collective protests, 85, 87, 93, 108–9, 111–12, 142, 144, 195n84, 196n94
comparative advantage, 19, 26, 131
comparative case studies, 14
Constitution of the People's Republic of China, 43, 46, 66, 77, 83, 169n82
corruption, 68, 70, 142, 145
counties, 50, 67–69; history of, 37, 67; number of, 37, 67
county-level cities, 37, 42, 46, 48, 50; number of, 44–45
county-ruling units, 7, 66
Cultural Revolution, 18, 19, 75, 78

Dalian, 38, 41, 43, 51, 95, 166n42, 203n55
Daqing, 19, 31, 74
Dazhai, 19, 31, 74
decentralization, 142, 143, 145; definition of, 20; of fiscal relations, 24–26; of foreign economic relations, 26–27; of investment, 23–24; of legislative power, 29; norms of, 19, 30–31, 52, 60, 74–75; in the Mao era, 18–19, 74; in the post-Mao era, 9, 11, 16, 20–29, 34, 71, 76, 90, 116
decollectivization, 8, 38
democratic centralism, 17, 73

democratization, 1, 53, 71
Deng Xiaoping, 80, 96, 108
deputy-provincial cities, 35, 38, 39–42, 48, 165n32
development zones, 26, 124, 125
"Develop the West" scheme, 27, 93, 94, 116, 124, 130, 132, 204n67
Discipline Inspection Commission, 81
diseconomies of scale, 2, 3
dual leadership, 81
dual sovereignty, 2
Du Runsheng, 106
dynastic collapse, 33

"emancipation of mind," 31, 74
encompassing policy, 90, 101, 189n16
enterprise income tax, 25
ethnic minority regions, 34, 35, 36, 66, 101, 110, 144
ethnic separatist, 5
extra-budgetary revenue, 24, 97, 192n40

factionalism, 88
Falungong, 5, 91, 93, 112, 114
federal system, 2, 77, 146, 147, 149n6, 199n14, 208n23
field office, 66
fiscal contract system, 24, 61, 83
fiscal transfer, 138–39, 144
Five-Year Plan, 22, 75, 118, 120
fixed-term rotation, 86
foreign investment, 24
foreign trade corporation, 26
four-tier system, 34, 66
France, 51, 146
free-riding, 118, 130
Fujian, 27, 42, 67, 101, 103

globalization, 1, 60
governance policy, 90
great administrative regions, 10, 18, 34, 35, 85, 129
Great Leap Forward, 18, 43, 185n33
gross domestic product (GDP), 24, 28, 62, 80

growth pole, 67
Guangdong, 27, 42–43, 49, 96–97, 101, 110, 135, 168n66, 168n73
Guangming Daily, 83, 99
Guangxi, 36, 78, 123
Guangzhou, 38, 40, 41, 49
guidance target, 21
Guizhou, 99, 103, 193n47

Hainan, 35, 64, 67, 101, 103; separation from Guangdong, 92, 96–97, 114, 190n17, 191n33
Han dynasty, 7, 37, 69
Hangzhou, 38, 42
Harbin, 38, 95
Hebei, 51, 68, 99, 135
Heilongjiang, 95, 100, 105, 106, 110, 123, 188n5
Henan, 67, 99, 102, 110
hidden information, 25
historical-analytic narrative, 14
historical atmosphere, 7
Hong Kong, 27, 35, 38, 64
horizontal interaction, 11, 13, 59, 64, 79, 115–16
household responsibility reform, 92, 100, 175n16, 188n5; as encompassing-governance policy, 103, 107, 113
Hubei, 101, 109, 167n51
Hu Jintao, 80, 93
hukou, 47
Hunan, 51, 68, 110
Hu Yaobang, 96, 106

implement(ing) according to local conditions (*yindi zhiyi*), 17, 19, 31, 73, 78, 106, 189n16
implementation slippage, 75
India, 146, 147, 172n107
Indonesia, 146, 147, 149n5, 172n107
industrial-commercial tax, 25, 83, 97, 98
information asymmetry, 57, 121, 131, 189n12
inspection trip, 80, 185n33
institutional adaptation, 12, 72

institutional resemblance, 80–81, 82, 86
institutional stability, 7, 35–37, 39, 52, 53
inter-local diplomacy, 135–37
internal cohesion, 3, 147
interregional trade, 115, 121, 131, 134, 140, 206n80
interview, 55
investigative instrument, 79–82
isomorphism, 19, 133–34
issue areas, 9, 11, 141

Japan, 27, 36
Japanese armies, 17
Jiangsu, 42, 43, 49, 99, 101, 110, 129, 131, 133
Jiangxi Soviet, 17, 80, 85
Jiang Zemin, 80, 93, 94
Jilin, 93, 95, 105, 110
Jinan, 38, 42
Jin dynasty, 7

key economic cities, 39
Kunming, 42
Kunshan, 49
Kuomintang, 17

land appropriation, 62, 70, 109, 144, 196n94
land reform, 16, 34
Latin America, 99
Lattimore, Owen, 15
leadership disunity, 59
leadership responsibility system, 112
level of analysis, 10, 20
Liaoning, 27, 42, 43, 95, 101, 105, 106, 110, 191n29
Li Keqiang, 5
Liu Zhongli, 99
local: concept of, 10, 173n1; defiance, 18, 31, 74; discretion, 9, 12, 19, 30, 60, 88, 90–91, 113, 141, 143–145; experimentation, 9, 17, 52, 71, 73; foot-dragging, 9, 31, 56, 64, 71, 75, 88, 89, 103, 114; interest, 58, 89

GPSR Authorized Representative: Easy Access System Europe, Mustamäe tee
50, 10621 Tallinn, Estonia, gpsr.requests@easproject.com

www.ingramcontent.com/pod-product-compliance
Lightning Source LLC
Chambersburg PA
CBHW021901020426
42334CB00013B/435